BRINGING
UNCLE
ALBERT
HOME

BRINGING UNCLE ALBERT HOME

A Soldier's Tale

DAVID P. WHITHORN

SUTTON PUBLISHING

This book was first published in 2003 by
Sutton Publishing Limited · Phoenix Mill
Thrupp · Stroud · Gloucestershire · GL5 2BU

This revised paperback edition first published in 2006

British Library Cataloguing in Publication Data
A catalogue record for this book is available from the British
Library.

ISBN 0 7509 4209 6

Typeset in 10/12.5pt Photina.
Typesetting and origination by
Sutton Publishing Limited.
Printed and bound in Great Britain by
J.H. Haynes & Co. Ltd, Sparkford.

Contents

List of Maps and Plates

Maps

Plate Section

Pte Albert E. Turley, 3rd Worcestershire (*Dean Forest Mercury*,
15 September 1916)
The Old Furnace, Blakeney, Forest of Dean (*Author's collection*)
Blakeney Parish War Memorial, All Saints' Church, Forest
of Dean (*Author's collection*)
All Saints' Church, Viney Hill, Forest of Dean
(*Author's collection*)
War Correspondents (*IWM Q1062*)
A Camp Scene behind the Lines, Mailly Maillet, 29 June 1916
(*IWM Q748*)
Enemy Barrage on the Thiepval Ridge (*IWM Q1057*)

List of Maps and Plates

Preface

At the beginning of this twenty-first century the terrible wars of the twentieth seem remote, belonging to a bygone era – somewhere, sometime before the swinging sixties. There are few, if any, veterans of the First World War left; the soldiers from the second are rapidly fading away. We watch the participants of the former living in a silent, sepia-and-white world, knowing they believed the politicians' lies and were slaughtered by the thousand on the fields of France by incompetent generals – and for nothing. Many people buy a poppy during November and observe two minutes silence for the fallen, although most knew neither the soldiers nor their times. Why? We might look at the long list of faceless names on local war memorials as we hurry by, but they are just names to us now, and old-fashioned ones at that. I wonder how long our respect for them will continue? What will happen when there are no veterans left to march past the cenotaph on Remembrance Sunday?

A quarter of a century ago I too could be counted among the 'knows-nothing and the cares-less' regarding the world wars. This was to change one rainy night when, for once, I didn't go for a 'night out'. Instead, I watched a television documentary entitled *The Battle of the Somme*. This one programme was to change my whole outlook on life, for ever. The hows and whys of this are not the subject of this book; let it be sufficient to say I have a passionate interest in the First World War, and the men who took part in it. I have read many books, talked with veterans and visited the battlefields many times. To the layman, I am an 'expert'; for myself, I realise only how little I really do know about this event in history. Yet, by studying it, I have found a purpose for my own life – to ensure that the First World War, the men who took part in it and what they achieved, are *never* forgotten.

This book is about the search for another man's life story, a man who fought and died in the Battle of the Somme – one faceless name on a church war memorial. This man was not a hero: he didn't win any medals for gallantry. He didn't leave a diary, poems, letters or anything by which he was remembered – not even a photograph. He does not even have a grave on which to lay flowers or to stand by and weep. Yet this man is very, very precious; and but for the chance of birth it could have been me or you who fell on that hillside, one sunny afternoon in August 1916.

It is not my intention to write a scholarly account of the history of events of over eighty years ago just to prove that I am an expert in military history: I am not interested in such intellectual competitions. Rather, I have sought to present my search for the past and from it to build a picture of the life and death of that one soldier killed on the Somme in 1916. The sources I have used are varied, and although I have some experience in accessing and using these, gained from twenty-five years of study, they are readily available for everyone to use. Following such guidelines as are provided in this book, I believe similar (and better) research can be performed by other people qualified with only the capacity and determination to succeed. In this way, the story of the men of 1914–18 will continue long after the last veteran has marched past the cenotaph.

To those who use this book for their own endeavours in this field, may you too, 'bring Uncle Albert home'.

Introduction to the New Edition

As I submitted the manuscript for *Bringing Uncle Albert Home* in the hope it might be published, I could not have believed the warm reception it would come to receive from both reviewers and a caring public. Nor could I imagine being asked to add updates for a paperback edition to be released in time for the commemoration of the 90th anniversary of the Battle of the Somme! An honour indeed.

Publication triggered more family memories, Albert's youngest sister, Elizabeth, was just 6 years old when he was killed. In the final years of her life (in the 1970's), she undertook a trip to the Somme battlefields to look for her brother's grave. Sadly, beyond this little is known neither about what information she had to work with nor what she found.

I have been able to include much new information. One reader recognised his own great-uncle listed in the Appendix and was able to supply me with letters from a soldier in the front line serving with Albert. Continuing to read soldier's accounts has provided other eye-witnesses to events and places in Albert's life. Searching through information, available at the National Archive in Kew, brought both highs and lows. Albert's service records, sadly, have not survived (along with 60% of such records destroyed by enemy action in the 1939–45 war). His 'medal index card' has survived indicating he served *only* with the Worcestershire Regiment, a point of importance in Albert's story. Reading original war diaries compiled by Territorial Force and New Army battalions only highlighted just how little detail is sometimes found in similar diaries kept by Regular battalions of the same regiment, such as the 3rd Worcestershire and 1st Wiltshire – my main sources of information.

Bringing Uncle Albert Home

To paraphase, '*to understand a man, first walk a mile in his shoes*'. I have not served in the armed forces. At times, I was acutely aware of this defficiency in trying to rebuild Albert's life, having to rely on only what I had learned from other soldier's accounts. With publication, I set out to make up for this. I joined the 'Great War Society'. Each member puts together the complete uniform and equipment of a Great War Soldier. Wearing this, he voluntarily undergoes military training according to contemporary manuals and '*lives*' the life of a soldier of the 1914–18 period, all, *except the fighting and the fear*.

I now know what it is like to wear the thick serge uniforms equiped with 1908 pattern webbing and kit (weighing the regulation 66lb or so!), not forgetting rifle and 'tin hat', to march miles in all weathers, even on the Western Front itself. I have fired the .303 Short Magazine Lee Enfield rifle on a range. I have lived in a trench, eaten bully beef and biscuit out of a mess tin with an oversize spoon taken from convenient storage in my right puttee. I now know basic drill and can '*form fours*' and '*present arms*' with the best. It would be true to say that I have learned as much (and more) about some aspects of the life of a Great War 'Tommy' as by over twenty years reading about it. I now have a greater understanding about many episodes described in the original accounts and have been able to bring some of these '*living-history*' experiences into this edition.

Finally, I have been contacted by many people having read Albert's story, now themselves inspired to trace their own relatives who fought in the Great War. Some of these, I have been able to help personally, and I have now lost count of the number of Great War soldier's stories I have helped to put together. Others too, have visited the Somme just to see Albert's name on the Thiepval memorial – one man asked for a set of detailed maps, he wished to lead a cycling party around the Somme following Albert's footsteps! It has been a truly humbling experience reading people's kind letters of appreciation. A member of Sutton Publishing's staff summarised peoples' reactions, '*We haven't had anything like this before, your book has simply touched everyone who has read it*'.

Introduction to the New Edition

Albert and his companions have passed away, 90 years is longer than an average lifetime and the Battle of the Somme is almost beyond living memory. For the soldiers who took part, the carved words on the South African memorial at Delville Wood, Somme, provide a testament for all generations to witness:

'Their ideal is our legacy, their sacrifice our inspiration'

Acknowledgements

This book could not have been written without the help of many people and institutions over a number of years. In particular, the author would like to thank:

The staff of the Worcestershire and Sherwood Foresters Regiment Museum, in particular: Maj D.W. Reeve MBE (Retd) Curator; Lt Col C.P. Love (Retd) Hon. Archivist; R. Prophet and J. Lowles, researchers, for supplying copies of records regarding the 3rd Worcestershire, details of which may be found in the Bibliography; and Lt Col A.L.O. Jerram MBE for reading the draft manuscript and offering useful advice.

The staff of the Royal Gloucestershire, Berkshire and Wiltshire Regiment Museum, in particular: David Chilton, Curator, and Maj P.J. Ball (Retd) for supplying copies of records, etc., regarding the 1st Wiltshire, details of which may be found in the Bibliography.

The staff of the Commonwealth War Graves Commission both for their assistance in tracing records and for continuing to maintain the cemeteries and memorials of the fallen of the world wars, which are an everlasting inspiration for all those who visit them.

The staff of the Photographic and Printed Book Archives of the Imperial War Museum for their assistance in identifying key photographs for this work and allowing me permission to reproduce them in this book.

The staff of the Naval and Military Press for permission to reproduce the trench maps from their publication *The Imperial War Museum Trench Map Archive on CD-ROM*. In addition, their other publication *Soldiers Died in the Great War* (also on CD-ROM) proved invaluable.

The staff of the History Centre in Worcester and the Public Library in Cinderford for their assistance in tracing relevant newspaper articles.

The staff of the Thiepval Visitors Centre who continue to preserve the memory of the soldiers commemorated on the Thiepval Memorial on a day by day basis.

The editor and staff of *The Forester*, successor to the *Dean Forest Mercury*, for permission to reproduce the photograph of Albert Turley.

Victor and Diane Piuk of Hardecourt-aux-Bois, Somme, for their hospitality, encouragement in this work, proof reading of the first draft of this book and so much more besides – including visiting a remote cemetery in the depths of winter to supply me with a vital photograph.

The nephews and nieces of Pte A.E. Turley for their memories and other members of my family who shared in many of the exciting discoveries. My wife Sarah, who managed to keep smiling no matter how many times we got lost driving and walking along the roads and farm tracks of the Somme.

Mr David Wicks for kindly supplying letters from his Great-uncle Pte. W. Pratt, 3rd Worcestershire.

The members of the Great War Society, for training and a unique comradeship which have both transcended the generations.

I would like to add due acknowledgement to the staff of Sutton Publishing for editing, production of maps and all their help in the publication of this work.

Finally, the greatest debt is owed to the soldiers themselves who found themselves caught up in the maelstrom of the Battle of the Somme during the summer of 1916. This book is humbly dedicated to their memory.

David Whithorn
Basingstoke, 2005

Author's Note

Capt H.M. Fitz Stacke, the author of *The Worcestershire Regiment in the Great War*, took particular pains in his Introduction to state that the title of a battalion of the Regiment was '*the nth Worcestershire*' not '*nth Worcesters*' nor '*nth Worcs.*', the title taking an 's' in neither the plural nor the possessive. This tradition has been upheld throughout this work, apart from direct quotations from other authors.

Overleaf: General map of the Somme Battlefield
Reproduced from Michelin Road Map of Northern France No. 236 (1:200,000), this map shows the location of all the villages mentioned in this narrative. Distances are given in kilometres. In total, Albert Turley marched approximately 50 miles (80 kilometres) around this area in his active service with the 3rd Worcestershire.

ONE

Fragments from France

EARLY DAYS IN THE FOREST OF DEAN

This story starts in the late autumn of 1994. A career change meant that I found myself living with my aunt and uncle in Lydney, on the edge of the Forest of Dean. My wife commuted each weekend along the M4 to spend time with us, and, we hoped, to plan our new lives together. However, the new job was not going well. My new 'section' comprised in total: a desk with chair, a company telephone with directory, a 17-inch colour monitor without computer, an absent manager and me. Company politics had generated a post that wasn't needed after all: there was simply no work to do. I spent hour after hour, day after day, staring into space, wondering how I ever got myself into this mess. Relief finally came after an apologetic telephone call to my old company. They would take me back, 'but it might take a month or so to sort out'.

Although I had known my aunt and uncle since I was a boy, visits to Lydney had been both short and infrequent. During my stay, our conversation was relaxed; they did their best to help me through these difficult times. They knew I had an interest in history and the First World War in particular. One day, quite unexpectedly, my aunt quietly said, in her Forest accent, '*I had an uncle killed on the Somme*'.

I had spent some years both researching the First World War and trying to put together the family tree. I was 'disappointed' to find that although many relatives had served in this war, all had survived, only to pass away before I was born or knew enough to speak to them about their experiences. Frequent springtime visits to the Ypres and Somme battlefields had allowed me to see the remains of those titanic battles, and to walk beside the gravestones of the thousands who fell. Yet as I walked there, I always wished there were one unique grave I could visit – of someone close, whose story I could tell to others.

My aunt, becoming as excited as I was, did her best to answer my ensuing barrage of questions. However, like the majority of people today, she only had memories of what she had been told: there was no one now alive who remembered her uncle as a living person. She remembered his name, Albert Edward, and he shared her maiden name of Turley. Albert's father, Moses, had built his own house, Old Furnace, and brought up his family in nearby Blakeney. However, she knew neither which regiment he served in nor when he was killed. She believed his name was on the war memorial plaque of All Saints' Church, Viney Hill, Blakeney.

Further conversations with my aunt and her elder brother, who had also spent his life in Blakeney, enabled me to piece together an all-too-common tragic story whose consequences had spanned much of the twentieth century.

Albert Turley was never talked about openly within the family as my aunt grew up – she had never even seen a photograph of him. They were simply told that 'he was under age and had run away to enlist with some friends, had got himself killed on the Somme, and broken his mother's heart'. Consequently, family members had been brought up with a deep distrust of the Armed Services.

However, there was much truth in this story. In November 1918, just after the Armistice had been signed, Albert's mother Mary had died. It was said she never recovered from the news of the death of her eldest son Albert. Knowing he would never come home, she had simply faded away, possibly succumbing to the Spanish flu epidemic prevalent at that time. Moses, now alone, had to bring up his children himself. In the 1920s, there was little work in the Forest for a mason, and certainly no money for luxuries. My aunt's father, Walter, had to give up a promising career as an artist to go down the local coalmine and bring another wage into the house. In 1939, Walter, having a reserved occupation, was exempted from military service in the Second World War. Similarly, Walter's own son followed his father into the mine, thus avoiding National Service. When my aunt married in the 1960s, there was concern in her family about my uncle, an RAF serviceman, then serving with the RAF in the Far East. The shadow of Albert's death on the Somme had been long indeed.

Returning to my empty office at the start of another week, I had the beginnings of an idea. I did not have much information – I had neither a regiment nor a regimental number – but it was possibly enough to find out where Albert Turley might be buried on the Somme. I knew the Commonwealth War Graves Commission handled both written and telephone enquiries from people who wished to discover details about relatives killed in either of the two world wars. The surname was uncommon, though not in the Forest of Dean, and I did have his full forenames. I knew that the Battle of the Somme was fought in 1916, between July and November. I hoped this would be enough.

I explained my situation to the Commission and was transferred to a kind lady who took down all the details I had on Albert. Minutes later she informed me that she had found him. The result was a surprise: '*Pte Albert E. Turley, 31327, killed in action 24/8/16, 3rd Worcestershire Regiment.*' Blakeney was in Gloucestershire: how had he ended up in the Worcestershire Regiment? The next information was not what I had been hoping to hear: '*Place of Commemoration, Thiepval Memorial, Somme.*' I thanked her, and put down the telephone.

Although I had read many histories about the Battle of the Somme, most had concentrated on the opening day of the offensive, 1 July 1916, when 60,000 British soldiers had fallen, for little gain. I had visited all the places concerned with this day, and knew the stories well. I also knew many significant dates associated with the capture of villages and woods as the battle progressed through the summer and into autumn. The date of 24 August did not tie in with any of these.

Having visited the Somme, I was also familiar with the Thiepval Memorial, a huge, multi-arched structure erected on top of the Thiepval Ridge. On it were inscribed the names of the 73,000

3

'missing' soldiers of the Somme. Being commemorated on this meant that Albert did not have a known grave. The Memorial covered the whole period and extent of the Battle of the Somme. As such, there would be no indication of the location or the circumstances of his death as can usually be inferred by the history of a particular cemetery.

Having found so much in such a short space of time, I was not ready to give up. My original notion to find the whereabouts of Albert's grave was now compromised. However, it would still be possible to take my aunt and uncle to see where he had served and was commemorated. I could also describe to them what had happened in that place. It would be the first time a member of Albert's family had made such a trip, or at least so we had thought at the time.

From the Commission, I now had Albert's regiment and regimental number. The next line of enquiry was to contact the Worcestershire Regiment Museum. I was put through to the archivist at the Worcestershire and Sherwood Foresters Regimental Headquarters, and asked whether it was possible to find out anything about Albert Turley, or where the 3rd Worcestershire were on 24 August 1916 and what they might have been doing on that day. He advised me to write in, as finding such details might take some time.

That evening, I explained to my aunt and uncle what I had found out about Albert. They were saddened to discover he had no known grave, but curious to know why Albert had served with the Worcestershire Regiment: did this confirm the family story that he had run away to join up? Between us, we composed the letter giving all the details we had. The letter was posted; all we could do now was to wait for a response.

It was only a matter of days before the reply came. The enclosures included photocopies of pages from *The History of the Worcestershire Regiment in the Great War* and a letter, in which we were informed that it was not possible to give a precise enlistment date. However, the number 31327 would have been issued in late 1915 or early 1916. This was a surprise: the family story telling of Albert running away to enlist with friends would have been more credible had the date of enlistment been August 1914. At the start of the war, following the prevailing patriotic spirit, many young men ran away to enlist, having lied about their age. Late 1915 saw the effective introduction of conscription under the Derby scheme, as the supply of volunteers had slowed to well below that required to maintain (and increase) numbers of troops at the front.

The regimental history gave accounts for all the Worcestershire battalions. Highlighted were entries for the 3rd battalion for 24 August 1916. On this day, in conjunction with the 1st Wiltshire, the 3rd Worcestershire had been involved in an attack on Lemberg Trench (this was later found to be an error, and should have read Hindenburg Trench). This position was situated on the Thiepval Ridge in the infamous Leipzig Salient, immediately to the south of the village of Thiepval.

The account revealed that the attack by the 3rd Worcestershire was successful, and the position was taken and held. Importantly, casualties had been few. However, one of these few had been Albert Turley. Apart from the names of officers and men who had particularly distinguished themselves, no other soldiers' names were mentioned. The names of the casualties were not given.

Also enclosed was a copy of one of the printed maps and photographs from the book. Originally the map had been hand-drawn and details of the positions of the trenches and the dates when the 3rd Worcestershire held them had been added. Unfortunately, there were few topographical features noted on the map, apart from the location of the villages of Thiepval and Authuille. The photographs depicted scenes in the trenches in and around the Leipzig Salient. In these trenches were soldiers of the 3rd Worcestershire making the best of things. One particularly poignant photograph showed a group of survivors from the attack on 24 August.

My time in Lydney was nearing an end; I had the confirmation of the start date for returning to my old job. It was with great pleasure that I packed my few belongings and wished the few friends I had made in my new job goodbye. It was sad to leave my uncle and aunt, as by now they had become to me much more than relatives, but we had agreed to have a short holiday together. At Easter 1995, just after the opening of the Channel Tunnel, the four of us set out for France. Our destination was a small hotel in the town of Albert, the gateway to the Somme battlefields. We had just one full day to visit the area, and we were fortunate to have the best of the early spring weather.

It was the first time my wife and I had taken people to visit this area. As good tourist guides, our first visit was naturally to the Thiepval Memorial to the Missing. We arrived there at about 9 a.m.; there were no other visitors. The place was peaceful, with only the sound of birds and a gentle breeze in the new leaves of the trees in the Memorial grounds. The surroundings could not have been more perfect. We left the car and walked up the dew-soaked lawn towards the towering Memorial. We climbed the stairs to the stone of sacrifice and looked out westwards over the cemetery with its 600 white stones – 300 crosses for French soldiers and the same number of gravestones for British soldiers – almost all 'inconnu' or 'unknown'. Further westwards, the morning sun shone on the opposite side of the Ancre Valley. In this patchwork quilt of fields, woods and small villages, here and there a wisp of smoke from a chimney indicated the start of another day for the living inhabitants of the Somme battlefield.

The Thiepval Memorial was so vast that the register of 73,000 names inscribed on it ran to many volumes. After sorting through them to find the 'Ts', we found Albert's name and the appropriate panel reference. The Memorial has the potential for sixty-four such panels, based on sixteen square pillars. Even knowing the panel number, finding the correct one still took a few minutes. Over 20 feet up, at the head of the panel, stood the title 'Worcestershire Regiment'. It did not take very long to find 'TURLEY A.E.' among the many, many columns of names. We left my uncle and aunt there for as long as they wished – this was their private time, when there was no need for a tourist guide.

From here, I had planned to take them to the site of the Leipzig Salient to show them where Albert had fallen. Using only the copy of the hand-drawn map, I attempted to line this up with the parts of the villages of Thiepval and Authuille that I could see, and to find the site of Lemberg Trench. Only now, with the benefit of hindsight, do I realise I was in error by nearly a mile. Still, the sight of open fields, with little or no cover, sloping up to the Thiepval Memorial, gave an appropriate perspective for that attack long ago.

The rest of the day was spent looking around the other major sites of the Somme battlefield. Returning to the hotel, we were very tired. My uncle and aunt had been deeply moved by the sights they had seen and the stories I had told them. They would not forget their visit to the Somme, remembering one family member and the thousands of others who had fallen there.

A PHOTOGRAPH

This could have been the end of the story. In reality, it proved only to be the beginning. Years were now to pass; the millennium came and went. Technology too was moving on. The advent and growth of the Internet appeared to coincide with a surprising resurgence of interest in the First World War, partly due to the fact that its last veterans were passing on. The war had also entered the National Curriculum and many new books on the subject were being published. The quiet country roads in northern France again saw British tour parties in cars and coaches looking for lost relatives and visiting the former sites of bitter carnage.

At home, I surfed the Internet and the ever-growing number of sites relating to the First World War. One day I found a Book of Remembrance. Among the entries was one from a Canadian, who, in addition to leaving the name of a relative believed killed on the Somme, asked if anyone could help him in his researches. Thus was to begin a long series of electronic correspondences, starting from an old photograph and a name (ultimately, this led to a corner of a field on the Somme and another name on the Thiepval Memorial). Importantly, I became much more experienced in sourcing and using historical information.

One quiet day, I cast my mind back to the trip we had taken to the Somme with my uncle and aunt to see Albert Turley's name on the Thiepval Memorial. There had been for us no photograph of the soldier we had been looking for, but I suddenly remembered from my recent studies that most contemporary local newspapers ran obituaries for fallen soldiers – and many even printed a photograph, usually of the soldier in uniform. I cursed myself for not having thought of this sooner.

I had no knowledge of newspapers, past or present, from the Forest of Dean. I contacted my aunt, who remembered there used to be three such newspapers, which had been amalgamated some years before. I asked her to contact the present newspaper to discover whether a newspaper archive relating to the Blakeney area for the period of the First World War still existed.

The reply from the *Forester* was better than I could have hoped for: not only did such an archive exist, but also a microfilm had been taken of it and was freely available for viewing at the Cinderford Public Library. With no more than a hope that Albert's parents had submitted an obituary for him, we hurriedly planned our next visit to the Forest of Dean.

I will be forever grateful to the unknown lady who gave up twenty minutes of her allotted time on the microfilm reader that Friday morning in Cinderford Public Library. We had arrived there on a cold morning, without a booking. It seemed our trip would be wasted, but the librarian explained our situation to the lady, who kindly gave way. The librarian loaded the spools for the *Dean Forest Mercury* for August/September 1916, and we were away.

This local newspaper carried the major points of the war news but really concentrated on local stories. The quaint adverts for all sorts of remedies and patent medicines were mixed with others relating to auctions of farming implements. Life in the Forest of Dean didn't seem to have been changed much by the titanic struggle taking place in the fields of France, in the high summer of 1916. However, included in the first week's edition of the births, marriages and deaths were indeed obituaries of local soldiers killed in the war. As well as a long write-up, each carried a photograph of the fallen soldier. Our excitement grew in anticipation, as week passed by week with the turning of the microfilm reader-handle.

As we reached the end of August and into September our spirits fell, as there was no sign of an obituary for Albert Turley. By now, our twenty minutes were nearly up. We knew we would have to stop soon. The last edition we looked at was that of Friday 15 September; and the final turn of the handle revealed a face I would have recognised even without the 'Pte A.E. Turley' written underneath. Although the library had not been totally silent, as it should have been up to this point – there was no possibility that it could have been afterwards.

The people of the Forest of Dean have always been a close-knit community. By now, everyone in the room knew what we had been hoping to find, and everyone, including the librarians, came to share in the discovery. There were several handkerchiefs in evidence. The poor lady who gave up some of her time on the machine looked bemused – no doubt she wondered if she would ever get back to her studies. Thankfully, we printed off a copy of the obituary and the photograph, and handed the reader back to her.

The obituary read as follows:

Dean Forest Mercury – Friday 15 September 1916
Pte A.E. TURLEY

It is with feelings of the deepest regret that we record the death of Pte A.E. Turley, eldest son of Mr and Mrs Moses Richard Turley, of the Old Furnace, Blakeney. The deceased soldier was called up in his group last January, and was with the Worcesters for about six months, after which he went to the front. He had been in the war zone exactly a month when his death occurred by a shell bursting in the trench. The gallant young soldier was only 20 years of age, and before enlistment followed the occupation of a mason, being for some time engaged in building the new School of Forestry, which has been erected near the Speech House. The sad news, conveyed to Mrs Turley by a letter from the chaplain, is as follows:-

Sept. 1, 1916.   Dear Madam – As a chaplain attached to the Worcester Regiment, it is with the deepest regret that I have to give you the sad news of the death in action of your son, Private A.E. Turley, Worcesters. Your son was in the trenches when he was killed, by shell, I hear. His death was instantaneous, and he can have suffered no pain. I am very sorry to say that conditions there made it necessary to bury him where he fell, but you can be sure that if it becomes possible later to mark his grave this will be done. The commanding officer, his company officers, and comrades all send you their deepest sympathy. I know well what a blow this must be to you, but I pray that God may give you the strength to bear it, and that you may be comforted by the thought that your son died nobly for King and Country, – With deepest sympathy, I remain, yours sincerely, (Revd) G.N. Evans.

As we read the letter from the chaplain, feeling some of the original pain his mother must have felt on first opening it, even my aunt was clearly relieved that he had been killed instantly, suffering no pain. To this, I could say little. In all the many obituaries we had read, the letters told the same story, that the soldier was killed instantly either by a sniper's bullet to the head or heart, or by a direct hit from a shell. To those who had died of wounds, the end had been swift, while receiving the best of care and without pain. In fact, being killed on the Somme seemed to be remarkably pain-free.

Above all, however, we had Albert's photograph – the first my aunt had ever seen of him. The resemblance between him and my aunt's father Walter, in a photograph when he was a similar age, was remarkable: they could have been twins. Yet there was something in the picture that just wasn't quite right. But our elation continued for the rest of the day as we discussed other points that had been raised in the obituary.

In the evening, I finally spotted the problem with Albert's picture. There was no question that the photograph was of Albert – the family likeness was beyond doubt. It was his cap badge that was wrong. Having no books with me, I could not remember what the Worcestershire Regiment cap badge looked like, but I did know that this could not be it. Although small and blurred, the lower part of the badge depicted a hunting horn, the emblem of a 'Light Infantry' battalion, and the Worcestershire was not a 'Light Infantry' regiment. The outline of the rest of the badge was unclear, but would be sufficient to make an identification when I got home.

According to the obituary, Albert had enlisted with the Worcestershire in January 1916, which tied in well with the information we had previously received from the Worcestershire Regiment archivist. He had enlisted by being 'called up in his group'. This clearly meant that he had joined the Army after being conscripted by the Derby scheme. This did not seem to fit with the family story of him 'running away to join up' – in truth, he would have had little choice. This also partly answered the question of why he served in the Worcestershire rather than the local Gloucestershire Regiment since he would have been placed where there was greatest need. Serving six months with the Worcestershire would have taken Albert through to mid-July 1916. He had served 'exactly one month in the war zone' before being killed, and, given the date of his death, this meant he had arrived on the Somme on 24 July 1916. All the pieces seemed to be fitting together.

The letter from the battalion chaplain seemed strange. First, it had been addressed to Albert's mother rather than his father. Possibly Albert's father had not wanted him to enlist in the Army, and encouraged him to try for a less hazardous branch of the Armed Services? There may have been arguments, leading Albert to choose his mother as 'next-of-kin'. Certainly such a personal letter to a bereaved mother, using the initials 'A.E.+ surname' of the deceased instead of his first name, also seemed odd. However, this would seem to be in keeping with the style of the rest of the letter, which read like a standard letter of condolence from someone 'doing his job'. (The truth of this only came to light later.) The fact that it had not been possible to mark Albert's grave on account of the prevailing 'conditions' gave a more realistic picture of the circumstances of his death. There had been no mention of this at all in the obituary: we knew Albert had been killed taking part in an attack.

Albert's obituary and photograph had been tremendous finds. My wife and I returned home content that we had discovered so much more and had given my aunt a visual piece of her family history.

A PROMISE MADE

That night I had almost forgotten about the strange cap badge. I only remembered it when my aunt rang us to check that we had reached home safely. While my wife continued the telephone conversation, I raced upstairs for my book and looked through the pictures trying to find the match to the blurred image on Albert's cap. After a few minutes I had found it: there was no doubt about it, the badge belonged to the Somerset Light Infantry. Why was Albert wearing this badge? Finding that Albert had been a member of the Worcestershire rather than his home Gloucestershire Regiment had been surprising enough – but what was this new link to Somerset?

The footnote on the page gave the full regimental name: 'Prince Albert's (Somerset Light Infantry)'. A cold shiver ran down my spine. Could this have been pure coincidence? Had Albert simply borrowed a spare hat, just to have his photograph taken? Or had wearing the cap badge belonging to a regiment bearing his own name have been somehow a message saying to those in the know, 'Look, *Albert* is in the Army now!' It seemed too far-fetched to believe. However, something more had stirred within me, and whatever the truth behind that cap badge I now began to realise just how much I had been able to piece together about Albert from so few sources, with seemingly so little effort.

I had read dozens of accounts of officers' and soldiers' experiences in the First World War, mostly written by the soldiers themselves, or their families, using surviving diaries and letters. Many contained photographs, some taken by the authors while serving on the Western Front. Albert had left no diary, no letters, not even a photograph. All I had started with was a name, and the fact that he was killed in the war. Exactly the same starting information was available to anyone from war memorials throughout the country. All these names were faceless. All were silent. Surely these thousands upon thousands had stories too? Stories that could be told, if somebody would just make the effort to piece together the fragments of what may still yet exist in records.

Since the start of my interest in this war I had wanted to trace the history of a soldier who had given his life for others. By so doing, I could demonstrate to people today exactly what had been sacrificed to give us the freedom we enjoy. I now had this opportunity. I thought again about Mary Turley, the mother who had died so soon after the end of the war. All she had was a letter telling her that her eldest son had been killed in action in France. His grave was not marked, so she would never have a chance to visit her son's final resting place – he would never be coming home to her.

I decided then and there to use all my knowledge of the war and the research skills I had acquired over many years to do my utmost to rebuild the story of this young man. In addition, in some way I could not yet see how, *I would bring Albert home* to the Forest of Dean, back to the family who had suffered so much through his loss.

THE QUEST BEGINS

In need of a starting place, I carefully collected all the copies of documents I had amassed so far. The most detailed accounts of the attack had naturally come from the Worcestershire regimental history. Yet I needed more, so once again I contacted the archivist of the Worcestershire Regiment, asking for other sources of information, in particular copies of the battalion diary, which he sent, together with relevant entries from the *Official History of the Great War* and a *History of the 25th Division*.

OFFICIAL HISTORY, VOL 2, 1916

. . . at 4.10 p.m. on the 24 August [1], after a special bombardment by the heavy artillery in which the trench mortars joined, the 3/Worcestershire and 1/Wiltshire (Br. General C.E. Heathcote's 7th Brigade, 25th Division) attacked and captured in fine style Hindenburg Trench, the chord of the Leipzig Salient. A smoke screen served to hide the movement from German observers in Thiepval, and the advance over the open followed the barrage so closely that the Germans, caught unprepared, were overcome with bomb and bayonet, after a brief resistance [2]. On the extreme left, however, beyond the road leading to Thiepval, the bombers of the Wiltshire were held up some distance from their objective. Consolidation proceeded under a German bombardment, which became intense just before 6 p.m. on 25 August, when the enemy trenches were observed to be crowded with men. A British barrage was called for and came down promptly with great effect, preventing the enemy counter-attack. At 7 p.m. on the 26th an unsuccessful attempt was made by 8/Loyal N. Lancashire (7th Brigade) to clear the western flank of Hindenburg Trench.

[1] – On 22 and 23 August began the relief of the [German] 16th, 24th and 40th Divisions by the Guard Reserve and II. Bavarian Corps., four divisions replacing three.

[2] – Two officers and 140 other ranks were captured. They belonged to the I and II Bns of the 93rd Reserve (4th Guard Division) which had just relieved the 28th Regiment. 'The time spent near Thiepval was one of the worst the division experienced,' says the divisional historian.

This account gave a useful synopsis of the attack. The pattern of events followed many such small attacks on the Somme, that is, artillery preparation, an infantry attack followed by a German counter-attack. It was evident that the attack was brief and quite successful. There had been fierce fighting during the capture of the Hindenburg Trench. The sickening possibility now existed that Albert had not been killed anonymously by a direct hit from a shell after going 'over the top' and crossing No Man's Land, but *personally* in the heat of hand-to-hand fighting. There was also the possibility that Albert had survived the original attack and had fallen to shell fire prior to the expected German counter-attack.

Fragments from France

The 25th Division in France and Flanders

On 23 August the Division extended its front southwards, the 3rd Worcesters, 7th Brigade relieving the left battalion of the 48th Division. Two days later the 7th Brigade delivered an attack with the Wilts and Worcesters on the main Hindenburg trench. During the day the heavy artillery carried out a bombardment of the line to be attacked as well as trenches and communication trenches in the neighbourhood in such a way as not to attract undue attention to the particular objective. At 4.10 p.m. on the 25th [sic] an intense artillery barrage was put down on the Hindenburg trench and a rolling barrage in front of it. Under cover of this the Wilts and Worcesters advanced and assaulted the position . . . The whole object was captured except a small portion on the left where strong opposition was met with in very broken ground and very little progress was made. At 4.12 p.m. two 'push mines' had been exploded and A Coy of the Wilts advanced down them to the enemy's trench. B and D Coys of the Wilts with the Worcesters on the right advanced across the open at 4.14 p.m. The attack was carried out in three waves, the number of men being employed being approximately one man per yard of objective. Our casualties were small and over 150 German prisoners were captured and a number killed. In addition a batch of about 100 German prisoners were caught and killed by their own artillery barrage. The success was largely due to the fact that the troops advanced well up to their own artillery barrage which was most effective in every way. They were materially assisted by a smoke barrage near Thiepval Wood which was designed to draw the enemy's fire in its direction and which undoubtedly succeeded in its object. Heavy bombing went on all day on the left sector and very little further progress was made. The whole of the Leipzig Salient was heavily shelled during the afternoon of the 25 August, causing many casualties. It had been intended to relieve the Wilts and L.N.Lancs. during the evening of the

25 August, as the former battalion had suffered heavy casualties during the preceding two days. The relief, however, could not take place as the Germans appeared to be massing for a counter-attack about 6.30 p.m., but if intended it was stopped by our artillery which at once put down a very effective barrage.

This account provided much more detail, confirming that the Germans had indeed heavily shelled their lost positions on the afternoon of the 25th both ahead of their counter-attack and seemingly earlier (on the 24th?) as they had killed 100 of their own troops who were 'prisoners'. Interestingly, this account was the only one that carried this last detail.

The Worcestershire regimental archive continued to provide valuable information, including the diary of an officer who had been present at the attack on 24 August. I began to realise that the attack made by the 3rd Worcestershire was inextricably linked with that of the 1st Wiltshire, and, by implication, that their regimental museum in Salisbury would now be another source of important information.

By now I believed I had acquired enough historical information to provide a factual account of what happened during Albert's service in France with the 3rd Worcestershire, culminating in the attack on the Thiepval Ridge on 24 August. But to bring these bare bones back to life, I needed eyewitness accounts. By the oddest coincidence this too would now come to light.

TWO

The Birthday Surprise

It was some time later, on a quiet evening, that I glanced along my bookshelves noting the many titles of books carefully amassed over the years on the First World War. One in particular, though in very poor condition and acquired some twenty years earlier, caught my eye: *The Battles of the Somme* by Philip Gibbs, a freelance war correspondent. It was a 1917 compilation of his 'heroic' despatches from the front, which had been syndicated in many of the newspapers of the day. I picked up the book and flicked through it, each paragraph full of exciting tales of 'derring-do' written in a style similar to today's tabloid newspapers. After the war, in his later work, Philip Gibbs had sought to make amends for these jingoistic pieces by exposing the realities of fighting (see Gibbs, P., *Now It Can Be Told*, Harper 1920).

I noted, by chance, that there was a piece on 25 August. As this date happened also to be my birthday, I gave it a little more attention. The piece was entitled 'The Attacks on Thiepval'. I scanned the first paragraph and saw Hindenburg Trench and Leipzig Salient. I didn't dare to believe that the attack on Thiepval described was actually the one in which the 3rd Worcestershire and 1st Wiltshire had taken part on 24 August; but as I read on I realised that indeed it was, albeit initially without specific mention of the units involved. By the time I had finished I realised that Gibbs had left behind one of the most detailed eyewitness descriptions of an attack on the Somme I had ever read. The quality of Gibbs' account made it very easy to imagine

what had happened that day to the 1st Wiltshire and 3rd Worcestershire.

Apart from the discovery of an excellent eyewitness account, important for my research into the 3rd Worcestershire, I also sadly realised that I had found the story of the last hours and minutes of Albert Turley's life. One of the figures Gibbs had seen going 'over the top' was Albert; perhaps one of those he had seen fall was Albert too.

Gibbs' *The Battles of the Somme* was published in 1917. Since readers might find difficulty in obtaining a copy, I quote the entire account verbatim, as a tribute both to the men who took part in the attack and also to Philip Gibbs himself. If some of his words were chosen to spare the feelings of those at home, they were few, and the poignancy of the article still shines through over eighty years later. The underlining is my own, and its importance will become clear later.

THE ATTACKS ON THIEPVAL
BY PHILIP GIBBS

August 25

1

The doom of Thiepval is near at hand. By a series of small, sharp attacks, in short rushes, after enormous shell-fire, our troops have forged their way across a tangled web of

Opposite: Trench Map of the Leipzig Salient (1)
Taken from map 57D SE4 edition 2B, dated 11/6/16. This map shows the British trenches facing the Leipzig Salient trench system. The positions are those of the opening of the Somme offensive on 1 July 1916. Note the position of the quarry, immediately to the south of the large 'R'. This was the site of the Leipzig Redoubt, the key to the Leipzig Salient defences. On this map the British trenches are named (usually with a Scottish reference), indicating the nationality of the first British troops to take over these positions from the French. The position of the Nab is also clearly defined, the vantage point of Philip Gibbs' eyewitness account of the attack of the 3rd Worcestershire on Hindenburg Trench.

trenches and redoubts until now they are just below the southern end of the village. They have bitten off the nose of the Leipzig Salient, and yesterday I saw them take the Hindenburg Trench and its strong point, which is almost the last of the defensive works barring our way to the south entrance of the village fortress.

On the west our trenches have been dug for some time through Thiepval Wood, within four hundred yards of this place, and on the east they have been pushed forwards to the left of Mouquet Farm; so that we have thrown a lasso, as it were, around the stronghold on the hill, from which its garrison has only one way of escape – by way of the Crucifix, northwards, where our guns will get them. That garrison is a death trap. The German soldiers must be praying for the end to come.

As I stood watching the place yesterday, from a trench only a few hundred yards away, it seemed to me astounding and terrible that men should still be living there. I could see nothing of the village for there is next to nothing left of it – nothing at all but heaps of rubbish which were once the roofs and walls of houses. But on the skyline at the top of a ridge which slopes up from the Leipzig Salient there still stand a hundred trees or so, which are all that is left of Thiepval. They stood black and gaunt against the blue sky, without a leaf on their broken branches, and all charred. The brown hummocks of the German trench-lines encircled them, with narrow strips of grass, vividly green, between these earthworks and below, falling away to our own lines, a turmoil of upheaved soil where a maze of trenches had been made shapeless by incessant shell-fire.

All through the afternoon, as all through the morning, and the mornings and afternoons of many yesterdays, our guns were firing in a steady, leisurely way, one shell every minute or two, at the ground marked out by the black tree stumps. They were mostly the shells of our 'heavies' firing from long range, so that for several seconds one could hear the long voyage of each shell, listen to the last fierce rush

20

of it over our heads, and then see, before the roar of the explosion, a vast volume of smoke and earth vomit up from the place between the trees where the enemy's trenches lay.

A friend of mine, sitting on some sandbags with his steel helmet just above the tops of some small thistles which gave friendly cover in our foreground above the parapet, said, 'Beautiful!' every time there was a specially big cloud burst. He is such a hater of war that his soul follows each shell of ours with a kind of exultation so that it should help to end it quickly. But I kept thinking of those fellows there, under that shell-fire.

It was only previous knowledge, explorations in German dug-outs, talks with men who have come living out of such bombardments, that made me still believe that there were men alive in Thiepval, and that before we take the place they may fight desperately and keep machine-guns going to the last. There was not a human soul to be seen, and the earth was being flung up in masses; but underground a garrison of German soldiers was sitting in deep cellars, trying to turn deaf ears to the crashes above them, trying to hide the terror in their souls, a terror invading all their courage icily, and looking into the little mirrors of long periscopes which showed them the vision of things above-ground, and the stillness of the British trenches, from which at any minute there might come waves of men on a new attack.

2

With a few others in the trench where I stood I knew that our men were to make another bound yesterday afternoon, though not the exact time of it. For nearly two hours I watched the bombardment, steady and continuous, but not an intense fire from all available batteries, and every few minutes I looked at my wrist-watch and wondered, 'Will it begin now?' Down below me was the hummocky track of our front-line trenches, in which the attacking parties had assembled. Only now and again could I see any movement there.

In our own trench some signallers were carrying down a new wire, whistling as they worked. A forward observing officer was watching the shell-bursts through a telescope resting on the parapet and giving messages to a telephone operator who sat hunched at the bottom of the trench with his instrument. A couple of young officers came along jauntily, swearing because 'these silly asses' – whoever they might be – 'never tell you where they are'. An Artillery officer came along for a chat, and remarked that it was a fine day for a football match.

3

It was a day when the beauty of France is like a song in one's heart, a day of fleecy clouds in the blue sky, of golden sunlight flooding broad fields behind the battle-lines, where the wheat-sheaves are stacked in neat lines by old men and women, who do their sons' work, and of deep, cool shadows under the wavy foliage of the woodlands.

Behind us was a ruined village, and German shells were falling into the corner of a wood not far away on our left, but the panorama of the French countryside beyond the edge of the battlefield was one of peace. Above our heads some British aeroplanes came flying, and the hum of their engines was like big bees humming. They flew straight over the German lines, and presently the sky about them was dotted with white puffs of shrapnel, and above the noise of the guns there was the high 'ping!' of the German 'Archies' as each shell reached up to those soaring wings, but failed to bring them down.

Another officer came along the trench and said, 'Good afternoon. The show begins in ten minutes.'

The 'show' is the name that soldiers give to a battle.

By my watch it was longer than ten minutes before the 'show' began. The leisurely bombardment continued in the same way. Now and again a German 'crump' replied, like an elaborate German guttural. Then suddenly, as though at the tap of a baton, a great orchestra of death crashed out. It is absurd to describe it. No words have been made for a modern bombardment of this intensity. One can only give a feeble, inaccurate notion of what one big shell sounds like.

When hundreds of heavy guns are firing upon one small line of ground and shells of the greatest size are rushing through the sky in flocks, and bursting in masses, all description is futile. I can only say that the whole sky was resonant with waves of noise that were long-drawn, like the deep notes of violins, gigantic and terrible in their power of sound, and that each vibration ended at last in a thunderous crash. Or again it seemed as though the stars had fallen out of the sky and were rushing down to Thiepval.

The violence of this bombardment was as frightful as anything I have seen in this war in the way of destructive gun-power. The shells tore up the German trenches and built up a great wall of smoke along the crest of the ridge, and smashed through the trees of Thiepval, until for minutes together that place was only to be known by tall pillars of black, and white, and brown smoke, which swayed about as though in a great wind, and toppled down upon each other, and rose again.

4

A voice at my elbow, speaking breathlessly, said: 'Look! They're away. . . . Oh, splendid fellows!'

Out of our front-line trenches scrambled long lines of men. They stood for a moment on the top of the parapet, waited for a second or two until all the men had got up into their alignment, and then started forward, steadily and in wonderful order. Some of the officers turned round, as though to see that all their men were there. I saw one of them raise his stick and point towards the ridge. Then he ran ahead of his men. They were on low ground – lowest on the right, in front of the parapet where I stood, but sloping up a little on the left by the Leipzig Redoubt.

<u>Beyond them the ground rose steadily to the ridge on which Thiepval stands</u>. Our men had a big climb to make, and a long way to go over open country, for four or five hundred yards is the very devil of a way to go when it is swept with shell-fire.

The enemy was not long in flinging a barrage in the way of our men. A rocket went up from his lines as a signal to his guns, and perhaps half a minute after our men had sprung over the parapet his shells began to fall. But they were too late to do any damage there. Our men were out and away. Some message seemed to reach the enemy and tell him this. He raised his barrage on to ground nearer his own lines, and his heavy 'crumps' fell rapidly, bursting all over No Man's Land. Now and again they seemed to fall into the middle of a bunch of our men, in a frightful way to see, but when the smoke cleared the group was still going forward. On the right of the line one great shell burst with an enormous crash, and this time there was no doubt that it had caught some of our men. I saw them fall in a heap. . . . Perhaps they had flung themselves down to avoid the shell splinters. Perhaps not one of them had been touched. It is extraordinary how men can avoid death like that.

Nothing checked the advance of the long lines of figures going through the smoke; not all the German barrage, which was now very fierce. The men had to cross one of those narrow strips of grass-land between the earthworks before they came to the first line of German trenches, and they showed up black and distinct against the green belt whenever the smoke of the shells bursting above them drifted away.

They were not in close formation. They went forward after the first few moments of advance, in small parties, widely scattered, but keeping the same direction. Sometimes the parties themselves broke up and scattered into individual figures, jumping over shell-craters, running first to left or right as the shriek of an enemy shell warned them of approaching death. I saw then how easy it is to lose all sense of direction in an attack like this, and the reason why many men sometimes go so hopelessly astray. But yesterday it was quite marvellous how quickly the men recovered their line when they had drifted away in the blinding smoke, and how the groups kept in touch with each other, and how separate figures running to catch up succeeded in joining the groups.

5

We watched the single figures, following the fortune of each man across the fire-swept slope, hoping with all our souls that he would get through and on. Then he would pick himself up when he fell face forward.

For a little while the men were swallowed up in smoke. I could see nothing of them, and I had a horrible feeling this time none of us would ever see them again. For they had walked straight into the infernal fires, and all behind them and all in front the shells were bursting and flinging up the earth and raising enormous, fantastic clouds.

It seemed an hour before I saw them again. I supposed it was only five or six minutes. The wind drifted the smoke away from the Thiepval Ridge, and there, clear and distinct to the naked eye, were the lines of our men swarming up. Some of them were already on the highest ground, standing, single figures, black against the sky. They stood there a second or two, then jumped down and disappeared. They were in the German trenches, close to Thiepval.

'Magnificent!' said a French officer who was standing close to me. 'By God, your men are fine!'

They were wonderful. The German barrages did not stop them. They went through and on as though proof against shells. Some men did not go on, and fell on the side of the slope, but it seemed to me there were not many of them.

In the centre of the German trenches was a strong point or redoubt, with machine-guns. It was one of those deadly places that have often checked one of our attacks, and cost many brave lives. But I could see that our men were all round it. One single figure was an heroic silhouette against the blue of the sky. He was bombing the redoubt, and as he flung his bombs the attitude of the man was full of grace like a Greek disc-thrower. A German shell burst close to him and he was engulfed in its upheaval, but whether he was killed or not, I could not tell. I did not see him again.

6

Up the slope went the other men, following the first wave, and single fellows hurrying after them. In a little while they had all disappeared. They were in the enemy's trenches, beyond all doubt.

New sounds of an explosive kind came through all the fury of gun-fire, which had slackened in intensity, but was still slashing the air. It was a kind of hard knocking in separate strokes, and I knew it was bomb-fire. Our men were at work in and around the German dug-outs, and there were Germans there who were not surrendering without a fight.

One fight took place on top of the parapet. A man came up and stood on the sky-line – whether an English soldier or a German it was impossible to see. I think a German, for a second after another man came up as though chasing him, and the first man turned upon him. They both had revolvers and fired, and disappeared. Other men were running along the parapets of the German trenches. They were ours, and they were flinging bombs as they ran. Then a curtain of smoke was wafted up in front of them again, and they were hidden.

From our own trenches another wave of men appeared. I think it wanted more courage of them even than of the first line of assaulting troops to go over that open ground. They had to face the German barrage and to pass over a way where many of their comrades were lying. But they went on steadily and rapidly, just as the others had gone, splitting up into groups, rushing in short rushes, disappearing in the smoke of shell-bursts, falling into shell-craters, scrambling up, and on again . . .

Another wave came still later, making their way to that ridge, where their comrades were fighting in the enemy's trenches. They too disappeared into those ditches.

Only in the ground near to me could I see any sign of life now. Here some of our wounded were walking back, and the stretcher-bearers were at work. I watched a little procession coming very slowly to our trenches with their stretchers lifted high. It was a perilous way of escape for wounded when the enemy was flinging shells all over the ground and there was no safety zone. Somewhere on our right a shell had struck a bomb-store or ammunition dump and a volume of smoke, reddish-brown, rose and spread into the shape of a gigantic query mark. Other fires were burning in what had been No Man's Land, and out of an explosion in the enemy's trenches there was flung up a black vomit in which were human beings, or fragments of them. <u>Over the ridge by Thiepval the enemy's barrage was continuous on the far side of the slope between our trenches on the west and the ground just gained</u>, and the top of the smoke-clouds drifted above the sky-line as though from a row of factory chimneys.

7

Suddenly out of all this curtain of smoke came a crowd of figures, leaping and running. They were Germans trying to get to our trenches, not in a counter-attack, but to give themselves up as prisoners, and to get some cover from their own shell-fire. Terror was in their attitudes, in their wild stampede and desperate leaps over the broken ground where the shells of their own guns were bursting. One great German 'crump' crashed close to them, and I think it must have killed some of them.

Then for more than an hour as I watched, other figures came back from the high ground towards our old front line, sometimes in groups of two or three, sometimes alone. They were our lightly wounded men, with here and there a German.

It was with a sense of horrible fascination that I watched

the adventures of these men, separately. One of them would jump down from the sky-line, and come at a quick run down the slope. Then he would suddenly stop and stand in an indecisive way as though wondering what route to take to avoid the clusters of shell-bursts spurting up below him. He would decide sometimes on a circuitous route, and start running again in a zigzag way, altering his direction sharply when a shell crashed close to him.

I could see that he was out of breath. He would halt and stand as though listening to the tumult about him, then come on very slowly. I wanted to call out to him, to shout, 'This way, old man! . . . Quick!' But no voice would have carried through that world in uproar. Then perhaps he would stumble, and fall, and lie as though dead. But presently I would see him crawl on his hands and knees, stand up and run again. He would reach our line of trenches and jump down, or fling himself down. Some cover at last, thank God! So it happened with man after man and each journey was the adventure of a man trying to dodge death. It was horrible to see.

High above the Thiepval Ridge there were perpendicular streaks of white smoke and light, strangely spectral, like tall thin ghosts wrapped in white shrouds and illumined in a ghastly way. I think they were the long tails of rockets fired as signals to the guns. The German black shrapnel and their green 'universal' shell was hanging in big puffs above the denser pall below, and there was the glint and flash of bursting shells stabbing through the wall of smoke.

Our aeroplanes were right over Thiepval all through the battle, circling round in wide steady flights, careless of the German anti-aircraft guns, which were firing continuously. Two hostile planes came out and our men closed about them, and flew to attack, but after a while the Germans fled back in retreat. The only observation the enemy had was from two kite balloons, poised well forward, but often lost and blinded in all the clouds.

So I watched, and knew, because our men did not come back from those trenches on the Thiepval ridge, that they had been successful. It was only the prisoners and the lightly wounded that came back. The assaulting parties were holding the ground they had captured in spite of all the shell-fire that crashed over them. They had tightened the iron net around Thiepval and had drawn it closer.

So at last I went away from the battlefield, back to the quiet harvest-fields flooded with the golden glow of the sinking sun, luckier than the men who had to stay, and ashamed of my luck. The enemy was flinging shells at long range. The harvest-fields were not quite so safe as they looked.

There were ugly corners to pass, shell-trap corners, where it is not wise to linger to light a cigarette. But hell was behind me, up there at Thiepval, where the storm of shell-fire still raged, and where, below-ground, the German garrison awaits its inevitable fate.

Reading the Gibbs account, it was clear that he had deliberately positioned himself to watch this particular event. He had known that an attack was to take place, but he did not know the exact timing and had waited the entire afternoon for it (hence his leisurely account of an afternoon's desultory shelling beforehand). He was not to be disappointed and his account of the 3rd Worcestershire and 1st Wiltshire going over the top and taking the Hindenburg Trench is admirably described. Gibbs' viewpoint, however, was limited, as he couldn't really begin to describe the actual taking of the trench, the consolidation and the wait for the inevitable German counter-attack. But as he walked back down the line, he had been clearly moved by what he had seen. Most of Gibbs' other despatches were compiled from conversations with the participants in the action: this attack he had witnessed for himself. What he couldn't have known at the time of writing was just how successful the attack had been. In fact, this action (particularly the subsequent repulse of the German counter-attack) was mentioned in an official communiqué by General Haig, the commander-in-chief of the British Expeditionary Force, specifically naming both the Worcestershire and Wiltshire regiments.

After Haig's communiqué had been released, Gibbs, as a witness to the attack, now found himself in a unique position to write further despatches, which would be readily printed by the newspapers in Britain, eager for more news. He produced two further correspondences regarding this attack on 26 and 28 August.

August 26

8

Following the official communiqué, I can now say that the troops whom I saw advancing so splendidly and steadily across a great stretch of No Man's Land to the higher ground round Thiepval were men of Wiltshire and Worcestershire. They deserve the honour that has been given them by Sir Douglas Haig in his report, because after their great assault they had to sustain last night a strong attack by Prussian Guardsmen, following a long and fierce bombardment. The courage of these English lads – among them being boys who once followed the plough and worked in the orchards of those quiet old counties – did not fail against the finest troops of the Kaiser's armies, and that phrase in the official communiqué which records their achievement is a fine memorial:

The success of our defences is largely due to the steadiness and determined gallantry of Wiltshire and Worcestershire men, who, in spite of being subjected to a very heavy bombardment, steadily maintained their positions, and repulsed the determined assault of the enemy.

As his despatch of 25 August had effectively described all that he had personally witnessed on the 24th, Gibbs now required fresh information. This would come from discussions with the colonel and officers of the units involved. [Later research indicated that these discussions probably took place with the 1st Wiltshire when they had come out of the line on 26 August and were billeted in Hedauville.]

The following despatch would therefore seem to be based on the actions of the 1st Wiltshire in the Leipzig Salient up to and including the main attack on 24 August. In fact, Gibbs didn't actually see very much of the 1st Wiltshire actions himself on the 24th and really only witnessed the actions of the 3rd Worcestershire. However, this point will be explained further below.

August 28

9

I have already described my own visual impression of the great assault made south of Thiepval by men of Wiltshire and Worcestershire, which I watched from a neighbouring trench. But there are still things to be told about this memorable achievement – as fine in its way as anything our men have done. The name of Wiltshire will always be specially remembered on the ground of the Leipzig Salient, which barred the southern way to Thiepval, for they were troops of this county who, as far back as July 8, captured the butt-end of that strong-hold, and, working with other county troops on their right, made the next advance, on August 22, which preceded the greater attack two days later.

That affair was extraordinarily fine and brief and successful. Twelve minutes after the attacking time, the Wilts men had gone across the one hundred yards of No Man's Land, captured the enemy's nearest line of trenches, and sent down their first batch of twenty prisoners.

The Wiltshires had only three casualties in getting across the open ground, though afterwards suffered more under the enemy's shell-fire. Most of the German dug-outs were blown in, but there was one big subterranean chamber which was not badly damaged, and wanted only a little work to make it a place of comfort for the new-comers. As their colonel [Lt Col S.S. Ogilvie] said to me today: 'It always gives us great pleasure to take lodgings in these German apartments.'

The attack on the Hindenburg Trench which I saw on

August 24 was complicated because the Wiltshires had to advance partly across the open – 300 yards of No Man's Land, which is no joke – and partly, on their left, through a network of trenches climbing the high ground from the Leipzig Salient to Thiepval.

It was necessary therefore to organise the attack so that those advancing over the open should not arrive at the Hindenburg Trench sooner than those worrying their way up through the broken earthworks, not at all an easy proposition.

Also before the Hindenburg line [sic] could be seized securely it would be essential to 'kill' a German strong point at a junction made in the Hindenburg Trench by a communication-way running up from the Leipzig Salient.

The penalty of not doing so would be certain death to many of our men by an enfilade fire of machine-guns. These are little details that worry the souls of commanding officers before they get the men over the parapet with thousands of bombs and the supplies of picks, shovels, sandbags, Lewis-gun 'drums', Very lights, and other material of war.

10

On the day before [23rd] the last attack on the southern way into Thiepval the enemy, who suspected bad things coming, tried to thwart our plan by hurling a terrific storm of shell-fire all over the Leipzig Salient.

He seems to have brought up new guns for the purpose, and his heavy five-point-nines 'crumped' the ground in all directions. But all this did not stop the Wiltshires and the Worcesters, who went on with their little scheme.

On Thursday afternoon last everything went like clockwork from the moment our artillery opened with the intense bombardment described by me in a former despatch.

The Worcesters attacked on the right, the Wiltshires on the left. Over the parapet they halted a moment, and then went forward in a steady and ordered way. I could not see

<u>the men working up through the trenches on the left until they sprang up to the crest of the ridge, but only those who went across the open</u>. The last eighty yards was covered in the quickest time, and soon after our shell-fire lifted off the German trench the Wiltshires and Worcesters were in among the enemy.

But not close together. There was a gap of fifty yards between the two parties, and in order to get in touch with each other they bombed left and right. It was at this moment a company officer[1] distinguished himself by great gallantry.

There were Prussian Guards in the trench, and they fought fiercely, using the gap as a bombing centre. Unless routed out this group of men might have spoiled the attack. The officer saw the situation in a flash, and was quick to get a rifle to his shoulder. He was a dead shot, and shot, one after another, five men who were trying to blow him to bits with their hand-grenades.

At the same time a sergeant[2] scrambled up into the open, and running along outside the trench flung his bombs at the enemy below, 'to rattle them', according to the description of his commanding officer. Another young soldier fired his Lewis-gun over the parapet and fired down into the trenches, so that the enemy had to keep quiet until our men were all around them.

The strong point by the Koenigstrasse had been rushed, and the Hindenburg Trench was ours.

11

Sharp and fierce fighting had carried the trenches on the left and captured a strong dug-out belonging to the German company commanders. Here also the Prussian Guards fought with great courage, firing up from their dug-outs and only surrendering under the menace of immediate death. One sergeant[3] here on the left walked about in the open with a cool courage and shot twelve Germans who were sniping from shell-holes. The ground was already strewn with their dead, killed by our bombardment, and over this graveyard of unburied men there was bayonet fighting and bombing until all the Prussians who remained alive became the prisoners of the Wiltshires.

There were several officers among them wearing the Iron Cross, and all the officers and men were tall fellows with their brand-new equipment, which showed that they had just come into the trenches.

Two captured machine-guns were turned against the enemy's line, with their own ammunition ready for use, and both the Wiltshires and Worcesters settled down in the new line, badly smashed as usual by our shell-fire, but with a lot of useful dug-outs still intact, to hold on under the inevitable retaliation of the enemy's guns.

All through the night there was a steady bombardment, but nothing of extraordinary ferocity. It was the usual night's 'strafe' in the neighbourhood of Thiepval, which is not really a nice place.

On the following day – last Friday [25th] – the hostile shell-fire increased. Five-point-nines were joined by eight-inchers, and, as one of the officers described it, 'every durned thing'. It quickened and strengthened in intensity until towards evening it was a hurricane bombardment meaning one obvious thing – a counter-attack. Our men were down in the old German dug-outs, grateful to their enemy for digging so deep and well, but it became most necessary to warn our 'heavies' that the Prussians were gathering for a smashing assault.

Runners were sent out to get back through the barrage if they had the luck, and several of these brave men tried and several failed, dying on the way. But one[4] had more than human luck. Owing to the appalling character of the ground, 'pitted and ploughed as though by a gigantic harrow' – it is his officer's phrase – the man lost his sense of direction, staggered and stumbled on through the smoke and over the shell-craters, and then – amazed – found himself looking over a parapet into a trench full of Germans with fixed bayonets. They were crowded there, those tall Prussians, awaiting the moment to launch their counter-attack.

The runner turned back. Before him the ground was a series of volcanoes, tossed up by German shells and British shells. He knew that he had to pass through our barrage and the enemy's barrage. The chances against him were tremendous. In his own opinion he had no more chance than a 'snowflake in hell'. But he ran back, dodging this death, and – came through untouched!

The 'heavies' did at last get the message and were quick to answer it. 'In three shakes,' said an officer of the Wiltshires, 'they were smashing the German lines to glory.'

Those tall Prussians crowding there were caught by this storm. Their trench became a ditchful of mangled bodies. Only a thin wave of men came out into open country, and of these not many went back.

The Prussian counter-attack was killed. The Worcesters and the Wiltshires held their ground around Thiepval, and their losses were paid for heavily by German blood.

This last despatch effectively tidied things up for Philip Gibbs, who then went to the south-east to describe the attacks on Delville Wood. He later returned to describe the taking of the remains of Thiepval at the end of September, thus 'missing' further attacks on the Thiepval Ridge.

Reading these detailed accounts fuelled my imagination. I was already planning a visit to the Somme battlefields, and to be able to stand on the spot where Gibbs had witnessed the attack of the 3rd Worcestershire, and to read his account again with reference to the landscape before me, would become a highlight of the trip.

As Gibbs had given only guarded references as to where he was actually standing when he witnessed the attack (possibly for security reasons), I highlighted all specific references to his location and to what he could actually see in geographical terms: these are the underlined parts of the texts above.

I also took both a copy of a contemporary trench map and a

modern French IGN 'Series Bleu' map (from which map coordinates are given) and studied Gibbs' account in more detail.

The Leipzig Salient covers the whole hillside immediately to the west of the village of Authuille up Thiepval Ridge northwards, named on modern maps as the fields 'les Couturelles' (477E, 5543.7N) and 'les Pommiers' (477.7E, 5543.8N). The easiest point of reference between the two maps was the site of the Leipzig Redoubt that partly occupied the site of an old quarry: such a feature would have been difficult to destroy totally, and its remains today are located at (477.2E, 5544.6N).

The following are my deductions from Gibbs' account:

a) On the west our trenches have been dug for some time through Thiepval Wood, within four hundred yards of this place, and on the east they have been pushed forwards to the left of Mouquet Farm.

Thiepval Wood was (and still is) known to the French as the Bois d'Authuille. This wood is away on the west, however, and much of the Leipzig Salient is well *over* 400 yards away. Some 400 yards to the *south* of the Leipzig Salient is the Bois de la Haie (confusingly also called Authuille Wood on British trench maps), which contained well-established British trenches that formed the original front line on 1 July 1916 and later provided the communication trenches up to the captured portions of the Leipzig Salient during the course of the Somme battle. Gibbs' references to the location Mouquet Farm are correct.

b) As I stood watching the place yesterday, from a trench only a few hundred yards away.

Gibbs was a few hundred yards away from the scene of the attack, watching from a British trench in the rear. This would probably mean from some point on the old British front line of 1 July.

c) But on the skyline at the top of a ridge which slopes up from the Leipzig Salient there still stand a hundred trees or so, which are all that is left of Thiepval.

The northern limit of Gibbs' view was the top of the Thiepval Ridge where a group of trees stood. Standing at any point in the

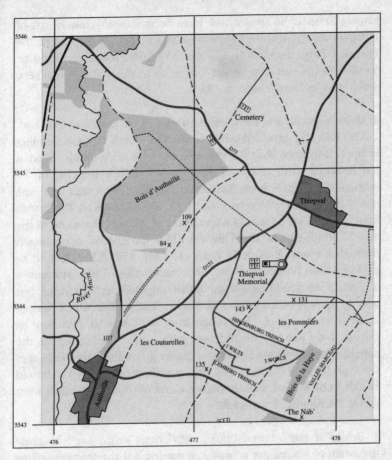

'Modern' Trench Map of the Leipzig Salient

A contemporary map of the area together with the French Cartesian co-ordinates referred to in the narrative. It is interesting to note how much of the devastated Somme battlefield has been rebuilt since its pre-war layout. Comparison with the previous map of the 1916 Leipzig Salient confirms this. One new feature, of course, is the Thiepval Memorial to the Missing. An old road to Authuille still passes through, although it now ends abruptly at the edge of the Memorial Park. In 1916 the road continued on from here, now it is just a farm track passing through 'points 143 and 135'. Also added to this map are the present locations of Lemberg and Hindenburg Trenches, although no outward sign remains of them.

Leipzig Salient, he would not have been able to view much of Thiepval village, since it lies beyond 'point 143', i.e. the top of the Thiepval Ridge located at 477.3E, 5544.0N. Today, it would be possible to see even less of the village, as modern Thiepval is very much smaller than it was in 1916.

d) Down below me was the hummocky track of our front-line trenches.

This reference provided Gibbs' position exactly. If he were standing in the British front line of 1916 with the edge of Authuille Wood, a few hundred yards away, all the British front-line trenches of 24 August would have been further *up* the hill. There was only one (safe!) place from where he could have looked *down* on the British front line and yet be within a few hundred yards of the scene of the attack. South-east of the Thiepval Ridge the ground slopes down through a copse, Bois de la Haye (477.8E, 5543.5N) – not to be confused with Bois de la Haie – to a small valley (Vallée Marceau – 477.9E, 5543.5N) known to the British originally as 'Nab Valley' but later to become better known as 'Blighty Valley'. This was a piece of 'dead ground', out of observation from the Germans, and used as brigade headquarters for the occupying units. Continuing up the opposite slope southwards to some higher ground was the position of the Nab itself (478.0E, 5543.3N), a little promontory in the old British front line, of slightly higher elevation than the British front line of 24 August. A perfect fit!

e) Behind us was a ruined village, and German shells were falling into the corner of a wood not far away on our left, but the panorama of the French countryside beyond the edge of the battlefield was one of peace.

From the Nab, the village behind would have been Ovillers-la-Boisselle and the wood would have been Authuille Wood. Gibbs would also have been able to look miles to the south-west, down Nab/Blighty Valley, past Aveluy and Albert to the peaceful lands beyond.

f) They were on low ground – lowest on the right, in front of the parapet where I stood, but sloping up a little on the left by the Leipzig Redoubt. Beyond them the ground rose steadily to the ridge on which Thiepval stands.

Standing at the Nab, Gibbs would have been directly behind the 3rd Worcestershire, attacking from the lower ground on his right, rising across his front to a position where the line dog-legged and continued to rise directly on his line of sight towards the Leipzig Redoubt. At this point, the 1st Wiltshire joined the 3rd Worcestershire. Gibbs had a perfect view of the 3rd Worcestershire, but could see little of the 1st Wiltshire; his limit of vision on the left would be the skyline containing the Leipzig Redoubt itself. Everywhere he looked the troops would be attacking across the open ground up the Thiepval Ridge.

g) Over the ridge by Thiepval the enemy's barrage was continuous on the far side of the slope between our trenches on the west and the ground just gained.

This part of the line would have been out of Gibbs' sight, containing the portion of the 1st Wiltshire attack he could not see from the Nab.

h) I could not see the men working up through the trenches on the left until they sprang up to the crest of the ridge, but only those who went across the open.

Here Gibbs admits he could not effectively see the actions of the 1st Wiltshire on the left. Only when they had cleared the maze of trenches that were left of the Leipzig Redoubt and carried on up the slope of the Thiepval Ridge would they have crossed his skyline and come into Gibbs' view from the Nab.

I had proved, to my own satisfaction, that the only place Philip Gibbs could have observed the attack on 24 August was the Nab, since this location was the only one that fitted all the stated facts (accepting some 'understandable' confusion about names of woods). The location made sense: it was close to the organisational centres of the units involved (Nab/Blighty Valley), it was out of harm's way (for a group of war correspondents – note the mention of a French officer present and a 'friend', quite possibly J. Irvine, a fellow journalist or even Ernest Brooks, the official photographer), and it would have given a good vantage point for at least part of the attack.

More importantly, for me, Gibbs' first despatch of 25 August related almost exclusively to the role of the 3rd Worcestershire in the attack of the 24th, of whom one would have been Albert Turley in his last action. I also knew that on my next visit to the Somme I could 'watch' the attack in my mind's eye, standing in the exact place Philip Gibbs had done, while reading his detailed account of that fateful day.

A birthday surprise indeed!

NOTES (additional to Gibbs' account)
From the 1st Wiltshire Diary – Recommendations for Awards:

[1] Possibly C.S.M. James – 'at the Leipzig Salient on the 24 August, this warrant officer displayed the utmost gallantry and qualities of leadership on an attack on the enemy's trench. He showed the finest example to the men under his command and by his initiative was largely instrumental in the consolidation of the position gained until he was severely wounded.' (Recommended for MM)

[2] Possibly Sergeant A.W. Loveday – 'at the Leipzig Salient on the 24 August. This NCO in an attack on the enemy trench displayed the greatest gallantry. On reaching the enemy trench he was mainly instrumental in gaining touch with the battalion on the right [3rd Worcestershire]. Despite the strenuous resistance offered by a party of the enemy [unreadable] of a bombing attack and his own personal bravery in jumping on to the parapet with a small party of men and attacking the enemy he compelled them to surrender. Throughout the attack showing great gallantry.' (Recommended for DCM)

[3] Only one sergeant was recommended for an award from the 1st Wiltshire for 24 August, citation as in.[2]

[4] Three runners, Ptes M.S. Clark, Stanley Miles and Harry Hancock were recommended for the DCM:

Clark: 'This man also showed great coolness, and carried messages from time to time during the heavy bombardment on the 24 August 1916, he was sent with a message and has not been seen since.' [He must have subsequently turned up, as he is not listed among the 1st Wiltshire killed on 24–6 August 1916.]

The Birthday Surprise

Miles and Hancock: 'Both men carried messages quickly during a very heavy bombardment on the night of the 25 August 1916, when all telephone wire were out [sic]. Both men were badly shaken with shell [sic] but showed great coolness and carried on with work until relieved.'

THREE

Reconstructing the Past

In this chapter I aim to reconstruct a historical diary of the events that Albert would have witnessed and been a part of. Albert himself left no diary of his service experiences with the 3rd Worcestershire. Neither are there any surviving letters from him, even to his family. The majority of books written about soldiers' experiences in the First World War derive from the survival of at least one of these documentary sources. Even the memories and stories of veterans became clearer when they still had the diaries they once kept and letters sent to loved ones at home. It would be difficult for me to use the words a young private soldier would have used in 1916, or to fictionalise a diary for the sake of realism. I am now much older than Albert was when he was killed in action; I have virtually forgotten what it was like to be only twenty, with experiences limited to those few short years of manhood. Moreover, my background would have had more in common with the officers in Albert's battalion than with the private soldier. Over the years I have studied this period the majority of accounts I have read have been written by officers, with a similar upbringing to mine. Hence I now feel myself hopelessly conditioned, and I see the events of the war through the eyes of the officer 'class'. The account that follows would be largely unrecognisable to Albert and his comrades in the ranks. In my defence, I believe the historical events Albert lived through are sufficiently interesting to stand in their own right without being falsely fictionalised. There are plenty of good fictional accounts of this war already.

This historical diary, constructed from many fragments, evolved as my own experience in using facts from original documents grew. In addition, I have now been able to add 'living-history' experiences from serving today as a 'Tommy' with the Great War Society. Although I have never suffered the fear of the unknown, the terror of actual fighting or faced death, I know what it is like to wear and live with Albert's uniform and equipment and to undergo many aspects of Albert's life away from the fighting zone. I know the comradeship of sharing an existence with similar 'Tommies', at times this being inseparable from that known by the original soldiers of 1914–18 themselves – in short, I have come to know Albert Turley much better and appreciate some of what he experienced.

At times, as I worked out the movements of various units and the interrelated timings of events, I became very close to understanding what the Battle of the Somme must have been like, sometimes too close: as I reconstructed the days leading up to Albert's death, I began to 'see' these events quite clearly in my mind, and had to stop writing many times, the tragedy and sadness being simply too great. Some of this personal perspective has been left in place.

Notes on the sources:
(1)   (3WD) 3rd Worcestershire Battalion Diary

(1WD) 1st Wiltshire Battalion Diary

(AJ 'date') The unpublished diary of Brigade Major Arthur E.C. Johnston. During July/August 1916 he was Brigade Major for the 7th Brigade, which incorporated both the 3rd Worcestershire and 1st Wiltshire. He had a soft spot for the 3rd Worcestershire, as this was the battalion into which he had been first commissioned in 1903.He would be wounded in 1918, in his convalescence he would 'tidy' his diary. He would return to command the battalion in the 1920s and continue his long association with the Worcestershire Regiment until the outbreak of the 1939–45 war.

(STK) *The Worcestershire Regiment in the Great War*, by Capt H.M. Fitz Stacke

(GG) *The Battle of the Somme*, by Gerald Gliddon (a topographical, meteorological and general history of the battle).

(WG) Report on actions 24/25 August, Lt-Col W. Gibbs, commanding 3rd Worcestershire. An original account, repeated in the 3rd Worcestershire Battalion Diary, but containing more details.

(SO) Report on actions 24/25 August, Capt. S.S. Ogilvie, acting commander 1st Wiltshire. Another original account containing much detail, oddly confused.

(2) Place-name spellings have been standardised for the sake of clarity; other spelling idiosyncrasies and grammatical constructions have been retained to preserve the contemporary and individual nature of the sources.

(3) Discrepancies relating to timings of events have on some occasions been resolved; in other cases this was not possible, and so a 'majority decision' was taken, although the alternative(s) are provided in each instance.

THE HISTORICAL CONTEXT

The majority of the historical diary that follows is written from an officer's perspective, for the simple reason that most of the above sources were originally written by officers. In order to obtain a better understanding of many details of the diary, it is first necessary to outline some aspects of everyday life for officers and soldiers in the war. In addition, it is necessary to understand some background history and details of British Army organisation in 1916.

Surviving accounts written by officers and other ranks often vary considerably, even when describing the same events and experiences. This was not only because of their differing social and educational backgrounds, and hence writing styles, but also because each lived their experiences from quite different standpoints. In the early twentieth century people not only recognised 'class' differences, they also accepted them and the role each 'class' was expected to play in all aspects of life, including warfare, believing that neither side would (or could) effectively cross this 'class' divide.

The private soldier may have known only a handful of men very well (probably those of his section, a maximum of ten men), the rest of his platoon (approximately thirty to forty men) reasonably well. Beyond this, at the company level (approximately 250 men) and higher, he may have only known those who could do him a favour, and those it was best to avoid. In the line, he and his section, led by a corporal or sergeant, would have been responsible for holding a specific bay in a trench (front, support and reserve trenches in parallel, linked by a non-manned, perpendicular communication trench). This would have involved the daily routine of sentry duty, the sharing out and consumption of monotonous rations, keeping the place as clean and tidy as practicable and sleeping. Apart from this, he would have been detailed to do what he was told, and be quick about it. At rest, out of the line, life would involve additional training and hard manual labour in support of the Royal Engineers among others. In the line the manual labour continued, such as digging new trenches or repairing the wire in No Man's Land at night, to protect the front line. When ordered to take part in an attack, his knowledge of the overall scheme of things would have been limited. He and his comrades would have been given orders for the attack and shown maps of particular objectives; he may even have been involved in a practice well behind the lines. When attacked, he would have to do the best he could to hold the trench and protect his life and the lives of his comrades.

The private soldier was not an uneducated man; the majority had the ability to reason for themselves. They were honest men, sharing the common misery of living in a ditch, risking their lives on a day-to-day basis. They were willing to make the best of any situation – if only they were given a chance by those 'up above'.

The officer, too, only knew a limited number of men really well. Depending on his rank, this would have varied from his fellow platoon and company officers to battalion and brigade commanders. A good officer would have known his platoon NCOs well, and probably knew his best (and worst) men too. Otherwise, in the line, his lot could be a lonely one. This he made up for when out of the line, when the battalion or company officers did their best to 'mess' together, trying to obtain the best food and to pride themselves in the entertainment of officers from other regiments. When in the line, the typical second lieutenant was responsible for the defence of the trenches held by all four sections of his platoon. In addition, he had to organise everything else, from stores (food and ammunition) to the mundane paperwork, which was the general bugbear of his life. In reality, his opinions didn't carry much weight in the overall planning of an attack. His job was to organise his platoon's part in the scheme, and ultimately to lead it over the top – usually from the front. He was spared the drudgery of manual labour and was provided with a batman to care for his personal needs. Another problem facing him from time to time was to reconcile and uphold orders sent from above, by people who understood the wider picture, with the views of his men, who understood the details only too well.

Keeping diaries was officially not allowed, for security reasons. Likewise letters home were censored. Thankfully large numbers of diaries were kept secretly; letters home were also kept and treasured by worried families. Individual battalions were obliged to keep a 'war diary' of their actions. The quality of the daily entries in these varied with the writer, the time he had available, his literary skills and his desire to do this routine job. After the war all these sources were used to compile regimental and other histories in order to provide a lasting account of those days.

The 3rd Worcestershire was a Regular battalion before the war and had been brought to France at the outbreak of war in 1914. Despite heavy losses in the opening battles, by July 1916, when Albert joined them, the rank and file would still contain a significant proportion of professional, pre-war soldiers. This would prove to be a mixed blessing. The professionalism of both the officers and men could quickly be instilled into new recruits, who would also benefit from an enhanced *esprit de corps* generated from many years of experience by hardened soldiers. On the other hand, it would be more difficult, as a newcomer, to be accepted by the 'old sweats'. Furthermore, as regulars such a battalion could be expected to be given more difficult objectives in an assault on the enemy.

On the larger scale the 3rd Worcestershire formed part of 7th Brigade along with 1st Wiltshire (another Regular battalion), the 10th Cheshire and the 8th Loyal North Lancs. The latter two were 'service' battalions, that is, they were raised at the outbreak of war in Kitchener's call for a 'New Army' of 100,000 men (and more). These had their own *esprit de corps* with officers and men coming from restricted localities. Despite being together for two years, these 'Kitchener men' were largely inexperienced in practical warfare, though at the battle of Loos in September 1915 a few divisions containing a majory of 'kitchener battalions' were decimated – the Somme battle of 1916 would also show tragically that patriotic enthusiasm was no substitute for experience. By July 1916 some brigades had been reorganised to provide a mixture of Regular and New Army troops to even out the differences in their respective battle experience. The actions and behaviour of the New Army battalions and troops were the despair of the regular officers and men, who in turn were regarded as rather standoffish by their New Army equivalents. The hard lessons learned at the opening of the Somme offensive would serve to unite them into very effective, battle-hardened composites for the later actions on the Somme.

On a higher level still three brigades were organised into a division. In the case of the 7th Brigade, this was the 25th Division. While this unit is too large and cumbersome to provide very much detail about the life and experiences of one private soldier, an understanding of the actions of an individual battalion, and indeed of the brigade, can provide much interesting information. The diary and history of the 3rd Worcestershire would provide the details most relevant to Albert Turley. In addition, information regarding the 1st Wiltshire would also be invaluable as this sister-battalion shared much of the life of the 3rd Worcestershire both in terms of tradition and usage during the Somme offensive. The records of the 10th Cheshire and 8th Loyal North Lancs would be less useful: these New Army battalions were 'paired' in the brigade in much the same way as the 3rd Worcestershire and 1st Wiltshire. During July–August 1916 they would fight as 'matched' pairs of battalions. In quieter times and sectors, one from each pair would be teamed together to 'improve' the New Army troops.

Bringing Uncle Albert Home

THE EXPERIENCES OF PTE A.E. TURLEY,
3RD WORCESTERSHIRE
JULY–AUGUST 1916

Part 1

The Background

1 TO 23 JULY

The 3rd Worcestershire were fortunate to miss the opening of the Somme offensive at 7.30 a.m., on Saturday 1 July. On that day 57,000 British soldiers fell, of whom 19,000 were killed. In fact, the battalion was out of the line and in reserve at Varennes, resting and listening to the continual roar of the guns, having marched up through Toutencourt and Harponville, setting off at 9.20 p.m. the previous night. (STK, 3WD)

On the 2nd orders arrived in the morning and the 3rd Worcestershire, along with the rest of 7th Brigade, were marched eastwards to Hedauville, staying until 9.30 p.m. From there, they went along the crowded, dusty roads to the assembly trenches in the south of Aveluy Wood, passing the convoys of wounded and survivors of the 1 July attack, only arriving there at 3 a.m. owing to the congestion. On arrival, the shell-fire in the front line above them suddenly increased as another British attack on the Leipzig Salient went in. This attack failed, and the 1st Wiltshire were rushed up into support, the 3rd Worcestershire remaining in the wood in reserve for the time being. (STK, 3WD, 1WD)

This was to be the 3rd Worcestershire's initiation into the Leipzig Salient trench system. This area had seen the only British 'lasting success' on 1 July to the north of the Albert–Bapaume road, which divided the Somme battlefield, as the attacking troops had gained a toe-hold in this strong German defensive work. The casualties had been severe, and the signs of this battle were all too evident. In fact, only the German front line had fallen: the support line was resisting all assaults. The shell-fire on the shelter trenches among the shattered tree stumps of Aveluy Wood was constant, and the 3rd Worcestershire expected to be moved up at a moment's notice. After dark on the 4th, the 3rd Worcestershire crossed the River Ancre and moved up into the Authuille support trenches. (STK)

The 1st Wiltshire held the captured German front line and were fighting in the maze of trenches in the Leipzig Salient. The Germans launched a sharp counter-attack before dawn on the 5th. The 1st Wiltshire held their line, but their losses were so high that C and D companies of the 3rd Worcestershire were brought up at midday to support them in the old British front line opposite the Leipzig Salient. A and B companies of the 3rd Worcestershire remained in the Authuille defences although later they were also moved up to support the 1st Wiltshire, who had made an attack in the salient and were being heavily counter-attacked. (STK, 3WD)

On the 6th A and B companies of the 3rd Worcestershire were relieved but this was a temporary move as they were soon forced to return, again to support the 1st Wiltshire. C and D companies joined them on 7 July, together with the 8th Loyal North Lancs. (3WD) The fighting in the Leipzig Salient was furious, with bombing fights up and down the captured trenches choked with dead and wounded. The whole was made even more ghastly by the rain that had turned the dust into a cloying mud. (STK)

At midnight on the 7th the 3rd Worcestershire were relieved by the 1/6th battalion of the West Yorkshires, and so returned to Crucifix Corner where they collapsed into 'the sleep of exhaustion'. For their endeavours in the Leipzig Salient, both the 1st Wiltshire and the 3rd Worcestershire received commendations in the Special Divisional Orders. (STK)

By 11 a.m. the following day the four companies of the 3rd Worcestershire found themselves together again in Aveluy Wood. Here they stayed until midnight when they were marched southwards the short distance to Usna Hill to support the actions at La Boisselle on the Albert–Bapaume road. (3WD)

The 3rd Worcestershire had not taken part in the formal attack in the Leipzig Salient, unlike their sister-battalion the 1st Wiltshire. Their role was a holding and supporting one, but no less deadly. The area would have been littered with the debris of the opening attack on 1 July, and No Man's Land carpeted with bodies. The fighting in the salient, in particular around the Leipzig Redoubt, had been bitter, with quarter neither given nor expected. The lack of ground gained does not reflect adversely upon the attackers; rather it is a tribute to the courage of the German defenders. The days spent in the Leipzig Salient by both the 3rd Worcestershire and the 1st Wiltshire would have given them sufficient qualification, in the eyes of higher command, to be used again here in the attacks at the end of August and the beginning of September.

The twin villages of La Boisselle and Ovillers-la-Boisselle, both German strongholds, sat on opposite sides of a valley known as 'Mash Valley'. Each had been a primary objective on 1 July but neither had fallen on that day. In fact some of the worst carnage occurred here, as troops had advanced in waves over the Usna Hill and up into Mash Valley only to be cut down in the crossed machine-gun fire from these villages.

The British attacks on 1 July had not been a complete disaster; ground was gained in the south of the battle area, particularly around the villages of Mametz and Montauban. After the 1st the attacks on the Leipzig Salient, described above, represent some of the last actions for some time in the north, as emphasis was switched to the south to exploit the gains already made there. To prevent future attacks in the south being outflanked in the west, it was necessary to continue the costly attacks up the Albert–Bapaume road towards and beyond the village of Pozières, the highest point on the Somme battlefield. In order to do this, it was first necessary to take and advance through the villages of Ovillers-la-Boisselle and La Boisselle.

On 9 July A and B companies of the 3rd Worcestershire moved into trenches just beyond the village of La Boisselle. The 8th Loyal North Lancs joined them that night, with C and D companies in support. (3WD) They could see across the valley to Ovillers-la-Boisselle and the efforts being made to take it. It was decided that an advance on Pozières up the Albert–Bapaume road would isolate the German garrison in Ovillers-la-Boisselle and force their withdrawal. Unfortunately, there was a shortage of artillery in this area of operations that would make any attack very costly, as it would be unlikely that all the German machine-guns could be knocked out without a heavy preliminary bombardment.

Here they stayed, holding the line until 13 July, undergoing nearly constant heavy shelling. The CO, Lt Col C.M.G. Davidge, was in fact wounded and command of the battalion was transferred to Maj W.B. Gibbs. Offensive actions in this area were given over to the two other battalions of 7th Brigade, namely the 10th Cheshire and the 8th Loyal North Lancs, the 3rd Worcestershire and 1st Wiltshire moving up, as required, to take advantage of the ground gained by these battalions.

From 13 to 17 July the 3rd Worcestershire sent out fighting patrols to support the attacks on Ovillers-la-Boisselle. (3WD) Their somewhat precarious position was greatly assisted by the larger British offensive that had begun on 14 July to the south on Bazentin Ridge. (STK) Ovillers-la-Boisselle was finally given up on 17 July as the remnant of the German garrison that held the ruins was hopelessly outflanked. (3WD) The 1st Wiltshire were in support, providing carrying parties (for supplies) for the 3rd Worcestershire. (1WD)

Johnston's diary entry for 15 July well describes the situation here:

Owing to the Brigade now being so weak (we had started with the battalions averaging 900–1,000 strong and now we're . . . about 180 per battalion), it was decided to relieve us by the 74th Inf. Brigade . . . Owing to our doing so well on the right, the Warwicks of the 48th Division, attached to us, were told to try and patrol across the open to POZIÈRES, but as soon as they tried to get out of the trenches, they were all knocked over by the Bosche machine-guns on our left [in Ovillers-la-Boisselle]. They also let a load of unfortunate Warwicks work down a communication trench between POZIÈRES and OVILLERS which the Bosche could enfilade for some way; the latter turned his machine-guns on to them and killed the lot (about 60). I wish the Higher Command would more often listen to the man on the spot. Went up to the trench held by the Regiment [3rd

Worcestershire] just in front of POZIÈRES, pretty warm spot but they were quite cheery. Our bombardment was boiling up for the people on their right to attack POZIÈRES, which ought to do alright unless the machine-guns are too much for us again. Our barrage behind the place is anyway making it very nasty for the Hun to bring up reinforcements. The 74th Inf. Brigade are going to take their turn at having a go at OVILLERS tonight together with the 143rd Inf. Brigade who are going for the trenches between it and POZIÈRES . . .

[later] . . . Apparently the 74th Inf. Brigade's attack on OVILLERS failed again, in much the same way and for the same reasons as ours did [lack of artillery support]. The 143rd Inf. Brigade however got their objective which puts them behind OVILLERS, so that the situation is rather interesting. (AJ 15/7)

On the 17th the 7th Warwicks relieved the 3rd Worcestershire. (3WD) The 1st Wiltshire had been relieved the day before and had spent the night beside the lake to the east of Albert. (1WD)

The remnant of the 3rd Worcestershire was eventually marched down the line for divisional 'rest', initially to Forceville for the night of 17/18 July – '*a dirty billet, but better than nothing*'. (AJ 16/7)

From here they went on to Beauval (3WD) –'*at 7 a.m. in heavy rain, which soon wet us through, via ACHEUX, LEALVILLERS, ARQUEVRES, RAINCHEVAL, BEAUQUESNE to BEAUVAL.*' (AJ 18/7). Here they stayed until the 20th (3WD) – '*a most excellent billet. Nice to get a rest and a change once more in a clean house, and to be in the midst of civilisation again, their [sic] being shops and all sorts of things here.*' (AJ 18/7)

On 19 July Johnston made a prophetic entry in his diary, which was to set the scene for an individual tragedy whose repercussions would last for the remainder of the twentieth century, for the Turley family at least:

Hope we shall get some drafts at once to fill the place of the 74 officers and 2,000 men we have lost the last few days.

Hear that we are definitely not to be sent north to take over a quiet bit of the line, but, as a compliment for what we have done, are being kept in these parts, shall be filled up with reinforcements at once, and will again take part in the 'great push', which is excellent news. (AJ 19/7)

From Beauval they marched to Authie and bivouacked nearby in the Bois de Warnimont until the 23rd. (3WD) Johnston's entry describes this march:

Left BEAUVAL at 2 p.m. and marched via TERRAMESNIL and SARTON to AUTHIE which we reached about 5.30 p.m. Hot day for a march but the men came along well except for the 10th Cheshires who are a despair to one – bad officers is the trouble I'm afraid. We are in an unexpectedly good billet. It is a great pity they move us about so much, we have now marched round three parts of a circle which would seem to be unnecessary, the men get no rest, and no training can be done. (AJ 20/7)

Even at Authie the men would get no real rest. Johnston again:

Have been told to send 1,000 men away on working parties with the Tunnelling companies in front; it means taking every remaining man in the Brigade away except a few specialists and senior NCOs. The men of course get no rest, training will be almost at a standstill, and it will be difficult to assimilate drafts as they come. In fact, if they want to get good value out of us in the next fight, I can't imagine the 'powers that be' doing anything more foolish . . . (AJ 21/7)

The next day, Johnston again confided his frustration to his diary:

The Brigade will therefore have spent its so-called rest marching in a circle on hot dusty roads from FORCEVILLE through ACHEUX, BEAUVAL, AUTHIE back to about ACHEUX in addition to having supplied 1,000 men for work the last two days. Some Staff officer ought to be hung for this, it is merely tiring out willing troops to no purpose. The quality of some of these drafts is not above reproach, and it is this, which I'm afraid may cause the breakdown of the great offensive. If we can go on replacing casualties with good material, and give the Huns no rest, we shall win through. If we had had compulsion [i.e. conscription], even 6 months earlier, we should have been able to make a certainty of this [offensive]; we should have had enough men and they would have had time to be properly trained. (AJ 22/7)

From here (Acheux) the 3rd Worcestershire marched to Mailly Wood to refit and absorb reinforcements. (3WD) The 1st Wiltshire had to wait for their 'rest' as they went to the front line at Hamel. They would receive their reinforcements directly into these front line trenches – a real 'baptism of fire'. (1WD)

The casualties for the 3rd Worcestershire for the month of July was as follows: officers – killed 6, wounded 8, missing 1; other ranks – killed 46, wounded 282, missing 38. (3WD)

This makes a total of 381 for the 3rd Worcestershire for the month of July 1916, practically 50 per cent of the fighting strength of the battalion. These were high casualties indeed for a battalion that had not made a direct attack on the enemy line. The Somme was beginning to gain its terrible reputation. The troops would have been physically and mentally exhausted from their actions in the trenches – the tortuous long march back to 'rest' would only have added to this. As a result of logistics, this finding was commonplace among all units engaged on the Somme.

On 24 July a band of new reinforcements arrived at Mailly Wood for the 3rd Worcestershire. Among them was Pte Albert Turley.

INITIATION – 24 JULY TO 6 AUGUST 1916

The 25th Division, of which the 3rd Worcestershire were a part, had been moved to the north of the Somme battlefield, to the 'quiet' lines in front of the village of Beaumont Hamel – the scene of one of the best known actions of 1 July 1916, undertaken by the 1st New-foundland Regiment. On this day, finding the communication trenches leading to the British front line crowded with wounded, this battalion had made its attack from the British support and reserve lines, having mistaken a German rocket signal for a British one indicating that the German trench had been successfully taken. The result was a catastrophe. The Newfoundlanders lost many men to the German machine-guns before they even reached the British front line, the remainder falling in No Man's Land; few made it any closer to the German lines. After the war the battlefield was purchased by the country of Newfoundland (then independent of Canada) and this park stands today as a living tribute to those men. The trenches are still visible, if mellowed by the passage of time.

The four depleted battalions of the 7th Brigade (the 3rd Worcestershire in conjunction with the 10th Cheshire, the 1st Wiltshire and the 8th Loyal North Lancs) now took turns in holding these lines. The battalions 'at rest' would serve to provide nightly carrying parties for the ones in the line. The aim was both to absorb new reinforcements into each battalion and to improve the British front-line positions in preparation for a future attack (which would eventually become the Battle of the Ancre in November 1916).

As Albert and his companions joined the 3rd Worcestershire on the 24th, he was fortunate to find the battalion 'at rest' in Mailly Wood, where it would remain until 29 July – unlike the 1st Wiltshire, which had gone straight into the front line. In some cases these new reinforcements may well have received a mixed welcome. Albert would have to wait for his baptism of fire, unlike his contemporaries in the 1st Wiltshire.

In his novel *The Middle Parts of Fortune* F. Manning describes the encampment at Mailly Wood as being behind the village of Mailly-Maillet in an angle formed by two roads, on a steep reverse slope which gave some protection from shell-fire, further enhanced by the provision of hastily dug shelter trenches. Although a novel, this book depicts a very accurate picture of the life of the private soldier during the Somme battle at this time (Manning served with the 7th King's Shropshire Light Infantry).

All new reinforcements were received with some scepticism. Until the Somme, all such had been volunteers. Albert and his party would have been some of the first Derby Men to arrive. They were considered as conscripts by existing troops, both Regular and Kitchener men alike, who wished to retain their identity as volunteers and would occasionally refuse to mix with the new men, believing that they would be better off without them. It would take another year – and the Battle for Passchendaele – to finally unite these disparate groups in time for the year of victory, 1918.

For Albert and many other youngsters arriving at Mailly Wood, any discrimination would have been unfair, given that they too had volunteered as soon as they had come of age. It was only by a trick of circumstance that they had been placed with older men who had been conscripted.

However, Albert had finally arrived at the front. He would have been able to hear the guns firing to the south and to see the flashes of light brightening the night sky. He would have found himself in his new section with unfamiliar faces. These men, doubtless tired after the events of the past days, may not have been too bothered about welcoming any newcomers.

Unfortunately, neither the 3rd Worcestershire diary nor history provides details of their activities from 24 July to 6 August other than that they were 'in Divisional rest at Mailly Wood' and later 'in trenches opposite Beaumont Hamel'. However, the 1st Wiltshire diarist and Johnston do give some details of this 'quiet' time to help provide a picture of Albert's first weeks on the Somme.

MONDAY 24 JULY
The day was overcast and very hot (maximum 23°C, minimum 13°C). Actions at Pozières, High Wood and Guillemont to the south of the Somme battlefield dominated matters. (GG)

The 3rd Worcestershire were at Divisional Reserve in bivouacs in Mailly Wood. (3WD) The 1st Wiltshire were in the trenches in front of the village of Beaumont Hamel receiving thirty-two new recruits in the line. (1WD) Johnston was with them, describing the conditions and attack here on 1 July:

. . . fairly good trenches and great facilities for observation. Went along the new trenches being dug in front of our own line; why on earth these weren't dug 4 months ago goodness only knows; result being that in the attack on 1 July our fellows here had some 500 yards to go to reach the German front line, which of course did not give them a chance; and now the building of the forward trench is difficult and costly. Heavy bombardment all day to the south, hope they are getting on. (AJ 24/7)

It is probable that Albert would have been assigned to his section of ten to twelve men led by a corporal or lance-corporal. Accommodation would have been in 'bell-tents', all the section sleeping in the same tent. To effect this, men slept radially with their feet to the centre pole. the section commander slept opposite and furthest from the draughty door. On the floor were spread the soldier's waterproof groundsheets. Their kit was placed at the head and thus provided a 'pillow'. Their rifles were stacked in guides around the centre pole (if not stacked elsewhere in camp). A single hook per man on the centrepole sufficed for his tunic etc. Woollen blankets (one or two per man, depending on season) were issued as covers, to be collected ('in bundles of twelve') the next morning, prior then to him laying his kit out on the groundsheet for an inspection. An oil lamp/candle sufficed for light and a coal brazier to keep out the worst of the cold in winter months. The latter was a mixed blessing as heads and shoulders froze and feet roasted. Taken short in the middle of the night either involved disturbing many men, or finding the other use for boots – after all, weren't you told it was supposed to harden your feet?

TUESDAY 25 JULY
The day was overcast and cooler (maximum 19°C, minimum 10°C). The actions at High Wood had ended for a time. The Germans had counter-attacked at both Longueval and Bazentin. However, the remains of the village of Pozières were almost entirely in British hands. (GG)

The 3rd Worcestershire continued in Divisional Reserve in

bivouacs in Mailly Wood. (3WD) The 1st Wiltshire held the line and reported a quiet day with only a few trench mortars falling on the front line. In the evening reserve companies were brought up to erect wire entanglements out in No Man's Land in front of the new British front line that they had been digging, and connecting the latter to the support line. (1WD)

Johnston, in the front line with the 1st Wiltshire, had a more 'interesting' experience:

In the trenches all the morning and early afternoon, quite quiet on our front. Went down again after dark to see to the wiring etc. of the new front line. Thought we might have some difficulty from the Minenwerfer [German trench mortar] the other side of the ANCRE and from machine-guns, but it turned out to be quite a quiet night except for some shelling further back which did not affect the working parties. On my way back through HAMEL and MESNIL . . . I got caught in a barrage of these new German gas shells; was on a bicycle so tried to push through it in the dark as quickly as possible; the gas was pretty thick but fortunately, unless one is caught asleep at the bottom of a dug-out, these gas shells are not so very dangerous unless one gets a concentrated mouthful of it into one's lungs. The gas seems to have rather a sweet sickly taste; got through it in about 3 minutes, and bicycled back to Bde. HQ without further incident, and had a good sleep. (AJ 25/7)

In camp, Albert and his new comrades would have suffered endless polishing of brasses and cleaning of kit followed by inspections leading to make-ups of various pieces of equipment, some being charged for out of a soldier's pay. The 'rest' day would typically start with drill followed by other forms of training in periods of 45–60 minutes, practical work (including range firing, bayonet practice and specialist training) as described below, alternating with lectures on new pieces of equipment (new gas masks and grenades were starting to make an appearance in summer 1916). Meals would be regular but monotonous with breakfast, dinner (at lunchtime) and tea. Afternoons and evenings *could* be free for sport, or trips to an *estaminet* for (better) food (usually egg and chips) and drink (weak beer with red and white wines as stronger, but more expensive, alternatives). A soldier's greatest problem here would be to find an estaminet host with change for his ubiquitous five-franc note with which all soldier's were paid! As importantly, sections of men would be detailed to take supplies up to the front lines each night – a hazardous and exhausting job. In addition more men would be involved with other heavy manual duties for other army units, notably the Royal Engineers.

WEDNESDAY 26 JULY

A hotter day, but rather windy (maximum 24°C, minimum 13°C). The ruins of Pozières finally fell, and the British now held the highest ground on the Somme battlefield. Actions could now proceed in the south, the left flank being secure and able to provide good observation over the whole battlefield. (GG)

The 3rd Worcestershire continued in Divisional Reserve in bivouacs in Mailly Wood. (3WD) The 1st Wiltshire reported German gas shells being dropped around battalion HQ together with lachrymatory shells in the village of Mesnil – the same ones that had caught Johnston on his bicycle. The 1st Wiltshire reported twenty casualties from the gas, but carried on improving the new trenches and also sending out nightly patrols into No Man's Land. (1WD)

Johnston was now to feel the effects of his decision to cycle through the gas cloud, being very fortunate to have met only tear gas. He went up the line again to view the working parties, and to meet some of the new recruits:

Am taking a complete rest as apparently this gas begins to be felt several hours after one has taken it: it affects the heart, and if one takes any violent exercise or exerts oneself unduly, it is apt to have serious consequences; otherwise it soon passes off; have rather a feeling as if I had got a weight on my chest, but otherwise am alright.

Went up to the trenches after dark, and had a somewhat eventful night. Bicycled up through MESNIL, which they started to shell just as I was passing through. Left my bicycle in HAMEL, and went up to see the working parties. These had as a matter of fact started out a bit too soon with the result that the Bosches spotted them and put a lot of stuff over; happened to get caught when I was out in the open getting through our old wire entanglements which was rather unpleasant. Found a crowd of men trying to come back, mostly new draft men who have never been under fire before. Headed them off and eventually got them on to their work, the shelling being behind on our old front line. The 1st Wilts did some very good wiring, and did not work badly on the whole with all these new men. Had considerable difficulty with the 10th Cheshires though, they are very shaky, I could find no officers, and I had actually to put the men on to their tasks myself and to stand over them to get them to work. Later the Bosche spotted our working parties, and gave us a baddish time with machine-guns and we had some casualties. Later I went to another party and the Bosche began 'crumping' hard just to our left. As usual the Bosche with his method, accuracy and thoroughness brought almost to a fault never altered his aim, and 'crumped' this place unmercifully, though as it happened there was no one there; if he had switched a short way right or left, lengthened or shortened, he would have done a lot of damage. It is uphill work with these new drafts in the ranks, the officers are inexperienced, the men undisciplined, half trained, and of course with [little] practical experience. They aren't a bad lot really, and when they have been blooded a bit, and had some discipline knocked into them, they will be all right; but it is not easy to do all this while actually in the trenches. Eventually got back about 3 a.m. (AJ 26/7)

It is probable that Albert would not have that much experience firing live rounds on a range up to now. His training would of course have included detailed lectures and practice handling of the parts of his rifle, how to strip and clean it (making sure of putting the piece of 'four by two' rag in the correct loop of his 'pull-through'!) and oil it, before he received any practical instruction on the use of it in action.

He would have been taught on the correct manner of '*charging the magazine*' (with five or ten rounds of ammunition) for delayed use and '*loading of the rifle*' (in the same numbers) for immediate use, before he ever fired a shot. Firing training would have been in the pre-war positions of standing, kneeling and prone firing positions. Although vital in open warfare and in an attack, standing on the firestep of a trench with support for his arms from the parapet would prove much easier. He would learn the standard method of bringing fire to bear on an enemy as instructed by his section commander. Firstly the *range*, e.g. '*at 400 yards*' at which he would set the backsight of his rifle to the appropriate distance. Secondly, the *target*, e.g. '*enemy soldiers emerging from left of wood*' at which he would check the direction indicated by the section commanders hand, take the safety catch off, load a round by working the rifle bolt and resetting the safety catch to on. Thirdly, the *number of rounds* to be fired e.g. '*five rounds*' at which he would bring his rifle up to the shoulder and release the safety catch. Finally, would come the *type of fire* e.g. '*rapid fire*' at which he would fire for all he was worth aiming at the target keeping his rifle in the shoulder for each shot, completing the number of rounds by working the rifle bolt, return to the loading position and reload to then await the next set of firing instructions. As a minimum, Albert would be expected to be able to fire fifteen aimed rounds in a minute. Well-trained soldiers could manage more than this, although it should be remembered that this procedure would involve at least one reload in the process. Marksmanship would be checked on the range and proficiency badges (and pay) would be awarded to the better shots. Now with the 3rd Worcestershire, this would be the time the section commander would find out about Albert's abilities and shortcomings, which would have to be put right very quickly.

THURSDAY 27 JULY
A hot day that started rather hazy but was to clear in the afternoon, (maximum 27°C, minimum 16°C), 8mm of rain fell. Attacks were renewed at Delville Wood and Pozières. (GG)

The 3rd Worcestershire continued in Divisional Reserve in bivouacs in Mailly Wood. (3WD) The 1st Wiltshire diary reported the German trench mortar shelling of the old British front line and the continued work in the line and the sending out of nightly patrols. They suffered further casualties as more men went 'down the line' suffering from the gas attack the previous night. (1WD)

Johnston too had a quiet day, taking two senior brigade officers around the front-line trenches.

As with his rifle, Albert would have had some training in the use of the bayonet. This weapon, above all others in the Great War, was held up by the Army hierarchy as being the attack-winning weapon – 'beloved of the British soldier'. In truth, the heyday of the bayonet had passed with the single-shot rifle which was useless after firing prior to a sometimes lengthy reload. It was believed the terrifying sight of a massed bayonet charge and the thought of 'cold steel' being rammed and twisted in your vital organs by a battle-crazed enemy would guarantee the ultimate success in an attack. In a world prior to the machine-gun, this was certainly true. Gruesome lectures entitled, *The Spirit of the Bayonet* aimed to instill the necessary blood-lust into recruits were part of normal training, '*three inches is adequate, six inches is better*' when it came to the thrust, coupled with the necessary final twist ensuring a fatal wound. In the Great War, only 2% of recorded wounds in hospitals were inflicted with a bayonet compared with 68% by shell fragments/shrapnel. Some authors claim this would show how ineffective the bayonet was. However, bayonets were deliberately aimed at the torso generally producing *fatal* wounds, whereas wounds by shrapnel were random and many were superficial. The standard British Wilkinson bayonet of the Great War consisted of 17″ of sharpened steel. For an infantryman in 1914, it was designed to be his last resort when facing a charging cavalryman. As events transpired, in a narrow trench, its length could prove more of a hindrance in close hand-to-hand fighting. The only saving grace here being the bayonets of his enemy were a similar length and equally awkward in a confined space.

Albert would have learned to thrust and parry with an experienced instructor. He then would have '*made his point*' into suspended sacks and rings in various configurations. Clearly, a sack could not fight back with a return thrust or fend an opponent off with a rifle butt. A sack did not have a ribcage where a bayonet might get stuck and become impossible to withdraw. A sack did not plead, scream and bleed when stuck. It did not stare back with bulging eyes in terror and agony with bloody hands clutching the exposed blade.

These basic lessons learned, Albert would then 'spar' with his comrades and instructor. Only then would he learn just how good he would be in a bayonet fight. Hopefully, the secret of bayonet-fighting would then become very clear, if matters degenerated to parrying and thrusting with an opponent your chances dropped to 50-50 (or worse!). Far better to treat your enemy as a sack and carry your thrust home first time, and not give your opponent any chance to parry at all. To always keep a round '*up the spout*', this could be vital, if only to fire and rip open a larger hole in an opponents chest from which to extract a bayonet that had become stuck.

The bayonet's fearful reputation was indeed well deserved.

FRIDAY 28 JULY

A hot but overcast day (maximum 25°C, minimum 15°C). A main part of Delville Wood and the associated village of Longueval fell, and fighting continued in the Pozières area. (GG)

The 3rd Worcestershire continued in Divisional Reserve in bivouacs in Mailly Wood. (3WD) The 1st Wiltshire had a quiet day, observing that a British artillery barrage had caught a German transport convoy travelling at night on the road from Beaumont Hamel to Beaucourt. (1WD)

Johnston again had a quiet day, taking another senior officer (Lt Col Sherbrooke, Royal Artillery) around the front-line trenches, reporting '*the Bosche very quiet*'. (AJ 28/7)

The 'rest' for the 3rd Worcestershire was over, as was the 1st Wiltshire's time in the front line, their tour of duty having resulted in one man killed and nine men wounded, in addition to those gassed. The 3rd Worcestershire replaced the 10th Cheshire and the 8th Loyal North Lancs replaced the 1st Wiltshire on the night of 28 July.

One weapon remained in Albert's standard armory, the bomb or hand-grenade. At the start of the war, the British did not have a hand-thrown bomb. Static trench warfare led to the development of such devices, the Germans already being well advanced with a explosive cannister attached to a stick for throwing. Simple and effective, this design remained largely unchanged through the war (although other designs were developed) and beyond. The first British design, the '*jam-tin*' bomb was just that, home-made from a discarded jam-tin filled with gun-cotton and scrap metal, the lid being refitted with a fuse which was manually lit. Various other designs were developed with varying success (and catastrophic failure!).

Albert would have been trained in the use of the Mark V 'Mills Bomb' of a design recognisable to British soldiers for generations to come. The bomb consisted of a cast-iron ball designed to fragment on detonation. The fuse was set by pulling a ring and throwing the bomb. this action released a lever which then activated the timed chemical fuse. Trained soldiers had to be capable of throwing the Mills bomb a minimum distance of thirty yards with accuracy.

Once confidence was gained this weapon, along with his rifle, the Mills bomb would become the infantryman's favourite weapon. Without exposing yourself to enemy fire when thrown, it could kill many enemy soldiers at once when they too were sheltered from direct rifle fire and at a distance well beyond the requirement for a bayonet.

Albert now had all the basic skills required to both attack and defend. The culmination of this would be to take part in mock attacks on practice trenches. This would allow the coordination of a platoon of men in the use of a variety weapons. In the valleys and woods around Maillet Camp, there would have been much opportunity to do just this.

It was now time for Albert Turley and his fellow new recruits in the 3rd Worcestershire to receive their baptism of fire in the front-line trenches before Beaumont Hamel. They had been fortunate to some extent, in that their time in Mailly Wood had given them an opportunity to receive at least some training with battle-hardened soldiers. As mentioned previously, there are no details of what the 3rd Worcestershire experienced in the line up to 6 August. It can be assumed that their duties would not have been dissimilar to those described for the 1st Wiltshire above. The diarist of the 1st Wiltshire now gives us a picture of their life at Divisional Rest in Mailly Wood; again, a similar series of experiences to those Albert Turley and the 3rd Worcestershire had just left behind.

SATURDAY 29 JULY

Another hot but overcast day (maximum 27°C, minimum 14°C). A German attempt to retake Delville Wood failed, and desperate hand-to-hand fighting was taking place to the north and east of Pozières windmill by the Australian divisions. (GG)

The 3rd Worcestershire took over the trenches at Hamel from the 10th Cheshire. (3WD) The 1st Wiltshire were relieved from the line by the 8th Loyal North Lancs, which was quiet except for some German shelling of Mesnil, and proceeded to Mailly Wood for a rest, arriving at 7 p.m. The rest was short-lived for some: fifty men were detached to assist the 52nd Tunnelling Company, no doubt for more manual labour. (1WD).

Johnston again had a quiet day in the heat taking another general on a tour of the front-line trenches, noting the noise of shell-fire to the south and the light shelling near HQ (presumably at Mesnil).

Albert's first day in the front-line trench had been quiet. After the heavy fatigues at Mailly Wood, which the 1st Wiltshire were now taking part in, this day may have seemed to him genuinely restful.

During their stay in the trenches before Beaumont Hamel, the 3rd Worcestershire companies would have been distributed to hold front, support and possibly reserve lines linked by communication trenches. After making their tortuous way up the latter (often shallow, often filled with water and mud) platoons and ultimately sections would undergo a formal 'hand-over' with the unit being relieved. This was a dangerous time (see below) with twice the number of men in the trenches, an enemy could double the casualties from a barrage of shellfire. Given the arrival time of the 1st Wiltshire at Mailley-Maillet camp, the reliefs must have occurred in daylight signifying this sector was indeed 'quiet'.

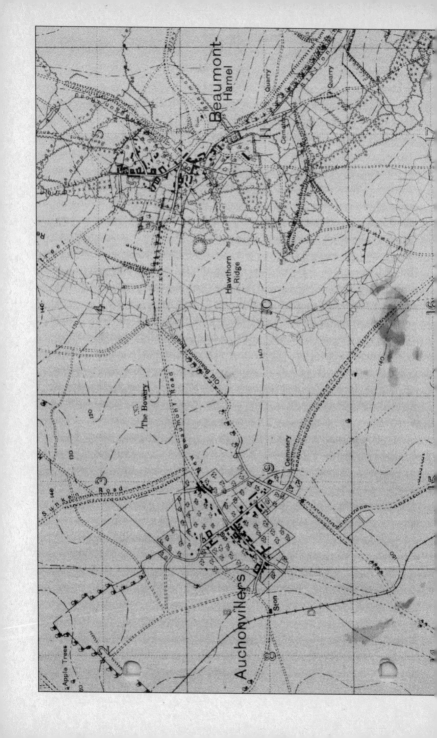

SUNDAY 30 JULY

Another very hot day with clear skies (maximum 28°C, minimum 14°C). Following progress at Delville Wood, the British made an attempt on the village of Guillemont, to the south of this wood and east of Trones Wood. Despite the ruined nature of the village and the short distance between the opposing lines, the German defences here would hold out until September. (GG)

The 3rd Worcestershire continued to hold the line in front of Beaumont Hamel. (3WD) The 1st Wiltshire, at rest in Mailly Wood, were allocated baths. (1WD) It was likely that the same privilege had been granted to the 3rd Worcestershire in previous days. Due to the bad living conditions, soldiers' bodies and clothes were invariably infested with lice. A bath would give them a chance to wash and have their clothes exchanged for clean ones – in theory. In practice, the 'clean' clothes often contained the eggs of lice along the seams, which would later hatch when worn, owing to the warmth and moisture of the body. New recruits would not have been exempted from these baths, and their 'genuinely' clean uniforms would have been exchanged – so these soldiers too would soon have to endure the misery of lice much sooner than might have been expected.

Johnston now had the chance to meet more new recruits, who were not having an easy time:

Another scorching [sic] hot day. Round the trenches as usual but nothing much doing except at night when the Hun Minenwerfers and guns from the THIEPVAL direction gave

Opposite: Trench Map of Beaumont Hamel

Taken from map 57D SE 1&2, this shows the British trenches to the west of the German ones surrounding the village of Beaumont Hamel. The British front line represents the positions immediately before the Battle of the Ancre in November 1916 when the new front line, partly dug by units of the 8th Brigade in July/August, had been completed. The Newfoundland Memorial Park occupies the area to the south of the village of Beaumont Hamel, incorporating the German defences around the 'Y Ravine' and the British lines in front of them.

our working parties a lot of trouble, causing casualties and stopping the work, particularly as these new drafts are not very steady yet. (AJ 30/7)

There were actually formal timetables issued for duties in the trenches, however local circumstances generally held precedence. Most activity took place at night when men, safely hidden by the dark, could emerge into No Man's Land to dig and repair trenches and construct wire defences. These men would have been protected by watching patrols, listening for signs of enemy workings and hostile patrols. It would be difficult to mask all the noise of working. With both sides busy on the same tasks, there was often an unspoken 'truce' and neither side would disturb the other. On the other hand, a sudden barrage or burst of machine-gun fire activated by the first side back could spell disaster for those left working in No Man's Land.

Albert was probably one of these men wiring out in No Man's Land, coming under trench mortar fire. However glorious he had imagined life in the front line to be, this was reality: he would now be under no illusions about his future life, or lack of it. The worrying part was that this was deemed a 'quiet' time.

MONDAY 31 JULY
An early heat haze and a tremendously hot day (maximum 28°C, minimum 15°C). Attacks continued at Guillemont, and the Royal Flying Corps bombed the village of Martinpuich to the east of Pozières. (GG)

The 3rd Worcestershire continued to hold the line at Beaumont Hamel (3WD), and the 1st Wiltshire remained at rest at Mailly Wood, organising training and sending groups of men on specialist courses at divisional schools in bombing (with hand grenades) in nearby Bertrancourt. (1WD) Although all soldiers knew the basic handling of their weapons, sections each had their 'specialists', who were used for the benefit of the whole platoon. Apart from outright specialists, such as Lewis-gunners (a Lewis gun was a light, portable machine-gun), these would include snipers, bomb-throwers, bomb-carriers and bayonet-men. The latter would also undertake night patrols in No Man's Land when rifle and bomb fire would have attracted unwanted indiscriminate artillery attention and machine-gun fire from both sides. It may have been too soon for Albert to become one of these specialists, unless he had previously shown a particular aptitude for any one of these skills.

The day-time for Albert and his comrades in the trenches was one of activity and rest. After a busy night's work, they would have returned in time for dawn. At this point there would be morning 'stand to'. All men in the front lines would stand on the fire-step and man the parapet with loaded rifles waiting, usually for an hour. Dawn and dusk were the favourite times for an enemy attack when this ritual took place. Following this, would be 'stand-down' when men would settle down to 'normal' duties. Firstly, this would involve breakfast which would have been brought up by support units (nominally warm from cookers in the rear). Generally this would have been a piece of bacon, some bread and (most welcome!) tea after a cold night in the open.

Other rations comprising meat (corned or 'bully' beef), cheese, bread or biscuit, vegetables (fresh if available or tinned), tinned fruit or more likely jam (the ubiquitous Tickler's 'plum and apple'), tinned butter, tea, tinned milk and sugar would also have been brought up in sandbags. Always mixed together for ease of transport, with tea and sugar tied off in the corners of the sandbag, the contents would generally suffer from soakings, mud and jute fibres. There were other tinned substitutes for the above which proved very popular, notably 'Pork and Beans' (effectively baked beans with a small amount of meat) and 'Maconacie's' (meat and vegetable stew). Such rations were divided within the section for the day. Fires of any kind were not usually allowed in the front line, but were in support as long as no smoke was discernable to provide a target for the enemy (although in 'quiet' times and sectors both sides observed an unofficial truce at mealtimes). A favourite here was the little 'Tommy Cooker', a tin filled with solid paraffin fitted with a cooking support. Albert would have been equipped with a very functional jack-knife, worn on a lanyard around his waist. As well as a blade for dividing rations etc., the knife had a can-opener and a curved spike, the latter used for easing knots and other piercing purposes. 'Old' soldiers usually attached an extra refinement with a button ring to the loop of the jack-knife, a 'crown cork opener' for beer bottles!

Johnston was given a temporary assignment south of the lines at Beaumont Hamel, gathering intelligence for a possible future attack near the River Ancre: '*I went down at once with some glasses, crawled about in the long grass, and found out pretty well all that is required.*' (AJ 31/7)

In the trenches, one daily event Albert and his comrades would certainly have looked forward to was the daily rum ration (if a battalion commander allowed it!). Intended for medical purposes to bring back life to bodies stiff after a night in the open, it was also used to provide 'dutch courage' prior to an attack. A tablespoon per man was issued into a soldier's mess-tin or cup by an NCO in the presence of an officer from an earthenware jar marked with the mysterious letters 'SRD' standing for Supply Reserve Depot (more commonly known to soldiers as 'Seldom Reaches Destination'!) As with the mail, heaven help the support party who lost this vital commodity!

TUESDAY 1 AUGUST
The weather was getting hotter (maximum 30°C, minimum 16°C). A German counter-attack to the north of Bazentin-le-Petit was repulsed.

The 3rd Worcestershire continued to hold the line at Beaumont Hamel. (3WD) The 1st Wiltshire continued their 'rest' at Mailly Wood with further training in bayonet fighting, musketry and shooting at range. More were being released to specialist schools. (1WD)

Johnston was attached to the 2nd Irish Guards for the day. They were up to dig preparatory trenches near the Ancre for a planned attack on Beaucourt and Beaumont Hamel. The night was not a quiet one: '*About the most noticeable thing of the night was the way our guns were shooting simply incessantly all night on the German trenches and all the roads and tracks behind the lines, which must worry them a good bit and cannot fail to cause a certain number of casualties.*' (AJ 1/8)

WEDNESDAY 2 AUGUST

The hottest day of the Battle of the Somme (maximum 31˚C, minimum 14˚C). A German counter-attack on Delville Wood was repulsed.

The 3rd Worcestershire continued to hold the line at Beaumont Hamel. (3WD) The 1st Wiltshire continued their 'rest' at Mailly Wood, this day carrying out practice attacks, providing a replacement detachment for the 52nd Tunnelling Company and supplying twenty men for an escort for German prisoners at Belle Église. (IWD)

Johnston was defeated by the hot weather: '*Took a day off and stayed in all day sitting out in the sun, and arranging various things on the telephone.*' (AJ 2/8)

Our modern mental picture of the Battle of the Somme is one of constant rain and thick mud – yet the opening of the offensive on 1 July had been a perfect summer's day (described by Siegfried Sassoon in *Diary of an Infantry Officer* as 'heavenly'). In this first week of August the heat was proving unbearable for all participants. In exposed trenches temperatures in the sun would have far exceeded the quoted 31˚C. Soldiers in the line would have had only their 'funk-holes' scraped in the side of the trench for shelter, and their thick serge uniforms would have been stifling. Thirst and the lack of water (brought up nightly in petrol tins, still tasting of petrol), exacerbated by the monotonous army rations of salty 'bully beef' and dry army biscuit, added to the discomfort. Worse still was the smell of putrefaction from the dead bodies still lying out in No Man's Land after the unsuccessful attack on 1 July. These bloated bodies, burned black by the sun, would have been further blackened by the plagues of flies feasting on this corruption (as well as swarming over the food the soldiers tried to eat). Life in the front-line trenches for Albert and the rest of the 3rd Worcestershire in these days would have been as near an experience of Hell as it would be possible to devise for living men.

And still, it was 'quiet' and the trenches 'cushy'.

THURSDAY 3 AUGUST

The hot weather continued with clear skies (maximum 30˚C, minimum 14˚C). Fighting continued west of Pozières and an explosion in the German-held village of Courcelette, presumably of an ammunition dump, caused a smoke cloud to rise to 2,000 feet. (GG)

The 3rd Worcestershire continued to hold the line at Beaumont Hamel. (3WD) The 1st Wiltshire continued their 'rest' at Mailly Wood, this day continuing their training on a new piece of ground further away from the encampment, possibly to prevent drawing too much enemy attention to the camp. (1WD)

Johnston was back on duty, escorting yet another senior officer around the front-line trenches.

Such a 'quiet' day in the trenches would have enabled the newcomers of the 3rd Worcestershire to write home about their first impressions of life in the trenches. Sadly, no such letters survive from Albert. However, since the first edition of this book was published, one such has come to light, from 29067 Pte. Wallace Pratt of the 3rd Worcestershire. From his regimental number, it is highly probable that he would have been in the same draft of reinforcements as Albert and would have probably have known him as well. His letter home is typical of that 'first' letter home (original spellings etc. retained):

> 29067
> C Company
> 12 Platoon
> 3 Battalion
> Worcester Regiment
> B.E.F.

Dear All at home,

Thanks very much for the letter, it's the first I have had since I've left England. We keep on shifting and of course that throughs the letters out.

We came into the reserve trenches Saturday evening. We sleep and have our food in a dug-out, during the day at different times we go out trench-digging. We get plenty of shells over us all the time. We were a bit nervous the first going off, but we soon began to keep cool.

You ask about parcels, well you can send me some cake or anything tasty that will keep, it will be a change. I expect Grannie has sent me a parcel, only I don't expect I shall get it on account of our shelling. Don't send big ones.

Each time you write you must enclose a piece of paper and an envelope, because I can't get any here. Don't worry about me I shall be alright.

Tell father I have been within 250 yds of the German lines. Ask him if he thinks that is close enough. If he doesn't I do.

I don't suppose you know what a Dug out is, well as near as I can explain to you, it is a wide trench with a roof over, and we have made it very comfortable, I will tell more next time.

So Good bye with love from your
Wallace X

This letter gives little away and therefore would certainly passed censorship by his officer. Set now in its historical context it reveals much more. There is no mention of the heat, the stench of decomposing bodies or other discomforts of trench life in front of Beaumont Hamel – he had yet to learn to use the familiar ironic phrase 'in the pink' written by nearly all soldiers in the Great War to mask the realities of life from loved ones at home. His trench-digging would have been confined to night-time and his estimate of being 250 yards from the enemy front line is confirmed in Johnston's account. Likewise his (and those others of the new drafts) first reaction to shellfire.

There are also more personal touches. His request for small parcels is justified. A soldier had to carry everything he owned on long marches (generally in excess of the 66lb, usually stated). Finding places to carry all the items from a large parcel within his equipment would have been difficult, and add to its weight. Quantities of perishable goods would have been another obvious problem. This is one very practical reason why soldiers generally pooled parcels from home. This sharing amongst members of the section ensured a near constant supply of 'treats' from home for all, and built comradeship.

The postal service between families in England and their loved ones 'somewhere' on the Western Front was a remarkable feat of organisation recognised as being of vital importance by the War Office to maintain morale. Letters took a couple of days, parcels usually arrived within a week. Despite Wallace's worries, very little went astray. Wallace's request for paper was quite genuine as all types of paper were short in the front line. When looking at survivals of correspondence between Great War soldiers and their families, there is generally a bias in favour of letters sent home from soldiers. It is not that a soldier's family did not write to him, it is just that well-read letters in the front-line could (and did!) serve one final, but very necessary purpose.

Sadly, Wallace would never elaborate to his family on the construction of his dug-out. He too, would share the fate of Albert Turley. Indeed, this letter was to be his last letter home.

FRIDAY 4 AUGUST
Slightly cooler (maximum 26°C, minimum 11°C). A successful day, as 2,000 yards of the main German second line to the north of Pozières was taken. (GG)

The 3rd Worcestershire continued to hold the line at Beaumont Hamel. (3WD) The 1st Wiltshire continued their 'rest' at Mailly Wood; the diarist, being hot and bored, concluded his entry with '*more training*' and '*nothing of importance occurred*'. (1WD)

Johnston, together with senior officers, revisited the Ancre Valley and completed a report to division at the 8th Loyal North Lancs HQ in Hamel. In addition to his concerns about the lack of training for the new drafts of men, he had clearly picked up information about the future plans for the brigade:

One never sees any of the Division people up in our trenches, and they therefore know next to nothing about the conditions up here. Hear we are to be relieved by the 6th Division, which is a pleasant surprise, though we are very comfortable here, except that the new drafts want training a lot, which of course cannot be done while in the line. We shall only be out 4 days, but it will be better than nothing. (AJ 4/8)

Some battalions prided themselves in their appearance in the front line e.g. Regular units. 'Clean' water was always scarce in the front line and usually reserved for drinking. Washing and shaving was therefore difficult and in lesser units than the 3rd Worcestershire may have been dispensed with. Men would have had to manage with a much-shared mess-tin full of water or tea to wash and shave in. Open razors were still the norm among soldiers, stropped on the reverse side of their leather trouser belt. Expensive safety razors with disposable blades could be sent out from home. Officers preferred the 'Valet Autostrop', a safety razor with a disposable blade that could be internally stropped to extend its life. Albert's youth may well have spared him this daily chore. However, one item that had to be kept clean was a soldier's rifle, brasses may have been allowed to tarnish (and they certainly would!) in the front line, but the rifle mechanism had to be kept spotless! It was also a 'crime' to go into action with a rusty bayonet.

Albert would have tried to sleep for much of the day in periods of maybe an hour or so at a time. Sections holding the bay of a trench were required to provide one (or two) look-outs on 'sentry-go' in two hour stretches all day and night. In the daytime a trench-periscope would be used, at night it would be relatively safe to look over the parapet directly. Support lines may have had dug-outs in which to shelter and sleep, in the front line normally 'funk-holes' were dug to just get the body inside, leaving the legs dangling in the trench. Soldiers mostly slept on the firestep in all positions with just their groundsheet for cover. Notwithstanding enemy and friendly artillery activity, with periodic tours by officers (at which all came to 'attention') for inspections etc. and other 'traffic' passing up and down the trench knocking limbs etc, getting any sleep at all could be quite difficult.

Despite this activity, for much of the time Albert would simply be waiting, trying to find something to occupy his mind. Staring at trench walls and the narrow sky line above would soon pall.

Time would simply drag by. Worse still, was being on sentry duty, two hours simply staring at the same view, desperately trying to stay awake when aching for a rest. To be found asleep on sentry duty was a court martial offence with potentially fatal consequences. Counting helped, barbs on barbed wire, trees on a distant hill, anything and everything just to stay awake and vigilant. At night, this would be worse. Innocent humps in the ground in daytime would become an enemy raiding party at night that you swear had just moved. Had that 'dead body' that the Very Light had just illuminated been there the last time? The desire to sleep would only increase, standing with the point of your fixed bayonet just under your chin might be painful if you dozed, but it could save your life!

SATURDAY 5 AUGUST

A much cooler day (maximum 20°C, minimum 9°C) with conditions still clear. The fighting, particularly by the Australian troops around Pozières, was nearing its conclusion and receiving commendations from Haig. (GG) The Australian divisions lost 23,000 men in capturing these positions. This part of the Somme battlefield, maintained in perpetuity by Australia, would become a permanent memorial to these brave men.

The 3rd Worcestershire continued to hold the line at Beaumont Hamel. (3WD) The 1st Wiltshire continued their 'rest' at Mailly Wood. (1WD) However, it was becoming clear to all the troops that a change was coming, the 1st Wiltshire devoting only two hours to training this day. All round there would be signs of clearing up, ready for the expected move.

Johnston was busy making plans for this relief. He would finish this day's entry with a cutting remark about the qualities of the new recruits filling the gaps in his four battalions:

Took some officers of the 6th Division all round the trenches in the morning. Went up again after dark . . . and saw the various working parties. Except for a bad ¼ hour about 11.30 p.m. with a Minenwerfer it was a fairly quiet night: quite a bit of progress was made with the work except that I'm afraid these new drafts don't know how to dig. (AJ 5/8)

Some of 'these new drafts', Albert Turley included, wearied by spending nearly a week in a blistering hot trench, had they but known it, had finished with digging forever.

SUNDAY 6 AUGUST
A warm day (maximum 24°C, minimum 11°C). Fighting continued east of Pozières and some ground was gained towards the village of Martinpuich. (GG)

It was a day of changes as the battalions of the 7th Brigade were withdrawn from the line. The 3rd Worcestershire were relieved in the front-line trenches before Beaumont Hamel by the 1st West Yorks. They then marched back to billets at Bertrancourt, a distance of 5 miles. Their losses had been heavier than their sister battalion when holding the line, with eight killed and eighteen wounded. (3WD) The 1st Wiltshire also moved from Mailly Wood, as the 11th Essex moved in, to billets at Bus-les-Artois. (1WD)

Johnston too was moving on, having handed over to the 18th Infantry Brigade. He rode back to Bus-les-Artois to join the 1st Wiltshire.

Albert's first tour in the trenches was completed. By now he would have learned first-hand the life of the soldier in the front line. He knew the work involved with the maintenance of the fire and support trenches, digging and wiring out in front of the British lines in full view of the enemy only shielded by the night. He had witnessed the horror, the sight and smell of dead soldiers rotting out in No Man's Land; he may even have witnessed some of his comrades being wounded or killed. He had known the long hours of boredom during the heat of the day, and the long hours of the night on 'sentry-go'. He would have also known fear, in the anticipation of an enemy raid on the trench at dawn and dusk 'stand to', and the shelling of his position – dodging up and down the trench to avoid the slow tumbling German trench mortars. He had, indeed, been 'blooded', yet he knew that holding the line was only a part of his future life. He knew that soon he would have to withstand a 'real' bombardment and take part in an attack or perhaps defend against one. This would be the true test of his training.

THE CALM BEFORE THE STORM – 7 TO 18 AUGUST 1916

MONDAY 7 AUGUST

Another warm summer's day (maximum 23°C, minimum 10°C). The British made a strong attack on the village of Guillemont; the Germans did likewise towards Pozières. Neither attack succeeded. (GG)

The 3rd Worcestershire stayed in the army camp at Bertrancourt, where further training was carried out. (3WD) The 1st Wiltshire remained at Bus-les-Artois. (1WD) Both villages were the sites of main dressing stations for the wounded; as a consequence both would have had sizeable military cemeteries. Apart from training, some time was given over to recreation. Soldiers of the 1st Wiltshire took on the Royal Army Medical Corps stationed there in a football match, winning the game 4–0. (1WD)

Johnston had spent the morning watching the troops training, but admitted to his diary that he had '*had a real slack day*'. (AJ 7/8) He does not mention whether he watched the football match!

TUESDAY 8 AUGUST

The weather again began to get hotter (maximum 25°C, minimum 11°C). Some gains were made in the pincer attack on the village of Guillemont, notably the ruins of the railway station to the north of the village. The matching attack from the south on Arrow Head Copse failed. (GG)

Both the 3rd Worcestershire and the 1st Wiltshire continued training their troops at Bertrancourt and Bus-les-Artois respectively. (3WD, 1WD) Typically, training would last all morning, giving some free time to the troops during the afternoon to avoid the main heat of the day.

Johnston had an enjoyable day, including in his diary an entry typical of the Regular pre-war officer:

Usual ride round in the morning [probably visiting individual battalion HQs]. In the afternoon went with the Gen[eral] and listened to the band of the 2nd Irish Guards who are in WARNIMONT WOOD – a real treat to hear a good Band once more; had tea with the officers. On the way back listened to the pipes of the Scots Guards, which was very nice too. It does one good to see all these Guardsmen about, fine big smart looking fellows, and there are any amount of them too. Dined with the Regiment [3rd Worcestershire] in the evening at BERTRANCOURT to celebrate Gibbs getting command; had a very cheery evening and had the Drums of the 2nd Irish Guards to play to us. (AJ 8/8)

Lt-Col W.B. Gibbs, the successor to Col Davidge, unlike Pte A.E. Turley would survive the attack of 24 August, but he too had less than one month to live.

WEDNESDAY 9 AUGUST
Another hot day (maximum 29°C, minimum 12°C). Following yesterday's successes, this day's attempt to take the village of Guillemont also ended in failure. (GG)

The 3rd Worcestershire continued their stay at Bertrancourt, continuing the training of the new recruits. (3WD) Probably, as with the 1st Wiltshire, they were also furnishing troops for fatigues. Four hundred of the 1st Wiltshire marched off at 5.25 a.m. for work between Mesnil and Engelbelmer, a gruelling task in the heat. The NCOs remaining in camp at Bus-les-Artois were treated to drill, led by a Guards instructor. The officers had an easier time, attending an exhibition of bomb-throwing at Divisional HQ. (1WD)

Johnston was feeling the heat, and had also heard news of another change: '*Another tremendously hot day. Apparently, the whole Division is being relieved by the Guards. I wonder if we shall be out long enough to really train these drafts.*' (AJ 9/8)

Having despaired at the actions of the new drafts in the line only a few days before, Johnston was finally hopeful that the officers and NCOs of the battalions would have a good chance to lick the new men into shape.

THURSDAY 10 AUGUST

A cooler, cloudy day (maximum 21°C, minimum 12°C) with heavy rain (4mm). To the south of the Somme battlefield, at Bois Français, King George V was visiting the troops. Only a few miles away British soldiers were making further advances beyond Pozières. The king would have clearly heard the shell-fire from this, and would himself have been well within range of the German artillery. (GG)

Both the 3rd Worcestershire and 1st Wiltshire continued the training of troops, the 1st Wiltshire again sending troops (500) for fatigues between Mesnil and Engelbelmer.

Johnston had a day's leave in Amiens, a large city less than 20 miles from the front line, where life was normal – or as normal as life could be so close to the war:

> Had a day's outing in AMIENS which was a pleasant change. Had a car placed at our disposal all day so drove with the Gen[eral] through ACHEUX, WARLOY etc. Got there about noon, had an excellent lunch and dinner at Godbars, did some shopping; quite refreshing to find oneself suddenly in quite a different atmosphere in the midst of crowded streets, trams etc. Had a look at the Cathedral, quite a fine building but all the choir and valuable wood work and pictures have been covered up with sandbags, also most of the best glass has been removed, I believe in case the Huns should shell the place or drop bombs etc. . . . Got back to BUS-LES-ARTOIS midnight. News good, we seem to be steadily gaining ground on all fronts. However we have much to do yet, and on this front the Bosche is keeping his best troops, and will fight to the death rather than retire. (AJ 10/8)

Amiens was safe for the moment; the city would become the focus for the major German offensive in the spring of 1918, but would not be taken. A quarter of a century later the cathedral and many other fine buildings would be bombed, causing much destruction and loss of life. However, contrary to Johnston's predictions, it would be the British who would do the bombing.

FRIDAY 11 AUGUST

A hot stormy day following a misty morning (maximum 25°C, minimum 15°C). (GG)

In the 7th Brigade it was a day of upheavals. The 3rd Worcestershire and the 1st Wiltshire – who had left 500 men behind for further fatigues at Bus-les-Artois – marched off to the village of Sarton via Louvencourt and Vauchelles, a distance of 6¼ miles. The 10th Cheshire and 8th Loyal North Lancs were billeted en route at Vauchelles. On arrival at Sarton, the men's feet were inspected – a regular event in the life of officers and soldiers alike. The officers were lectured by the CO. (3WD, 1WD)

Johnston was involved with the organisation of these moves, but remained in 'bad billets' at Vauchelles. He, like all the other senior officers, was very busy this day, as the king, on his tour of the Somme battlefields, would be passing through Sarton the following day. The 3rd Worcestershire and 1st Wiltshire, as senior battalions of the brigade, would be there to witness this and give him a cheer.

Albert Turley, who hitherto had probably not ventured far from his home in the Forest of Dean, was now 'somewhere in France', preparing to greet his sovereign and commander-in-chief. After his time in the trenches, and the days out of the line undergoing exhausting training and fatigues, the next day would be the highlight of his army career.

SATURDAY 12 AUGUST

A hot day (maximum 28°C, minimum 18°C) with some rain (1mm). Fighting continued to the northwest of Pozières, as the British advanced this day on a mile-long front. (GG)

Both the 3rd Worcestershire and half of the 1st Wiltshire would have had early morning inspections and formed up along the main road passing through the village of Sarton. The remainder of the 1st Wiltshire rejoined the battalion later in the day, unfortunately missing the whole event. (3WD, 1WD)

Johnston gives the best picture of this eventful day:

Went down to SARTON where we lined the streets. The king arrived at 10.30 a.m., shook hands and spoke a few words to the senior officers, and then drove on in his car through the troops who gave him a good cheer. The Prince of Wales was with him and looks splendid, quite the typical healthy young Englishman. Everybody likes him immensely, and one hears that those who are looking after him have a time of it, as he is always going up in front if he gets half a chance. (AJ 12/8)

It was a fleeting visit, but no doubt one that those present would not forget. The troubles in the then Prince of Wales's later life were still twenty years ahead. For the troops, after this parade it was back to the normal life associated with being 'down the line' – endless training and fatigues.

SUNDAY 13 AUGUST

A hot but thankfully breezy day (maximum 27°C, minimum 15°C). 'Munster Alley', a notorious German trench beyond the village of Pozieres, finally fell to the troops of the 15th Division. (GG)

The day, although a Sunday, was not a day of rest for the 3rd Worcestershire and 1st Wiltshire. Training would continue, after a voluntary church parade at 9 a.m. for the 1st Wiltshire, in the form of a circular route march via Theivres and Orville. It was felt that the ordinary rank and file would become lazy, inefficient and difficult to manage if they were not kept busy doing something. (3WD, 1WD)

Johnston, on the other hand, was excused: '*Another scorching* [sic] *hot day. Did a little work in the office and wrote letters.*' (AJ 13/8)

MONDAY 14 AUGUST

A showery day (2mm rain) but still very warm (maximum 25°C, minimum 15°C). (GG)

Both the 3rd Worcestershire and 1st Wiltshire remained at Sarton training, this day concentrating on bayonet-fighting, bombing and company drill. (3WD, 1WD)

Johnston was excited – he had heard a rumour:

Rode down to SARTON in the morning. Am possibly going to command a battalion, a magnificent job but one of great difficulty and responsibility in these days of few and inexperienced officers, semi-trained NCOs, and raw recruits sometimes of not too good material. (AJ 14/8)

This rumour would prove to be fact.

TUESDAY 15 AUGUST
A warm day (maximum 24°C, minimum 14°C) with heavy rain in the evening. The king returned to England from his visit to the Western Front. (GG)

It was a day of movement for the 3rd Worcestershire and the 1st Wiltshire as they were marched down the straight Roman road via Raincheval to Puchevillers, a distance of 5½ miles. The 1st Wiltshire set off in companies from 6 a.m., making good time, the final company arriving in the huts there at 8.30 a.m. (3WD, 1WD)

Marching . . . the most common means of mass troop transportation in the Great War. Although Albert would have spent much of his training being steadily hardened to march increasing distances with increasing loads, such a relatively short march on a hot day would have been far from a pleasant stroll. His uniform was designed to both keep him warm at night and be comfortable (to an extent) in the heat of the day. This started with his underwear consisting of a stout set of vest and long underpants. The temptation to cut down the latter was resisted as they prevented chaffing on the march. Above this was a thick flannelette shirt and woollen serge trousers held up by canvas braces and a leather belt. On his feet were woollen socks and nailed regulation boots weighing 2lb each. Keeping the mud out of his boots and usefully supporting his lower leg muscles he wore puttees, spirally wound long lengths of material. His boots would have been tied in a manner not generally found today. the single lace tightened and wound around the ankle of the boot so that the securing knot was at the back. Ensuring his puttee started at the fifth pair of holes in his boot, they would wind neatly around the ankle giving them a smooth appearance at the front. On top, he wore his tunic, again of thick woollen serge. In hot weather, the wool acted as a wick drawing moisture away from the body to be readily evaporated. After a march, his woollen clothing would actually be relatively dry. However, the cotton parts (notably his pockets, tunic/trouser linings and inner surfaces of his webbing) would be soaked and wretchedly uncomfortable.

A soldier carried everything he needed on his person and in his equipment. The design for this was based on the 1908 pattern webbing which was so designed to be put together (from many individual parts) to suit the stature of an individual soldier. When correctly assembled, the whole was perfectly balanced and, despite its weight, could be safely worn unbuckled at the waist with no danger of it falling off.

Most of the weight would be in Albert's large pack, carried on his back. His small pack, containing other personal items would be another (though lesser) weight on his left hip. Given the list of what the large pack was supposed to contain, it is difficult to see, when faced with this large pile of equipment, how it is possible to fit it all in, let alone make the pack look neat! No published book I have read explains how it was done. The secret has thankfully survived through oral tradition. It is quite easy when shown how and, with practice, there is space to spare! The vital part is to fold and roll up the greatcoat which goes in first and *sideways*. This is then beaten into the four corners and a central hole forced down the middle. At the bottom is then put the items that are not readily needed i.e. spare socks and 'cap comforter' (a sealed knitted tube, the length of a small scarf (or comforter) which when internally rolled and folded becomes a useful warm cap!). On top of this went his '*mess-tin and lid*' in its cover, the space inside being useful dry storage for that cake from home, spare cigarettes and paper. On top of this goes the holdall containing washing equipment, razor, comb, polishing kit and spare laces. Here too, should be his knife, fork and spoon. Kept here for inspection purposes, it was far better to keep utensils in the front pocket of his small pack where they were easier to get at if needed. At this point, the 'hole' is full. All that remains is to push the '*hussif*' or 'housewife' (a folded pouch of thread, needles and spare buttons) down one side and to lay the folded wash towel flat on the top. Here too, could be laid the folded groundsheet, though it was better to keep this in the small pack too, or under the outside straps of the large pack. If allowed, another good place was under the epaulette to spread the weight of the rifle sling on the march (see below). The side flaps were then folded in and the main flap of the large pack brought down and secured.

By now, Albert may well have learned a few 'tricks' to make long marches more bearable. On each front, he wore five ammunition pouches each filled with fifteen rounds of ammunition. 'Old' soldiers would have kept the two outermost only partly filled (if filled at all). This prevented the constant rubbing of the bulging pouches on the tender inside of his upper arm. In '*marching order*', his cased entrenching tool helve would normally be worn on the right hip under his waterbottle. In '*battle-order*' this was moved to be attached to his main straps at the small of his back under his (also relocated) small pack (his large pack being left behind in an attack). Here, it was more comfortable, saving the constant rubbing against his right hip. He would have made sure his bayonet scabbard/entrenching tool handle was pushed as far back on his left side as possible, otherwise they would constantly hit his left thigh at every step. His most useful equipment: groundsheet (doubling as a waterproof cape), cigarettes etc., food and spoon would have been placed where they were easiest to get at and maybe not where they should be *by the book*. An awkward feature was his waterbottle, strapped into a carrier and fixed to his belt. Soldiers selected a slack fitting carrier (or made one so), otherwise it would need a friend to get the bottle out and certainly need one to put it back in! Strangely, a cup was not an issue item, the mess-tin lid serving (rather inadequately) for this purpose. Most soldiers 'acquired' a metal cup, then attached it on the outside of his small pack under the fastening, next to his ration bag. Despite the added weight of his 'tin-hat' (or 'Brodie'), it provided far better head-cover from the sun and rain than the formal (sweaty) 'SD' cap and allowed a cooling draught over the top of his head. By 1916, gone was the stereotype of the elegant, smartly dressed British soldier of 1914 –

the 'rag-bag' collection of 'Tommies' with no two being dressed exactly the same was now the norm, at least near the front line.

Despite this, marching was not comfortable. The 2˝ shoulder straps, bearing most of the weight of the equipment would begin to dig in to muscles and collar bone and 'hunching' the shoulders and pulling the straps forwards would only bring temporary relief. On the march, troops mostly '*marched at ease*' when they carried the rifle as seemed fit (they would '*march at attention*' with the rifle '*at the slope*' through villages and past other units – 'Regular' units i.e. 3rd Worcestershire, making a particular point of this). Most soldiers slackened the rifle strap and carried it conveniently over the shoulder where the regimental shoulder title on his epaulette would then hold it in place if he needed both hands. This too, soon caused an ache as the weight of the rifle (9lb) bore down on its much narrower webbing sling onto the shoulder joint. Thankfully at will, he could alternate shoulders and carry the rifle at point of balance in his hand parallel to the ground, '*at the trail*'.

Keeping going on the march was not only physically demanding but mentally challenging too. Normally, marching in '*columns of four*' meant that for the middle two soldiers, the back of a head and rear equipment provided much of the view. Looking at the ground was not a good alternative, it gave the false impression of speed which rapidly developed into dizziness. Soldiers at the outsides could at least look sideways and enjoy the view, but got the worst of any soaking when a passing lorry went through a puddle! To add to this, soldiers were required to '*keep in step*' and in better units (Regulars) '*maintain dressing*' too. The former would soon become automatic and monotonous, deviation in the latter meant clipping the heels of the soldier in front or being clipped by the soldier behind, either soon brought a 'distant' soldier back to attention and a few choice words from the senior NCO marching alongside.

Each hour, ten minutes rest would be given for soldiers to relax, take a drink, have a smoke etc. Surprisingly, this short period was generally enough to 'cure' most problems, at least for a while. In the latter stages of a long march, march discipline might be relaxed. Usually, the final stretch would be done '*at attention*', the soldiers then anticipating final arrival at their destination.

On this day, Johnston set off later, possibly riding with the 3rd Worcestershire. His mind, however, was on other matters:

> The Brigade marched through RAINCHEVAL to PUCHEVILLERS once more, where we have a pretty good billet: a short march and we got in by 10 a.m. The G.O.C. Division has written to the authorities strongly recommending me for the Command of a battalion. I wonder which one I'll get. Stayed in all afternoon. (AJ 15/8)

On 28 August Johnston was made temporary Lieutenant-Colonel and put in charge of the 10th Cheshire. This was a double irony: first, this 'New Army' battalion was one of those Johnston cruelly deprecated in his earlier diary entries; secondly, it is also probable that he missed taking charge of his 'Regiment', the 3rd Worcestershire, by only one week.

Arrival at the village of Puchevillers meant more than simply further routine training. As well as being a main railhead for the supply of ammunition and the recovery of the wounded from the Casualty Clearing Station there, here there were fields containing full-scale trench systems. These were used to practise attacks. If Albert and his fellow replacements had wondered what all these days of extensive training were for, then he now had his answer. Even if Albert hadn't been told the place or the date, it was clear that he would soon be taking a very active part in the relentless Battle of the Somme.

WEDNESDAY 16 AUGUST
A warm (maximum 24°C, minimum 13°C) but wet day (2mm rain). The British advanced both west and south-west of the village of Guillemont. However, the German garrison was still valiantly holding on, and would continue to do so for some time yet. (GG)

Both the 3rd Worcestershire and 1st Wiltshire continued their training at Puchevillers. Two companies of the latter spent the day on the practice trenches in the fields near the road to Marieux. (3WD, 1WD)

Johnston was still preoccupied: 'Dull day. Went for a short ride in *the morning. No news.'* (AJ 16/8) He and the troops of the 7th Brigade would now be in for a rude awakening: the time for training was over.

THURSDAY 17 AUGUST

The weather was changing, this day although still warm (maximum 23°C, minimum 12°C) being a mixture of showers and bright spells. (GG)

For both the 3rd Worcestershire and 1st Wiltshire, the training had been completed. Both battalions moved off and marched 'up the line' via Harponville to Hedauville, a distance of a little over 8 miles. The 1st Wiltshire set off by companies at 5-minute intervals at 6 p.m., finally arriving in billets at 10 p.m. (3WD, 1WD, STK)

Johnston witnessed this at first hand, possibly again with the 3rd Worcestershire. However, he for one knew their ultimate destination:

> On the move once more up this time, moving in the late afternoon through TOUTENCOURT, HARPONVILLE, VARENNES to HEDAUVILLE getting there about 8.30 p.m. Hear we were to go into our old friends the trenches in and near to the LEIPZIG SALIENT first thing tomorrow morning. Very short notice, and gives no one any chance of reconnoitring; however it is ground we know, and as there is going to be an attack tomorrow afternoon just on our right, it is necessary to get our relief over early. Everything rather a rush as battalions did not get here till about 11 p.m., orders for the relief etc. had to be got out, and battalions had to start again 5 a.m. (AJ 17/8)

One of the battalions waiting for relief was the 7th Warwickshire (48th Division). Corporal (later Captain) Henry Ogle (MC) on this day was there with a ration party based in Bouzincourt, taking much needed supplies up to his battalion in the trenches in front of the Leipzig Salient. He has left behind an account of his journey up into those trenches following the route Albert was to take a few hours later:

The battalion was in the line near the north-eastern edge or corner of Authuille Wood. The approach was by road and communication trench which skirted the southern side of the wood along a steep slope. At the top, the slope eased off after the corner of the wood was reached and the turn led north to a broad spur on which the Germans had made the Leipzig Salient works. . . .

. . . It was on the night of 17 August . . . that our party set out with rations and stores for D company in the line. We passed the thundering big guns in the valley and began to climb. the Battalion was due out the following night. It began to look as if Jerry was expecting our relief to take place on this night, for well placed shells fell on the way up and there had been none the other nights . . .

. . . D company was in the front line, such as it was, and after some scrambles we reached their headquarters to find their part of the sector in that state which we had come to regard as 'quiet'. But this was not to last any longer, for we had hardly delivered our loads and assembled to return when we heard the well known distant whine, increasing in volume and intensity with fearful speed, then deepening into an overwhelming roar, as a salvo of 5.9s [a German medium-sized shell] plunged into the ground in front of the fire-trench at an angle, the nearest shell bursting exactly under the parapet. The resulting crater breached the parapet and filled the trench. the four explosions were almost simultaneous and heralded a barrage which must have been designed to catch the relief, which they evidently expected, when our trenches would have been full of arrivals and departures. . . .

. . . We heard a frightfully sudden *whizz-bang!*, followed in rapid succession by three more which all skimmed the parados [the back of a trench] and exploded just behind. . . . Next came the shriek and droning roar of another salvo of 5.9s descending nearer to the communication trench by which we had just come and by which we hoped to depart. These explosions must have covered the noise of a gas shell or two, for from the support line came the ding-dong-dong-dang of the gas alarm. . . . There was nothing we could do but wait for a lull long enough to get away in. . . .

. . . We had not much longer to wait. Away on our left the uproar seemed to increase. Suddenly it was all over. It may have lasted five minutes, probably much less. Had there been a relief in progress the casualties would have been heavy . . . I think we only got the thin fringe of the shelling. There were shouts for stretcher bearers from several quarters elsewhere but we had come through untouched. We were all ready and lost no time in getting away.

Albert had a lucky escape it would seem, though in the days to come, the 3rd Worcestershire would lose many men to such sudden barrages in front of the Leipzig Salient.

As the entries for the past two weeks reveal, Albert Turley, at least, was not an example of 'cannon fodder'; he was not thrown into a useless attack without having been trained. On the contrary, he had received training with some of the best soldiers available at the time. He had been under fire in the front line, albeit in a quiet sector, to accustom him to life in the trenches and to the sounds of shell-fire. There was little else now that he could be taught: from now on he would have to take his chances along with seasoned troops, NCOs and officers. This would be Albert's first attack. Should he survive, he knew that any remaining prejudice there may still have been against him and the other Derby Men would be ended. But first, he would have to survive.

Many of Albert's comrades would well remember their earlier experiences fighting in the Leipzig Salient. Albert would probably have heard their stories on the march when the news of their final destination filtered down to the rank and file. One can only speculate as to the emotions Albert felt as he arrived in the rain and dark at Hedauville that night, tired and wet through; but in the distance he would have seen the flashes of guns to the east bringing the Thiepval Ridge across the valley brightly into relief. Here was his destiny – a far cry from the peaceful hills and valleys of his childhood home in the Forest of Dean.

Reconstructing the Past

THE EXPERIENCES OF PTE A.E. TURLEY,
3RD WORCESTERSHIRE
JULY–AUGUST 1916

Part 2

Over The Top

18 TO 25 AUGUST

FRIDAY 18 AUGUST

An overcast day and cooler (maximum 23°C, minimum 13°C) with a little rain (1 mm). Further British attacks near the villages of Guillemont and Ginchy were successful, but an attack by the 33rd Division on High Wood failed – this area too was continuing to hold up the overall advance. The character of the Somme battle was beginning to become one of attrition, ground gained was becoming less important than numbers of Germans killed. (GG)

The 3rd Worcestershire and 1st Wiltshire left for the front line in the Leipzig Salient early in the morning. The 3rd Worcestershire at 5 a.m., the 1st Wiltshire after an initial party of 100 men, by companies, starting at 7.45 a.m. Their route would likely have taken them through the village of Bouzincourt and down into the Ancre Valley to cross the river at Aveluy and enter the Authuille Wood trench system at Crucifix Corner, exactly where the 3rd Worcestershire had left it the previous month. The relief for both battalions went quietly and was completed by midday, the 3rd Worcestershire relieving a battalion of the West Yorkshires on the left of the 1st Wiltshire. The positions in the Leipzig Salient had changed little since both units had last been here in the line in early July. The 1st Wiltshire reported a quiet day, with only a few enemy trench mortars falling on their left front. (3WD, 1WD).

The general plan was to restart operations in this area with a joint offensive by units of the 25th and 48th Divisions. The latter had taken over the Ovillers-la-Boisselle area after the 25th Division had left it in mid-July. By mid-August, the Ovillers Spur was in British hands. It was time for another try for the fortress of Thiepval. (STK)

Johnston was up in the front line, with the 3rd Worcestershire:

Went down to our old HQ in BLIGHTY VALLEY near
AUTHUILLE WOOD in the morning. Relief went off easily.
Did not go out in the afternoon owing to the attack going
on, on our right. It seems to have gone awfully well, as we
got all our objectives and 500 prisoners with only very small
losses ourselves. We got a good deal of the retaliation but
little damage done. (AJ 18/8)

Albert would have noticed the difference in atmosphere in these
trenches; this was not the quiet sector that Beaumont Hamel had
been. The attack, described by Johnston, would not have been
clearly visible from the 3rd Worcestershire on the left of the Brigade
front. The 1st Wiltshire, however, would have had a better view of
what was to come.

SATURDAY 19 AUGUST
The weather was set overcast and cooler (maximum 23°C,
minimum 10°C) with rain (2mm). (GG)
    Local operations continued on the far right of the 3rd
Worcestershire. Although not directly involved, they still took
casualties from retaliatory shell-fire (8 wounded). (3WD, STK) The
1st Wiltshire, nearer the action on the right, had a quiet day and
were settling in to the routine of holding an active part of the
British front line. A (left) and C (right) Companies were in the
front line with D Company in the reserve line and B Company in
support in Oban Avenue behind their battalion HQ. (1WD) The
3rd Worcestershire have left no similar details of their
deployment, although they would have been similar to the 1st
Wiltshire, i.e. two companies in the front line, one in support and
the other in reserve.
    Johnston gives a picture of life in these trenches:

Went round the trenches with the Gen[eral]; rather wet
owing to last night's rain but apart from this I have never
seen trenches handed over in such a state, and the people

before seem to have no idea of keeping the place clean, and there were few signs of work having been done except in the LEIPZIG SALIENT. (AJ 19/8)

Complaints about the poor state of trenches handed over are common in officers' accounts. Soldiers were only too keen to go back 'down the line' to take much trouble in tidying up after themselves. Trench stores, particularly ammunition, had to be formally handed over, together with intelligence information relevant to the sector. Relieving battalions wisely went into the trenches loaded with such provisions in addition to their own heavy equipment.

SUNDAY 20 AUGUST

An overcast but better day weatherwise (maximum 23°C, minimum 13°C). In response to earlier British attacks, the Germans counter-attacked on the Thiepval Ridge – probably against units of the 48th Division. (GG, STK)

The 3rd Worcestershire and 1st Wiltshire continued to hold the line. The 1st Wiltshire reported a fairly quiet day with enemy mortars intermittently falling on the front line and around the battalion HQ. (1WD) The 1st Wiltshire lost one man killed and the 3rd Worcestershire lost one man wounded. (3WD)

For Johnston, things were now getting hectic:

Very busy day getting ready for these two attacks we are going to make, and the Gen[eral] is sick with a bad chill on the liver. Took Gen. Bainbridge round the trenches first, and then went up again for most of the afternoon. In the morning our Heavy Artillery did us a lot of harm by firing short; as usual they try and shoot off the map or have observers miles behind the line, they have no real idea where their shells are going; it has always been the way with these Heavy Gunners wherever one goes, and until they are made to come up they will never make accurate shooting. The Field Gunners are ever so much better. Got pretty heavily shelled by the Bosche in the afternoon and all our communication trenches got well knocked about.

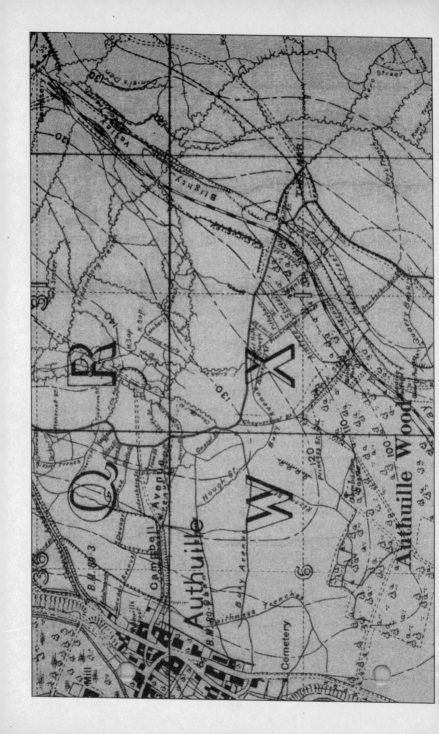

Rather a nuisance where there is so much traffic and so much stuff to carry up to prepare for the attacks in this trench warfare. Have been presented with the Croix de Guerre, which is a pleasant surprise. (AJ 20/8)

Johnston had had an awful day, having not only to organise things for the forthcoming attacks but also to cover for a sick general. The infantry and artillery had a long tradition of mutual distrust, the former often accusing the latter of 'dropping short'. In the First World War, artillery units employed a Forward Observation Officer (FOO) in or near the front line to report on the accuracy of shooting and direct fire onto new targets by telephone, or runners when the telephone lines were broken, which happened frequently, especially during artillery bombardments.

Both the 3rd Worcestershire and 1st Wiltshire diaries reported a quiet day, the former with only one man wounded. Any British shells dropping short and the later German bombardment must have indeed been concentrated on the communication trenches between the rear area and the front/support lines.

There may be another reason for British shells falling short, especially if Johnston was right about gunners firing 'off the map'.

The British issued trench maps for all parts of the Western Front, with updates as required. These had been based on French

Opposite: Trench Map of the Leipzig Salient (2)
Taken from map 57D SE4 edition 3A dated 1/9/16. This edition has many interesting new features compared with the previous map. The old German lines, now held by the British, are named, and both Lemberg and Hindenburg Trenches are clearly marked. Note the new communication trenches across the old No Man's Land linking up the old British front line with the captured positions. The road between the Nab and 'Campbell Avenue' has disappeared, probably the result of the relentless shelling of this tortured ground. Note also the difference in the positions of the contour lines in the Leipzig Salient, in particular the '140m' line has 'moved' southwards to the north of the Quarry/Leipzig Redoubt from above the large 'R' on the 2B edition. Blighty Valley is now named and a new light railway has evidently been constructed along it to the rear of the British positions.

originals, but were updated with British names for geographical features. The position of German trenches was also detailed, as were known or suspected defensive works, such as machine-gun posts. These were used to plan infantry attacks, and provide the necessary initial distance/elevations for artillery bombardments – to be verified by the FOO *in situ*. It was therefore vital that these maps were kept up-to-date as new information came to light.

The Imperial War Museum has issued a large number of these trench maps on a single CD-ROM. This allows detailed study of most actions on the Western Front. For security reasons, details of British trenches were usually omitted from the originals, although all known German trenches and features were shown. However, in areas such as the Leipzig Salient at this time, the British held some of these German positions previously identified, thus it is possible to discern the actual position held by the 3rd Worcestershire.

This CD-ROM has two maps for the area involving the Leipzig Salient for this period (Ovillers: 57dSE4 2b and 57dSE4 3a), dating from 11/6/16 and 1/9/16 respectively. Although the latter would not have been available to the troops on 20 August, it is clear that the edition number has increased from 2b to 3a.

Looking at the maps it is easy to identify captured German trenches as they change from red to blue lines. New trenches are also equally obvious as is the disappearance of roads, which may have been due to the action of long-term shell-fire.

However, there is a less apparent difference between them. On the 2b map there is a 140-metre contour line running across the north side of the quarry at the centre of the Leipzig Redoubt. On the 3a map, this contour line is not in the same place; in fact the 140-metre contour line lies further northwards, up the Thiepval Ridge. Inspecting other contour lines in the area reveals there is a 5-metre difference in recorded elevations between the 2b and 3a maps everywhere in the Leipzig Salient. Modern French maps confirm the elevations as given on the 2b edition trench map. This would suggest revisions of the map following 2b, and possibly the one in use on 20/8/16, may have had an inherent error. Further investigation revealed that there were such maps released between 2b and 3a. These were 2c on 1/7/16 (and 19/8/16) also a 2d

(Secret) edition on 1/9/16 in addition to the 3a released on the same day. Sadly, copies of these other editions are not held within the Imperial War Museum's archive. It is likely it will never be known which map the heavy artillery used this day.

Any initial calculations of British shelling relying on the editions of the map after 2b thus may have been in error by 5 metres. This error is comparable to the difference in elevations of Lemberg and Hindenburg Trenches on the Thiepval Ridge. Such an error could account for artillery shells dropping short on this day. The 'problem' would have been cleared up very quickly by a FOO – if he were indeed present. [It is also interesting to note that the attack on 3 September q.v. failed partly due to a problem with the artillery 'not lifting' – maybe this too was due to a faulty map and lack of observation.]

The receipt of the Croix de Guerre by Johnston would at least have cheered him up. He knew that the first of the attacks was the following afternoon; success would depend on the ability of the troops taking part and his own preparations.

MONDAY 21 AUGUST
A warm day (maximum 22°C, minimum 9°C). (GG)

This day Albert Turley would witness, and assist in, an attack on the Thiepval Ridge. There is some confusion regarding the actual date of this attack. With the exception of the 1st Wiltshire battalion diary, which puts these events on the 22nd, all the other sources unquestionably place them on the 21st. For the purposes of this narrative, the majority view is upheld.

On the immediate right of the 3rd Worcestershire in the Leipzig Salient trenches were the 1st Wiltshire and further again to the right (possibly out of sight) were the 1/4th Gloucestershire of the 48th Division. For the 1st Wiltshire, the attack would be made by C and D Companies, with B Company moving up in support from Oban Avenue to No Man's Alley. The British artillery had been shelling the German lines all day; this bombardment would reach its height at 6 p.m. A little later the troops would go over the top and up the Thiepval Ridge to attack the German trenches (Lemberg Trench). The rapid progress of the 1st Wiltshire was such that they actually ran into their own barrage before it lifted. The attack was successful, and the captured trenches were consolidated. In retaliation, the Germans shelled the British held trenches all night. (1WD). The total casualties in these days for the 1st Wiltshire had been ninety; records however reveal only two of these were killed in action, although some may have died of wounds later.

The 3rd Worcestershire had not only witnessed this attack, they provided supporting fire in an attempt to keep down the heads of supporting German units. They too suffered casualties in the retaliatory shell-fire, losing at least three killed together with eleven men wounded including one officer. (STK)

Johnston gives much more detail for this attack, in particular the part played by the 1st Wiltshire:

Up in the LEIPZIG REDOUBT most of the day making final arrangements for the attack. At 6 p.m. our guns put a 3 minute bombardment onto the German Trench, under cover of which two companies of the 1st Wilts got out of their trenches, lined up for the assault, and pushed out their snipers in front into crump holes from which they shot at any German sentry who ventured to look over. As the barrage lifted the 1st Wilts charged over; as a matter of fact they started a bit too soon and actually stopped and stood up in the middle of No Man's Land until the barrage lifted when they hopped into the German trench. That men should stand quietly in the middle of No Man's Land like this showed that they were well in hand and well disciplined; it was also a great compliment to our Gunners who shot magnificently, and there was not a single short round. The result was that the 1st Wilts were into the trench before the Germans knew anything was up, the sentries were bayoneted at once, and the rest of them bombed in their dugouts or taken prisoner. The fumite bombs were excellent for clearing dugouts except that they usually set the woodwork alight and the occupants were buried and burnt to death; this was rather a pity as one wants to use these dugouts oneself after capturing the trench. About 50 prisoners were taken and about the same number killed. On the right of our attack where we were close up to the Hun trench in which they had a block, we tried a 'push pipe machine' for the first time with great success. It is a contrivance which bores a pipe at the rate of 18 yards an hour underground under the German trench, the pipe is filled with ammonal, and as the boring makes no noise the Huns have no idea of its presence. When the 1st Wilts started, this was touched off and in addition to blowing up the German block, it made a ready made communication trench in their line, up which our bombing parties rushed on to the astonished Bosche. The Division on our right attacked at the same time, and although they did not quite get all they wanted, took a good many trenches and over 100 prisoners. The latter were all a very sorry crew, they say they have been shelled incessantly, get no sleep and not too much food, and I think they were all very glad to be taken prisoner. (AJ 21/8)

This account serves to help dispel another modern misunderstanding of British military tactics of the First World War, which holds that military command did not learn from their mistakes and repeatedly used tactics that resulted in failure and heavy loss of life. On 1 July, thousands of men had walked across No Man's Land after a preliminary bombardment that had lasted a week. The results had been very heavy casualties with little ground gained. This was due mainly to:

a) Lack of the correct *heavy* artillery required to cut the barbed wire defences and destroy defensive strongpoints.
b) Overconfidence in the effect of the long artillery bombardment used by lighter artillery pieces, leading commanders to believe that there would be no German resistance to the infantry attack.
c) Distrust of the attacking soldiers' abilities, who were overloaded with equipment and ordered to walk across No Man's Land in ordered formation.
d) Resilient German trench defences, adequately protecting the German defenders until the time of the attack.
e) Failure of attacking troops to 'mop up' surviving German defenders in dugouts, who on rising up to the 'captured trench'

overpowered the few British defenders left behind. They then were presented with easy targets, that is the backs of the lines of British attackers passing on into the German support lines.

f) Inflexibility in the plan of the attack, which was built on unfailing and continuing success by the attacking troops. The artillery barrage designed to protect the attacking troops was lost if they failed to keep up with the 'timetable'.

In this attack, note the improvements in tactics to overcome the above points:

a) Heavy artillery was used to adequately cut the German wire and destroy defensive strongpoints.

b) The bombardment prior to the attack was very short and concentrated on the German front line. This gave both the element of surprise to the attacking troops and served to limit the abilities of the defending German troops, which were expected to have survived, and still be in considerable force.

c) The soldiers, although still attacking in a wave, rushed across No Man's Land up to their own barrage, and thus were ready to leap into the German trench to take it once the barrage had lifted. Soldiers, too, had individual tasks according to their speciality (refined in the previous weeks of training), for example, snipers to keep down the heads of the defenders, bayonet men to lead the attack in the trench on the sentries and finally the bombers to clear the trench and dugouts.

d) The British had learned through painful experience the strength of German trench defences. In this attack, they were using new technology, for example the 'push pipe' to help overcome it.

e) 'Mopping up' was now taken very seriously. Fumite bombs consisted of a canister of white phosphorous, wax and petrol. These, when thrown into a dugout, would detonate and emit jets of liquid fire. This would serve to incinerate the dugout and any defenders therein.

f) The objective of the attack was limited to the capture of single trenches and defensive systems; there was no plan to 'push through to Bapaume'.

It was hardly surprising that the German defenders were all too willing to be taken prisoner. This attack had been completed in a matter of minutes with devastating effect. One is only left to speculate what might have been achieved on 1 July had similar tactics been used.

One feature of this attack, as Johnston mentions, was that the battalion on the right, the 1/4th Gloucestershire, had not achieved '*all they wanted*'. This unit, part of the 144th Brigade of 48th Division, had been heavily involved in the fighting south of Thiepval on the Ovillers Spur between 13 and 16 August. They had been relieved to Bouzincourt for the 17th, but had been brought back into the line for this attack, and presumably more. It was clear that they were now exhausted, more units of the 'refreshed' 7th Brigade would now have to shoulder the burden of attacks in the Leipzig Salient.

Albert had witnessed all this – the fury of the bombardment, troops going over the top, sounds of hand-to-hand fighting to the death, the destruction of dugouts – knowing that men were being burnt alive inside them, the retaliatory bombardment by the Germans of his own position. What must he have thought? One thing was for certain: having taken part in the weeks of training and watching the training being put into deadly practice, he would have realised that he and his battalion would very soon be undertaking a similar venture.

TUESDAY 22 AUGUST
Another fine day (maximum 22°C, minimum 11°C). Haig was becoming concerned at the time being taken to capture the village of Guillemont. The stout German defence of these ruins was slowing down the whole British advance on the south of the Somme battlefield. (GG)

The 3rd Worcestershire were still holding the Leipzig Salient trenches to the left of the 1st Wiltshire (3WD, STK). Consolidation of the newly captured trenches was continuing by the 1st Wiltshire and 1/4th Gloucestershire with bombing fights up and down shared trenches until both sides established a block that could be adequately defended. Despite the continuing fighting, the

1st Wiltshire had just one man killed this day, but the number of wounded is unknown. British and German shelling continued throughout the day. For the 3rd Worcestershire this would result in nine casualties of whom one was killed. Following the British success there would come the expected German counter-attack. Falkenhayn, the German commander on the Somme had ordered that all ground would be held to the last man. Each British attack was to be followed with a counter-attack irrespective of the value of any ground lost. Indeed, the British on the Somme, would 'only be allowed to advance over the bodies of the German dead', a phrase used by Falkenhayn's subordinate, Fritz von Below. Casualty figures for the Battle of the Somme vary, but together the British and French lost approximately 600,000 men. The Germans lost almost exactly the same number, due in part to Falkenhayn's strategy. German generals could be 'bunglers' and 'butchers' too.

Johnston had a very busy day:

> In the trenches all the morning and along our new captured ones – our artillery are certainly making an awful mess of the Hun trenches, and it is good to see that even some of the deep dugouts get damaged. After lunch brought up the G.O.C. Division up to the salient for a hurried visit. Stayed up myself making arrangement for our next attack. Got well pounded on my way back as the Germans put up a barrage, and eventually counter-attacked chiefly against the people on our right, but without success. (AJ 22/8)

The heavy artillery had done its job well. On the rolling uplands, the clay soil (responsible for the infamous 'Somme mud') overlaid chalk deposits. These allowed for easy excavation of deep (40ft) dugouts that were practically shellproof. The Germans had used the two years they had held this previously quiet front wisely, and had constructed extensive underground defence works capable of holding battalions of men in relative safety. Many were interlinked and provided with home comforts including wood-panelling, comfortable beds and electric lighting. The British had also used the chalk sub-strata to their advantage; they had constructed mineshafts underneath the

German lines. These had been filled with explosive and detonated before the attack on 1st July, with mixed results.

For the soldiers in the line in the Leipzig Salient, there would be little chance of sleep as the shelling was almost continuous. One or more sentries would be posted in each section of trench, looking out for both trench mortars and a now expected German counter-attack. As well as the noise and the fear, soldiers would have experienced the horror of seeing comrades killed and wounded by the shell-fire, as well as the necessary disposal of parts of shredded humanity in sandbags afterwards. Food and water supplies consisted of what the troops had brought into the line with them, and at night these could be replenished by the troops in reserve (10th Cheshire and 8th Loyal North Lancs.). The previous tour of the 3rd Worcestershire and 1st Wiltshire in the quiet trenches before Beaumont Hamel would now be largely forgotten. On top of the fatigue associated with holding the line day after day, they knew that another attack would soon be launched.

WEDNESDAY 23 AUGUST

A fair day (maximum 22°C, minimum 12°C). German counter-attacks continued unsuccessfully near the village of Guillemont. The first batch of 12 'tanks' had arrived on the Somme. It was hoped that these 'secret weapons' would be able to break the stalemate of trench warfare on the Somme. But they would be not be used until the middle of September, when it would be a case of too few, too soon losing the element of surprise for these potential war-winning weapons. (GG)

The 1st Wiltshire continued to hold the captured trenches in the vicinity of the Leipzig Redoubt, probably relieved that the continuation of the attack on the Thiepval Ridge was now to be delayed. German shell-fire was sporadic; the British continued to bombard the German trenches to good effect. The 1st Wiltshire lost at least five men killed, and an unknown number wounded. (1WD)

The delay was caused by the acceptance that the 1/4th Gloucestershire, after making several successful attacks and resisting all German counter-attacks in the past few days, were now too depleted to undertake yet another attack. The 1st

Wiltshire were still strong. However, pairing this battalion with a much-weakened one may have jeopardised the next attack. It was decided to withdraw the 1/4th Gloucestershire from the Leipzig Salient and bring the 3rd Worcestershire around the back of, and through the 1st Wiltshire to take over the newly captured Lemberg Trench from them. This hasty relief and holding of the Lemberg Trench was completed by 9 a.m. and was very costly, the 3rd Worcestershire losing fifty-four men of whom at least five were killed. In turn, the battalion in reserve, the 10th Cheshire, would replace the 3rd Worcestershire and support the forthcoming attack from the left flank. It was now up to two battalions of 7th Brigade, the 3rd Worcestershire and the 1st Wiltshire, to continue the attack on the Thiepval Ridge. (3WD, STK)

On the verge of taking over the 10th Cheshire, Johnston now had his work cut out in reorganising the planned attack at the shortest notice to now include the 3rd Worcestershire:

> The attack postponed, and the line re-arranged so as to enable us to take on a bigger objective. We now have 3 full battalions in the line, and had a very busy day making dumps of bombs, S[mall] A[rms] A[mmunition], R[oyal] E[ngineer] material and other arrangements in the new bit of our area [the 3rd Worcestershire frontage]. Lively shelling all day, and yet again our Heavies observing well behind the line fired into us. (AJ 23/8)

For Albert and the rest of the 3rd Worcestershire, things had been bad, but now they had become much worse. They were about to hold the part of the British front line which had only just been consolidated and was still under imminent threat of a German counter-attack. What was more, information from both officers and NCOs together with the looks and best wishes of the exhausted survivors of the 1/4th Gloucestershire informed the soldiers of the 3rd Worcestershire that they would be going over the top to take the next German line (Hindenburg Trench) on the following day.

Today, it is difficult to find circumstances that would provide us with similar emotions to those Albert Turley and the rest of the new recruits to the 3rd Worcestershire must have been feeling on 23 August. Exhausted through lack of sleep and carrying endless stores for an attack, they knew they would take part in the attack the following day – their first. Plans for the attack had been recently changed. There would be little time to discuss the finer points of the attack, the role of each man. Only the general direction of the attack would be clear, and they knew that somehow their extreme left would have to keep in touch with the 1st Wiltshire.

Life that day would indeed have been hectic. A mixture of hurried meetings, trying to map the original plan of the attack involving the 1/4th Gloucestershire onto the units of the 3rd Worcestershire. Organising the actions of companies and platoons would have involved all the officers, and this would need to be organised at the section and individual level by the NCOs. Sorting out the supplies and equipment ready to go over the top would have been chaotic. In addition, they also had to hold the line against everything the Germans could throw at them during the day. If this lot had fallen to a less experienced unit, it is likely that the whole attack may have been postponed or cancelled. Given the 3rd Worcestershire were a Regular battalion, recently re-fitted, this would not be an option. Pte Albert Turley would certainly have benefited by being with such a unit during the training behind the lines in the previous weeks, but now he would have to put all that training into practice and take his chances along with the rest.

Although it is impossible to know for certain, Albert would probably have been told or even invited to stick by an experienced soldier in the attack. For him, the haste associated with the reorganisation of the attack may have actually been beneficial by not giving him time to think about what might happen the following day. He may have reassured himself by knowing he was with excellent and experienced troops. Most soldiers believed that the worst would always happen to someone else, and there was always the chance of a '*Blighty*', a minor wound that would take them home – longed for by many.

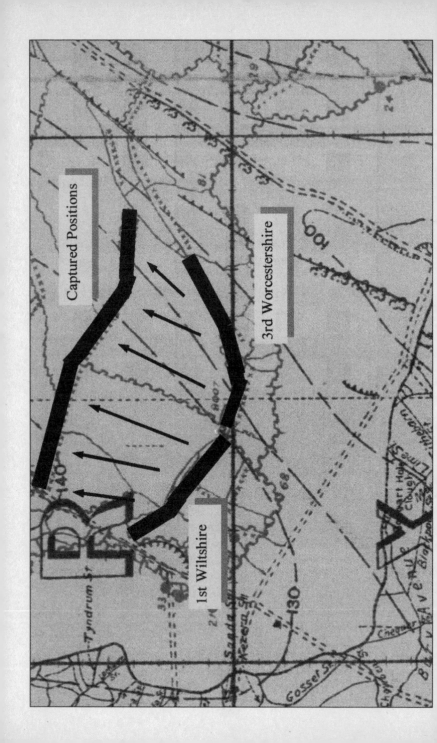

Captured Positions

3rd Worcestershire

1st Wiltshire

THURSDAY 24 AUGUST

A hot summer's day (maximum 25°C, minimum 12°C). This day there was further British progress in the northwest part of Delville Wood. German counter-attacks west of Ginchy were repulsed. (GG)

In the diary of the 3rd Worcestershire, the entry simply reads, 'Battalion attacked and captured German trenches' (3WD). There is a reference to a description of the attack with an attached map. Although the original operational order and map are now lost, Gibbs' report (WG), previously also thought lost, has now been found – contained as an appendix to the 3rd Worcestershire War Diary, kept within the National Archive at Kew. The report starts:

> On the morning of the 23rd the battalion took over trenches R31 b 90–62 and X1a 79–X1b 91, the 1st Wilts being on our left and the 1st Bucks of 48th Division on our right. (WG)

Opposite: The Attack on Hindenburg Trench 4:15 p.m. 24 August 1916
On this enlargement of the trench maps covering the Leipzig Salient, the positions of the 3rd Worcestershire located on the right of the 1st Wiltshire in Lemberg Trench are clarified. In front of them, and up the slope of the hill, was Hindenburg Trench, which was taken and captured in a matter of minutes. Both battalions continued to hold the captured positions through the night of the 24/25 August and survive the counter-attack by the Prussian Guard on the following day. Other points to note include the centre of the attack and the flanks. On the right, the 3rd Worcestershire had the simpler flank to capture and consolidate. On the left, the 1st Wiltshire had a maze of trenches to overcome, which was not achieved. Ultimately this would prove costly and lead to the failure of the next attack from these captured positions on 3 September 1916. In the centre of the attack, the distance between the British and the German positions was the greatest, giving the British soldiers here the most ground to cover as they crossed No Man's Land. During the attack, the 3rd Worcestershire naturally deviated to the right and, conversely, the 1st Wiltshire to their left. This led to a 50 yard gap, in the centre of which was a German strongpoint. This was probably located where the (then disused) trench running across No Man's Land intersected with Hindenburg Trench, a position normally defended by a machine-gun. Only rapid deployment of a Lewis gun team and bombing along the trench top from both sides saved the situation on the day.

Capt. Ogilvie (though signing himself at Lt-Col), acting CO of the 1st Wiltshire, also left behind a detailed report of the fighting this day as an attachment to their War Diary. Curiously, there are particular errors in this account with respect to the date for the attack (given throughout as July rather than August). Other interesting corrections are found in the margins of this document, written by others, presumably at Brigade HG. He starts:

> On the 23rd July [sic] I received oral instructions that the Regt. should be prepared to assault and capture the German trenches R31c 46-76-97-07-26. All preparations were accordingly made and supplies of Bombs and SAA were secured and forward dumps of RE material were made. On the night of 23/24 July [sic] orders in writing were received confirming the previous oral instructions. Two companies of the 8th Loyal North Lancs were put at my disposal for the attack. Later the same night orders were received postponing the attack. The date of the attack was finally fixed for the 25th July [sic] zero being at 4.10pm. (SO)

The topography of the next German lines to be attacked varied from a maze of shelled trenches on the left of the 1st Wiltshire, to a single trench (Hindenburg Trench) continuing across both the 1st Wiltshire and 3rd Worcestershire fronts. This difference was due to the left of the line of attack being what remained of the old German front line and support line of 1 July. Hindenburg Trench had then been a single communication trench leading up to these lines. The direction of this new attack was effectively perpendicular to this old communication trench, which by 24 August had become the new front line with communication trenches of its own, running northwards. All the attack would be uphill, the distance being 50 yards on the extreme left to approximately 300 yards on the right, in front of the 3rd Worcestershire.

The plan for the attack would be similar to that carried out by the 1st Wiltshire and 1/4th Gloucestershire on the 21st, i.e. a

Pte Albert E. Turley, 3rd Worcestershire: note the 'incorrect' cap badge later identified as that of Prince Albert's (Somerset Light Infantry). (*Dean Forest Mercury*, 15 September 1916)

The Old Furnace, Blakeney, Forest of Dean. The house was built by Albert Turley's father Moses Richard, a stonemason, and apart from some minor modifications there has been no change since 1916. Note the curious method of construction, the front wall being of brick laid frog-side-out. (*Author's collection*)

Blakeney parish war memorial, All Saints' Church, Forest of Dean: a fine stained-glass window and white marble tablets inscribed with the names of the fallen from both world wars. Albert's name and regimental details are on the lower portion of the upper tablet. (*Author's collection*)

All Saints' Church, Viney Hill, Forest of Dean, not to be confused with the church of the same name a few miles away in the centre of Blakeney. This cemetery contains the Turley family burial plots. Inside the church there is a polished brass memorial plaque with the names of the inhabitants of Viney Hill and surrounding communities who fell in the First World War: Albert is also commemorated here. (*Author's collection*)

War correspondents. Taken on 17 September 1916 by Lt Ernest Brooks, this picture shows Philip Gibbs of the *Daily Chronicle* (right) together with J. Irvine of the *Morning Post* (centre) watching an aerial combat. Note the unknown French officer on the left, quite possibly the same man who commented to Philip Gibbs how well the 3rd Worcestershire had 'gone over the top' on 24 August. (*IWM Q1062*)

A camp scene behind the lines, Mailly Maillet, 29 June 1916. Although taken by Ernest Brooks before the opening of the Somme offensive, this scene resembles that which greeted Albert Turley at Mailly Wood as he finally joined the 3rd Worcestershire on 24 July 1916. (*IWM Q748*)

'Enemy barrage on the Thiepval Ridge'. This 'innocent' photograph from the IWM archive, taken by Lt Ernest Brooks, has a nominal date of September 1916. The location suggests that this picture has been taken from 'the Nab', where Philip Gibbs witnessed the attack of the 3rd Worcestershire. If this is the position, the trench under fire higher up the Thiepval Ridge would be Hindenburg Trench. Using a hand lens it is possible to discern darker grey specks of men approaching this trench from the lower one (presumed to be Lemberg Trench). The drifting smoke from the 'enemy barrage' looks more like fires from burning dug-outs than actual shell-fire. Despite the date given for the photograph, it is possible that the picture was taken in the late afternoon of 24 August, and thus represents the actual attack by the 3rd Worcestershire. Philip Gibbs and Ernest Brooks were working together at this time, and the taking of an action shot to back up the narrative would make sense from a modern journalist's viewpoint. Shockingly, what this photograph may have unwittingly preserved is Albert Turley and many of his comrades of the 3rd Worcestershire at the point of being 'killed in action'. (*IWM Q1057*)

The king's visit to the Western Front, August 1916. Here King George V and Maj Gen H. Hudson are reviewing troops of the 25th Brigade, 8th Division, in the village of Fouquereuil on 11 August 1916. There is no picture of the king's visit to Sarton on 12 August, when he reviewed the 3rd Worcestershire and 1st Wiltshire, but this photograph gives an excellent representation of what Albert would have witnessed that day. (*IWM Q957*)

View of the Thiepval battlefield, showing the general area associated with this narrative. Few trees have escaped destruction and the ground is broken. Although the exact location of this photograph (also bearing a nominal date of September 1916 and again taken by Ernest Brooks) is unknown, conditions in and around the Leipzig Salient in front of Thiepval would have been similar for the 3rd Worcestershire in August 1916. (*IWM Q1077*)

Men of the Wiltshire Regiment advancing to the attack at Thiepval. This remarkable photograph (taken by Ernest Brooks) of British soldiers 'going over the top' on 7 August 1916 would not correspond to the experiences of the 1st Wiltshire, since on this date they were behind the lines at Bus-les-Artois. However, the place of the attack may well have been within the Leipzig Salient at Thiepval. Unlike many well-known photographs of the Battle of the Somme that are considered to have been faked, this one appears genuine. It would be in a scene such as this that Albert Turley would have taken part as the 3rd Worcestershire advanced up the Thiepval Ridge on 24 August. (*IWM Q1142*)

Relieved troops of the 1st Wiltshire. This photograph, taken by Ernest Brooks at Bouzincourt, shows officers and men of the 1st Wiltshire after their return from the fighting at Thiepval. The faces of many of these men show the strains of fighting in the Leipzig Salient more clearly than words can ever express.
(*IWM Q1145*)

The 1st Wiltshire with the spoils of war. Again taken by Ernest Brooks, these men of the 1st Wiltshire at Bouzincourt, after only a few hours of rest and a good meal, have cheered up sufficiently to pose for a standard patriotic photograph. Here the men show off their captured German equipment, including *Pickelhauben* (spiked helmets), forage caps, bayonets and hand grenades. (*IWM Q1103*)

The 1st Wiltshire playing football. This photograph, again taken at Bouzincourt by Ernest Brooks (probably on 31 August), shows the survivors of the attack on the 24th resting and waiting to return to the Leipzig Salient for the repeatedly postponed follow-up attack. Many of the soldiers in this photograph would not survive the attack on 3 September. (*IWM Q1108*)

The 3rd Worcestershire with the spoils of war. The original caption to this photograph (purportedly taken at St Quentin) in the IWM archive gave the date as April 1917. The same photograph is identified in Stacke's *The Worcestershire Regiment in the Great War* as being taken on 27 August 1916 at Hedauville. Further investigation revealed that the 3rd Worcestershire were resting and being refitted on the Franco-Belgian border in April 1917; they were therefore nowhere near St Quentin and certainly had not just taken part in an action capturing German booty. The badges on the German *Pickelhauben* are mainly Prussian. All these factors would seem to indicate the correctness of Stacke's identification. The sergeant in the front row is clearly wearing a bracelet, which would have carried a stamped aluminium identification disc containing the same details as the fibre discs the soldiers wore around their necks. If more soldiers had had such aluminium discs then subsequent identification of bodies would have been much easier. The 'old soldier' in the second row (the only one still wearing his 'tin hat') bears an astonishing resemblance to J. Irvine, war correspondent of the *Morning Post*, already identified in an earlier photograph! (*IWM A1981*)

Maillet Wood, 2001. Here Albert Turley joined the 3rd Worcestershire on 24 July 1916. Mailly Wood Cemetery, in the foreground, contains many British graves; once there were also French graves, but these were relocated after the war – usually unofficially and at private expense. (*Author's collection*)

Newfoundland Memorial Park. The trees mark out the extent of the park and, equally effectively, the British positions of July/November 1916. The road on the right begins at Auchonvillers and passes by the park towards the village of Hamel. Communication trenches stretching from the foreground running into the trees would have allowed the troops relatively safe access to these front-line positions. Albert Turley would have come along these communication trenches for his 'baptism of fire' in July/August 1916. (*Author's collection*)

British advance positions, Beaumont Hamel. This preserved trench, situated in the Newfoundland Memorial Park, was dug as a jumping-off position for planned future attacks on the village of Beaumont Hamel. It is situated several hundred yards into No Man's Land beyond the British front line of 1 July 1916 and would conform to the descriptions by Brigade Major A.C. Johnston as being typical of trenches dug by units of the 3rd Worcestershire, 1st Wiltshire and 10th Cheshire during July/August 1916. For me, this part of the Memorial Park will now always be 'Albert's Trench'. (*Author's collection*)

The road through the village of Sarton in 2001. Here, on 12 August 1916, the 3rd Worcestershire and 1st Wiltshire lined both sides of the road to cheer the passage of King George V on his tour of the Western Front – a highlight of Albert's life. (*Author's collection*)

Puchevillers. This quiet village behind the lines was used for training in the summer of 1916. The limestone church tower situated at the highest part of the village is original and would have been a well-known landmark to the soldiers using this place as a billet in August 1916. (*Author's collection*)

Hedauville, another quiet Somme village. Being nearer the front-line positions, this village witnessed much destruction. The majority of the houses here are quite modern, surrounding a pleasant village green. Here, Albert Turley would have spent the night of 17/18 August (his last) before 'going up the line' for the final time. (*Author's collection*)

The Ancre Valley, seen from the top of Bouzincourt Ridge, showing Albert's route to the British front-line positions on the morning of 18 August. The road dips down to the village of Aveluy astride the River Ancre. On the hill to the left is the Thiepval Memorial to the Missing, then the strong German defensive position around Thiepval Château. Before this and to the right are the British positions hidden by Authuille Wood. The open ground between them is the site of the Leipzig Salient. From this position Albert would have had his first view of the positions he would never leave. (*Author's collection*)

Lemberg Trench (1), from the site of the Lemberg Trench itself looking north towards the Thiepval Memorial. The Hindenburg Trench is situated just 300 yards away at about the limit of the ploughed field. This view shows the open nature of the ground facing the 3rd Worcestershire on 24 August – there would be little or no cover aiding the men who went over the top from this position, Albert among them, their only protection a lightening barrage falling on the Hindenburg Trench as they advanced. (*Author's collection*)

Lemberg Trench (2), looking right from the previous (1) position along the edge of the Bois de la Haye, marking the line of the Lemberg Trench. On the afternoon of 24 August this line would have been full of men of the 3rd Worcestershire waiting to go over the top. (*Author's collection*)

Lemberg Trench (3). Looking left from the previous (1) position, the Lemberg Trench stretched up the barren slope towards the right of the group of trees that marks the site of the Leipzig Redoubt. Chalk marks indicate the position of the battered Lemberg Trench and shell-craters. Approximately halfway towards the Redoubt, the 3rd Worcestershire met the 1st Wiltshire, whose own positions then continued through the Redoubt and beyond the skyline. Here too, on the afternoon of 24 August, men anxiously awaited their orders to go over the top. (*Author's collection*)

Thiepval Ridge from the Nab. This is the view that Philip Gibbs would have had of the attack of the 3rd Worcestershire on 24 August 1916. The valley in the foreground is Nab or Blighty Valley. The centre of the Lemberg Trench (from where previous photographs were taken) is at the intersection of a vertical line extending from the top of the telegraph pole in the foreground with the horizontal line made by the boundary of the barren fields on the far hillside of the Thiepval Ridge. The present growth of the Bois de la Haye, on the right, obscures the lines of 3rd Worcestershire men advancing in lines up the slope to the Hindenburg Trench that Philip Gibbs would have seen only too clearly that day. (*Author's collection*)

Ovillers Military Cemetery, with the grave of Sgt Frederick Pocock of the 3rd Worcestershire, who died of wounds on 24 August 1916. (*Author's collection*)

Puchevillers Military Cemetery, with the grave of Harry Westwood of the 3rd Worcestershire, who died of wounds on 25 August 1916. The cemetery also contains many graves to 1st Wiltshire men who also died of wounds following the attack on the Hindenburg Trench. (*V. Piuk*)

Serre Road No. 2 Military Cemetery. Containing over 7,000 gravestones, this is the largest British military cemetery on the Somme battlefield. Pte Hughsia Ruddock and Sgt John Griffin are buried here, both having been killed in action with the 3rd Worcestershire on 24/25 August 1916. (*Author's collection*)

The Thiepval Memorial to the Missing. Designed by Sir Edwin Lutyens and finally opened in 1932, this memorial dominates the battlefield. It enshrines the 73,000 names of the 'Missing of the Somme' including Albert Turley's and many hundreds more of the Worcestershire and Wiltshire Regiments. *'At the going down of the sun . . . we will remember them.'* (*Author's collection*)

Lonsdale British Military Cemetery. This cemetery is the closest to the Leipzig Salient and contains a majority of graves to unknown soldiers. Here also, buried side by side, are Pte Arthur Calderwood and Pte Robert Reeves of the 3rd Worcestershire, both killed in action on 24 August 1916.
(*Author's collection*)

Bray Military Cemetery is a small cemetery situated in the south of the Somme battlefield, containing Pte Harry Davies and Pte Roland Rose, whose bodies were interred here in 1924 – the last of the named graves to those who fell with the 3rd Worcestershire on 24/25 August 1916. However, alongside these are two other soldiers of the Worcestershire, one possibly being Albert Turley.
(*Author's collection*)

Wreaths at Thiepval. Our wreath, with Albert's photograph, the map of the Leipzig Salient and the list of the fallen of the 3rd Worcestershire from their successful attack on Hindenburg Trench, lie on the Stone of Sacrifice.
(*Author's collection*)

rapid bombardment followed by a swift infantry attack to capture and consolidate the trench. The bombardment would be carried out by heavy and light artillery and Stokes (trench) mortars, and would commence at 4.10 p.m. The infantry would also start the assault at 4.10 p.m. The intense barrage on the German front line would last 2 minutes, after which it would lift to the rear German positions. At the same time, at 4.12 p.m., it was expected that the infantry would have reached the German line and be ready to rush it and capture the trench. (1WD)

Capt Ogilvie gives the starting positions for the 1st Wiltshire:

The disposition of the troops was as follows: A Coy on the Left, half D Coy in the centre and B Coy on the Right. The remaining two platoons of D Coy formed the carrying parties for D and B coys, and a platoon of C Coy was lent to O/C A Coy to assist in carrying, as the labour Coy had already suffered heavy casualties. The three remaining platoons of C Coy were held in reserve in Don Street. The two companies of the LNL were used to garrison the line. The attack was somewhat complicated by the fact that B & D Companies were making an attack from trench to trench while A Company was bombing up trenches on the left flank. The distance to be covered was about 300 yards and the troops received orders to advance under the barrage of our guns. (SO)

It can be assumed that the plan for the attack for the 3rd Worcestershire was very similar in timing, artillery preparation and infantry assault. There is evidence from Philip Gibbs' account and a surviving officer's letter (see chapter 4), as witness to three waves of infantry assault for the 3rd Worcestershire. In this case, there would have been two assaulting companies followed by two further waves, each of a single company. Possibly, the nature and complexity of the maze of trenches forming the left flank of the 1st Wiltshire objective was the reason behind the extra company of men being used in their first attacking wave. It would also be the area in which two 'push-pipes' or 'jacks' would be used to form ready-made trenches into the enemy lines.

Lt-Col Gibbs' edited account of the 3rd Worcestershire action runs as follows:

> At 4.10pm on 24th the battalion advanced to attack on [Hindenburg] trench and was completely successful, the ground gained on right exceeding objective . . . . and a barricade erected. Owing to the advance being carried out very close behind our barrage no difficulty was experienced in crossing No Man's Land, practically the only casualties being caused by our own barrage owing to some men going too far ahead. The enemy found our men on top of them before they could man the parapet or get their machine guns into action. The enemy offered a stout resistance in the trench and here most of my casualties occurred in bomb fighting. The enemy suffered severely, the whole of a machine gun detachment which tried to get their gun on parapet . . . . were shot down by one of my Lewis Guns which was very quickly brought up on to a traverse and did great execution down the trench. The enemy bombed inwards vigorously . . . . but his bombing parties were destroyed or driven back within half an hour. Barricades were formed at these points and the enemy abandoned the position. (WG)

Philip Gibbs' account earlier in this book gives a very graphic picture of what happened on the afternoon of the 24th. The men of the 3rd Worcestershire he had seen fall, crossing No-Man's Land, seemingly had been casualties to British shellfire, a tragic (but all too often) consequence to brave men 'keeping up to their own barrage'.

Capt Ogilvie describes the actions of the 1st Wiltshire at the start of this attack:

> The hostile trenches were bombarded during the day and at 4.10 p.m. an intense fire was opened on the objective gradually lifting so as to clear the trenches by 4.15 p.m.

At 4.10 p.m. B & D Coys left their own trenches and advanced 150 yards to a line of petrol tins previously put out to mark where the men should form up for the assault.

At 4.12 p.m. the jacks were exploded and A Company advanced down them to enemy trenches.

At 4.14 p.m. B & D Companies assaulted from line of petrol tins and at 4.15 p.m. reached and captured the enemy's trench. The trench held a considerable number of enemy who showed fight and some brisk fighting ensued. The enemy in the trench were killed or made prisoners while those who tried to leave the trench and return to their lines in rear were all shot. Touch was almost immediately got with the 3rd Worcestershire Regt. on the right and A Coy on the left. The carrying parties . . . . kept the front line supplied with all that they required. (SO)

Despite success by both battalions on capturing the Hindenburg Trench, the 1st Wiltshire had been held up on the extreme left in the maze of trenches, Capt Ogilvie:

On the left, A Coy experienced great difficulty from the outset. The enemy concentrated immediately an intense fire on their trenches causing heavy casualties. They were, however, successful in their attack on the trench leading up the old road. . . . In the trench on the extreme left . . . they met with resistance from the beginning and failed to progress further than about 50 yards. (SO)

Johnston became involved and left behind an excellent account of the start of this attack:

Rather heavy shelling during the morning, and when I had been along the trenches the [3rd Worcestershire] Regiment had got to assemble in [the right part of Lemberg Trench] and found that the Germans could overlook all of them and was sniping down them very badly (had one of the closest shaves I've had in my life), the prospect did not look promising. To make matters worse the enemy's shelling increased in the afternoon, and their machine guns on the right swept the trench the 1st Wilts were assembling in and killed a couple of officers. However, in spite of this, the two battalions got ready and at 6.10 p.m. [sic] our guns started a very intense barrage on and behind the objective for 2 minutes during which time our fellows, in spite of the enemy's shelling, got out of the trenches and formed up for the assault. At 6.12 p.m. [sic] the barrage was slowly lifted and the infantry followed up close behind it. That they did this successfully from such an awful starting point, kept direction over very rough ground, and advanced over 300 yards of open ground, at any rate showed that the men were of the right stuff and well disciplined: the artillery too was accurate and our fellows were into the German trench close behind it and before the Bosche was ready for them, with the result that the trench was gained with comparatively slight losses. About 150 prisoners taken and a great many more bayoneted or bombed in their dugouts; some dugouts were set alight by the fumite bombs which was a pity as the flames made a good target for the enemy's artillery besides rendering them useless for our use later on. On the left, the 'push pipe' fellow blew up a couple of his pipes which did tremendous damage wrecking two bits of German trench and completely burying a whole street of German dugouts. One corner on the extreme left however held the 1st Wilts up, and the situation was obscure. (AJ 24/7)

Capt Ogilvie had no doubts as to the reasons behind the failure of his attack on the extreme left:

I ascribe this lack of complete success to the following causes:

(a) The heavy casualties caused by the hostile shelling just prior to the attack (the officers and several NCO's became casualties at this time).

(b) The pipe-forcing jacks were exploded too soon so that

the assaulting troops had to proceed slowly down the trench in order to avoid running into our own barrage instead of taking the objective at a rush. The explosion of these jacks has the effect of a small mine and at once brings every one of the enemy from his dugout so that it becomes absolutely vital to rush the trench immediately after the explosion with the greatest possible speed. (SO)

It was clear that despite everyone else's enthusiasm for these 'push pipe' devices, Capt Ogilvie had not been impressed from the outset:

RE superintended two pipe-forcing jacks which had been put at my disposal for the purpose of blowing up the blocks in the two enemy trenches on the left flank. Owing to the fact that one of these had been fortunately [!] exploded by a shell, sticks of ammonal had had to be laid near the block under cover of darkness the previous night. (SO) (A note added to Ogilvie's account made it quite clear that the 'push pipes' had definitely <u>not</u> been under his control.)

Now, because of the hold up on the left, Johnston now went up to see for himself and became personally involved as the attack drew to a successful close:

I went up to see. Had a rough journey up and also going along the captured trenches. Found the men in great form and work going well, fire-steps already cut, sentries and machine guns in position watching for any counter-attack, a certain amount of material had already been got up, and the men were hard at work building up sandbag revetments etc. and digging out the trench where blown in. We had taken over 700 yards of German trench and advanced about 300 yards over an open glacis, but thanks to the artillery barrage close in front, the enemy did not get their machine guns up in time, also a barrage of smoke and lachrymatory shells on our right covered that flank so that our losses were not very high – about 80 per battalion – which considering the number of Germans put out of action and the length of trench captured, was very good. (AJ 24/8)

Lt-Col Gibbs also made reference to the effectiveness of the fumite bombs:

> Fumite and smoke bombs were flung down entrances of dugouts and a considerable number of enemy were destroyed in certainly 2 dugouts by these bombs, remainder surrendering, about 80 prisoners, including wounded, being taken. (WG)

He then went on to describe the final dispositions of the 3rd Worcestershire following the successful attack:

> The position was completely in our hands by 5.30 p.m. Two machine guns were captured and large numbers of rifles, equipment and bombs. The Wilts Regt. gained their objective on the left and communication was established [on the right] . . . with 1st Bucks Regt.
>
> The captured position was extensively damaged by our shell fire and practically no fire trench remained. Consolidation was pushed on at once and all night, a strong post with Lewis Gun being built. The captured machine guns were also erected on the parapet and made use of, a good supply of ammunition being captured. Two guns of 7th M.G. Coy were also established in my front. (WG)

The 1st Wiltshire sector continued to see fighting for the rest of the evening, particularly on the extreme left:

> Heavy bombing went on all day in this left sector with varying fortune but only slight progress could be made. Consolidation of the trenches gained was proceeded with all speed. (SO)

The attack had been practically a carbon copy of the one carried out on the 21st with a similar successful result. The tactic of a rapid intense bombardment, allowing the infantry to catch up and surprise the enemy before moving off, was soon to become perfected as the 'creeping barrage'. Here both the artillery and infantry moved forward together, the former leading the latter. This tactic was very effective in an attack against several lines of trenches.

The 1st Wiltshire diary also mentions the hold up on the left of the line in the maze of trenches. However, the rest of the objectives for both the 1st Wiltshire and 3rd Worcestershire fell immediately. Casualty figures tend to vary between records, the 1st Wiltshire deemed their casualties 'heavy', with 320 men lost including 6 officers (1WD). The 3rd Worcestershire diary provides 158 casualties, of whom 25 were killed, one being an officer; both these values being much higher than those given by Johnston.

Stacke's history of *The Worcestershire Regiment in the Great War* provides further descriptions of individual events:

. . . the morning of 24th August passed without notable incident. The sun blazed down while final arrangements were completed for the attack on the enemy's position in front; a strongly fortified line known as the 'Lemberg Trench'. At 4.10 p.m., the British artillery suddenly opened up a devastating barrage fire, and the Worcestershire and Wiltshire climbed out of their trenches and advanced. Covered by the barrage, the two battalions closed up to the enemy's line; then, as the guns lifted their fire, they dashed in with bomb and bayonet. The enemy made a stout resistance and there was much desperate fighting. At one point a German machine-gun detachment tried to get their gun up on to the parapet, to enfilade the trench. Lance-Corporal W. Shenton, the leader of a Lewis-gun section, quickly hoisted his Lewis-gun on to a traverse. It was a matter of seconds between them, but the British weapon just got into action first. The German machine-gunners were shot down and their machine-gun was captured [L.Cpl. W. Shenton was awarded the DCM].

A fierce bombing fight followed up and down the trench. From both flanks the enemy came pressing inwards to retake their lost ground; but the Worcestershire bombers held them back. Small bombing parties led by 2/Lieut. W.S. Knowles and 2/Lieut. G.P. O'Donovan [both awarded the MC] fought desperately on the flanks of the captured trench until the enemy's efforts died away and the gain was secure [the battalion captured 2 machine-guns and 80 prisoners].

Then, under a storm of heavy shells, all ranks set to work to entrench and consolidate the captured trenches. The enemy were too disorganised to attempt any immediate counter-attack and during the night the entrenchment was satisfactorily completed. Major G.S. Briscoe showed great courage in leading carrying parties forward across the open and in directing the work under fire until he was hit [Major G.S. Briscoe was awarded the DSO].

In spite of the fierce bombardment, much gallant work was done by the signallers of the Battalion. Sergt F.D. Jowett maintained communication between the captured trench and the previous line for over five hours. He was wounded, but stubbornly refused to leave his work until he was again hit and disabled [he was awarded the DCM]. (STK)

Careful study reveals that this account was derived mainly from the recommendations for gallantry awards that accompanied the Battalion diary.

In all these accounts there is no mention of the 50-yard gap that emerged between the 1st Wiltshire and 3rd Worcestershire as revealed in the Gibbs account, which was subsequently captured from both ends. There was German shelling for the rest of the day (1WD), as might have been expected. Now it would be only a matter of time before the German counter-attack was launched.

Somewhere hidden among the details of this successful attack on the Hindenburg Trench, partly masked by the 'heavy' or 'light' casualty figures, was the death in action of *one* soldier, Private Albert Edward Turley of the 3rd Worcestershire – late of Blakeney in the Forest of Dean, eldest son of Moses Richard and Mary Turley, aged just twenty years.

It will never be known exactly what Albert's end was – maybe this is no bad thing. He could have fallen to a sniper before going over the top, been blown apart by a shell burst crossing No Man's Land, shot down by a German soldier defending his trench, strangled, bayoneted or bombed during the hand-to-hand fighting in the Hindenburg Trench or killed by a shell during its consolidation. Given that all the accounts agree that there were very few casualties in actually crossing No Man's Land – the chances are that his death would have occurred somewhere in the Hindenburg Trench itself.

What is almost certain is that Albert, like all the others, would have spent the hours and minutes of that afternoon simply waiting for 'zero hour' in the Lemberg Trench. Having spoken to several veterans who went over the top on other occasions, I know that this anxious waiting time would be soon forgotten in the adrenaline rush that occurred as each soldier showed himself above the parapet, exposing himself to the enemy's fire. Few veterans ever chose to relate what their thoughts were in the minutes before climbing the scaling ladder – most looked away in a watery stare and remained silent. Most had written their last letter, given it to a friend – believing that he would survive, or leaving it in the trench for it to be posted to grieving loved ones at home. No one wanted to show outward signs of fear; some talked loudly out of a false bravado, most were quiet saying silent prayers and, just before zero, chose to shake the hand of a friend and wished him the best. In the end, they would go over the top together, into the unknown.

Despite Albert's only recent arrival to the 3rd Worcestershire, he was truly one of them as they went to capture the Hindenburg Trench that sunny August afternoon. In all the records and memorials there is no distinction between pre-war 'Regulars' and himself as a 'Derby man'. He was simply one more among the best and finest soldiers of that day. Whatever his end, I should like to think he was among his comrades who cared for him, and he was not alone – who, of any of us, can ask for more when the time comes?

I could have ended this 'diary' here, with Albert's death. However, to bring the account to a fitting conclusion, I shall continue until the 3rd Worcestershire left the line a few days later, as a tribute to the battalion's achievements in July–August 1916 on the Somme.

FRIDAY 25 AUGUST

An overcast day but quite hot (maximum 27°C, minimum 16°C) with heavy rain (8mm). The whole of the shattered remains of Delville Wood fell into British hands, six weeks after the South Africans first entered it and unbelievably held it for seven days in face of incredible odds. (GG)

After the successful attack on the previous day, the captured positions were still under imminent threat from German counter-attack. This was particularly true on the extreme left where the 1st Wiltshire held parts of the maze of closely packed trenches. In contrast to the captured Hindenburg Trench, which the 3rd Worcestershire were holding, the nearest Germans were only a matter of yards away from men of the 1st Wiltshire behind a defensive block.

For the 3rd Worcestershire, dawn would be the most likely time for such a counter-attack, however none came:

The enemy made no effort to attack during the night, but patrols approached at dawn on 25th inst., one of whom was shot within 50 yards of my line. (WG)

The night too had been quiet for the 1st Wiltshire:

That night passed quietly but the next day the whole of the Leipzig Salient was shelled with the utmost persistency and from about 2.30 p.m. with great intensity. (SO)

The 1st Wiltshire diary also tells of continued shelling from both sides throughout the day and the steady consolidation of the captured lines. Two companies of the 1st Wiltshire, probably in the Hindenburg Trench, were relieved by two of the 8th Loyal North Lancs., enabling these troops to move back to the old front line (Lemberg Trench). However, the fighting was not yet over.

The extreme left was proving very difficult to consolidate and it was decided that the 1st Wiltshire should make another attack at 6 p.m., using the troops now in support in Lemberg Trench, to finally drive the Germans out of the remains of the shattered trench system as Capt Ogilvie describes:

> At 6 p.m. I had ordered a further attack on the extreme left but this could not be carried out owing to the terrific [enemy] barrage on the trenches. It is my firm conviction that the enemy were contemplating a very serious counter-attack at about 6 p.m. that day and that it was only frustrated by the very intense fire of our heavy artillery at this time. The speed with which the Heavy artillery got on was due to the use of pigeons carrying the message at the required hour. (SO)

Indeed, this timing coincided with the German preliminary artillery bombardment and counter-attack. The German barrage prevented these 1st Wiltshire troops moving up to the left in time for their attack, the latter being now being cancelled. (1WD) In the margin of Capt Ogilvie's report was another note by probably an Artillery commander '*I don't think anyone waited for the pigeons on this occasion, we all let fly as soon as we saw the objective gained [by the enemy]*' (SO)

In fact, this counter-attack was directed across the whole of the captured Hindenburg Trench. On the right, the 3rd Worcestershire were ready:

> The captured position was shelled heavily during the afternoon of 25th and at 5.30 p.m. the whole of the sector occupied by the battalion was bombarded intensively, the enemy massing in his trenches for the attack. He endeavoured to get onto the parapet but immediately came under our machine gun fire and shortly after our Artillery barrage was brought on to his line . . . . completely stopped his attack. One of my men actually went on to the enemy's parapet at about 7.30 p.m. and found him still 'standing to'

in the trenches with fixed bayonets. All attempts to attack completely failed and the enemy was unable to approach my parapet owing to the accuracy of our Artillery fire. (WG)

Stacke's account described their involvement in greater detail:

. . . the enemy's guns bombarded the captured position. The bombardment was most trying to men exhausted by twelve hours of battle; but the troops stood it gamely, cheered on by the example of their young officers [2/Lieuts. H. King and S.P.J. MacDonald being awarded MCs and 2/Lieut. J.B. Barron adding a bar to his]. Any target afforded in the enemy's trench was at once dealt with by burst of fire. A counter-attack was expected, and arrangements to meet it were perfected.

At 5.30 p.m., the enemy's guns burst forth with a terrific fire, and the glint of crowded bayonets in the trenches opposite told of the impending assault. But the British artillery was ready; and a barrage even fiercer was loosed upon the German trenches. Peering from our own front line amid the crashing shells, the soldiers of the 3rd Worcestershire waited for the German attack; but no attack came. It was impossible for anything human to live in the open, and the enemy's trench beyond was being pounded to pieces. Gradually, the shelling died down, and at dusk [actually 7.30 p.m.], a daring patrol crept forward from the trenches of the Worcestershire and made their way from shell-hole to shell-hole, across to the opposing line. They found the German trench smashed and broken, filled along its whole length with killed and wounded. But amid their stricken comrades a remnant of the enemy were still holding on, still waiting with fixed bayonets for the order to attack. They were the 5th Grenadier Regiment of the Prussian Guard.

No further counter-attack was attempted, the fighting died down . . . (STK)

However, in other parts of the 700 yards of captured trench, the German counter-attack had fared better, though ultimately it was a costly failure. Johnston had witnessed this:

> Went all round the captured trenches in the morning, enemy shelling pretty heavily, and they were evidently boiling up for a counter-attack; however the men were full of confidence and said they were ready for anything. In the afternoon the shelling intensified, and our casualties were heavy; about 6 p.m. by which time all our telephone lines were cut, we saw 3 green rockets go up which is our SOS signal, so we knew the long expected counter-attack had come; fortunately we had got our artillery to quicken up a few minutes before, and now they turned it on at intense rate so that we had our line covered by an intense barrage. For some time we could get no word back, the smoke obscured the view, and it was therefore an anxious time. However, we had complete confidence in the old 1st Wilts and 3rd Worcesters, and they did not fail us; we got news eventually that they were all right though they had lost very heavily. The Bosche came over in two places but did not get far, and as the trenches they were trying to start from were being pounded by guns of all calibres, they must have lost heavily. Our losses too were very heavy I'm afraid, and both the 1st Wilts and 3rd Worcesters each lost about 200 men during the day; they got an awful shelling but stuck it out well. . . (AJ 25/8)

The Germans were acting under strict orders from their higher command, as described previously. The continuous attack and counter-attack by the British and Germans respectively, together with worsening weather and ground conditions, would give the Battle of the Somme its ghastly reputation, for all time.

There had been occasions where the deliberate display of a mass of glinting bayonets above the trench parapet, by an attacking unit, would be used to demoralise the enemy defenders. Any such display of bravado would give up any chance of surprise and would be met by an intense and accurate artillery bombardment. The effects of this on an overcrowded trench would be devastating, and reduce the effectiveness of any subsequent attack. Furthermore, the breaking up of an attack in this way would serve to give heart to the defenders. Stupidity was not monopolised by either side in the First World War, nor was courage.

None of these accounts gives a true picture of the nature of the bitter fighting in and around the captured Hindenburg Trench this day (such descriptions come later). However, the casualty figures give one picture, although there is still much confusion. Johnston's figures of 200 for each of the 1st Wiltshire and 3rd Worcestershire may be an overestimate and reflect the nature of defending a counter-attack on a 700-yard front by two battalions. The 1st Wiltshire diary gives no figures of casualties for this day; the 3rd Worcestershire had forty-seven casualties of which nine were killed (1WD, 3WD). Careful study of the modern records reveals that one officer and six other ranks of the 1st Wiltshire and six other ranks of the 3rd Worcestershire were killed in action. However, there are no detailed figures for the wounded which Johnston would have incorporated into his figures.

What was beyond doubt was that both the 1st Wiltshire and 3rd Worcestershire, especially the former, were now exhausted. Johnston goes on:

. . . After dark we relieved the 1st Wiltshire who are now down to about 200 strong, but fortunately it turned out a quiet night compared to the day though the enemy's shelling by no means ceased. (AJ 25/8)

SATURDAY 26 AUGUST
Another hot day (maximum 27°C, minimum 16°C) with heavy rain (7mm). (GG)

It was now time for the exhausted 3rd Worcestershire to be relieved from the front line. they had had another night under fire:

Beyond continual and heavy shelling of sector held by battalion the situation remained unchanged until battalion was relieved on 26th. (WG)

At 7 a.m. the remaining men of the 1st Wiltshire were relieved by the two other companies of the 8th Loyal Lancs. They formed up at 'the Bluff' and began the march back to Hedauville at 1.20 p.m. where they rested. (1WD). Likewise the 3rd Worcestershire were relieved by the 8th Border Regiment; they too moved back to Hedauville. (3WD)

Following this successful action the battalion commanders would have received congratulatory telegrams, sent up the line by Lt-Col E.M. Birch, General Staff, 25th Division, now preserved in the National Archives:

The [25th] Divisional Commander wishes particularly to congratulate the 3rd Battalion Worcestershire Regiment, 1st Battalion Wiltshire Regiment and Royal Artillery for their excellent work. (3WD)

Following from Reserve Army – Please inform 25th Division that the Army Commander is very much pleased by the capture of the HINDENBURG Trench. He is particularly glad to hear that the casualties are slight. This shows that the preparations were thorough and reflects great credit on all concerned. (3WD)

As can be seen from these, the popular stereotype of the Great War British General as uncaring and believing his men to be mere 'cannon fodder' was simply not the case. His position was an unenviable one, he would have to bear the responsibility for the deaths of his men, for the rest of his life.

On the Thiepval Ridge, the position on the extreme left was still unclear. Both the Germans and British found themselves with sharp salients into the opposing lines, each being able to fire into the backs of the other. It was decided to carry out another attack on the German positions. Johnston's entry:

A very quiet day fortunately, and we were able to be relieved by the 75th Infantry Brigade, except that we left the 8th Loyal North Lancs. in to do a small attack in the left hand corner of the LEIPZIG SALIENT. They did it at 6 p.m. but had no luck, very rough ground, they are short of officers and few trained NCOs . . . (AJ 26/8)

This final unsuccessful attack by the 7th Brigade in the Leipzig Salient cost twenty-one other ranks killed in action and an unknown number of wounded. This failure would prove very, very costly later on.

AFTERMATH

Both the 1st Wiltshire and the 3rd Worcestershire moved back to 'rest', firstly at Hedauville and thence to Bouzincourt on 28 August. The Divisional Commander reviewed the survivors; he thanked the men for their successful efforts in the Leipzig Salient. An official photographer took the picture of the 3rd Worcestershire survivors, but found it more difficult to do so for the 1st Wiltshire because of the weather, which had now turned to heavy rain.

In the days to come, it became clear that the battalions of the 75th Brigade required some help in continuing the attacks in the Leipzig Salient in the worsening conditions. Due to their previous success in this area, the 1st Wiltshire and 3rd Worcestershire were now temporarily detached from the 7th Brigade and requested to assist with operations in the Leipzig Salient from 31 August.

The wet weather was now affecting ground conditions in the front line. Both the depleted 1st Wiltshire and 3rd Worcestershire maintained their role in reserve, the planned attack being delayed on a daily basis, until 3 September. The troops passed the time with a little physical training and football competitions.

It was also a time to write letters home. One such, of the many written on 1 September from the Revd G.M. Evans, would fall on the mat of The Old Furnace, Blakeney, in the Forest of Dean. On opening it, Mr Richard Moses and Mrs Mary Turley would learn that their eldest son, Albert, had been killed in action, instantly by a shell in the front-line trench. The shadow of grief, which would be cast over the family for the rest of the century, had now fallen. Normally, such a letter would have been preceded by a telegram; it may have in this case – we will never know.

The family of Wallace Pratt, killed alongside Albert received a letter in addition to an official one, from his platoon corporal (original spelling etc. retained):

> 12 Platoon C Coy
> 3 Worcester Regt.
> B.E.F.
> France

Dear Sir,

I very much regret to say that Pte W Pratt fell in action on the 24th. He played no small part in the wonderful attack which the Battalion made on that day. All the men in the Platoon with me express their sympathy with you in your great loss though he died the glorious death of a British soldier fighting for his king and Country. He helped to uphold the Regiment he belonged.

The parcel you sent him was divided among the platoon he was in as when a man gets wounded or killed the parcels are divided.

> *Yours truly,*
> *Cpl WR Strange*

Condolence letters were normally written by company/platoon officers, one from an NCO is rarer and is usually more sincere. Here is a letter written by one who was in the thick of the attack on 24 August, now detailed to sort out parcels and letters sent from home to the members of his platoon, now without a recipient. There are no details of how Wallace died, the truth, unsaid, is hidden behind a most fitting epitaph that can be extended to all the soldiers of the 3rd Worcestershire who fell in the attack on Hindenburg Trench.

On the Somme, there were no new replacements for either

battalion as there had been in July; there was simply no time to train them.

The remnants of both units went back into the front line in the Leipzig Salient trenches – the same ones as those they had so recently left. There was one difference: this time the 3rd Worcestershire (being the stronger battalion of the two) was in the centre facing the German salient. The 1st Wiltshire were on the right of the 3rd Worcestershire protecting the flank. On the left of the 3rd Worcestershire were the 2nd South Lancashire attempting to take the German salient from the east.

Orders were changed on the night of the 2/3 September. For some reason it was decided to reduce the front attacked by the 1st Wiltshire. Strangely, this meant that there now would be a gap between the right of the 3rd Worcestershire and the left of the 1st Wiltshire. In fact, both flanks of the 1st Wiltshire would now be 'in the air'. To match this change in orders, artillery bombardment schedules were now to be altered.

Only hours later, at 5.10 a.m. on the wet morning of 3 September, the infantry attack commenced after a heavy bombardment. This time there was no repeat of the successful lightning attack of 24 August. On forming up in No Man's Land to attack their objective, the 1st Wiltshire found themselves under a German artillery bombardment with little or no cover. In addition, machine-gun fire from both unopposed flanks cut into the lines of advancing men. Some men reached and entered the German trench only to be forced out again by a British bombardment that for some reason had 'failed to lift'. The survivors were forced to retire, and few would make it safely back to their own front line through the German machine-gun fire. On the left, both the 3rd Worcestershire and 2nd South Lancashire reached the German trenches, only to find that they had been levelled by the British bombardment. Here too, there was no shelter from the increasing German counter-barrage. They held as long as they could, again before the few survivors were forced to return to their own trenches.

The attack had been a disastrous failure with heavy casualties for both the 1st Wiltshire and the 3rd Worcestershire (including both battalion commanders, Lt Col W. Gibbs of the 3rd Worcestershire being killed). The survivors of both units were brought back to Bouzincourt where a solemn muster roll was held on 4 September.

The once proud 3rd Worcestershire that had entered, after the opening of the Somme battle, into the Leipzig Salient and had fought in three actions there, had now been effectively destroyed. Indeed the 3rd Worcestershire, again being refitted, would not rejoin the Battle of the Somme until early October. They would fight again in the Thiepval area, but removed from the Leipzig Salient, together with units of the 10th Cheshire now commanded by Lt Col A.C. Johnston.

The character of the battalion changed again: there were even fewer of the old sweats, and more Derby men replacements, with their own camaraderie. Many of the soldiers who had fallen in the attack on 24 August would be forgotten as successive actions again reduced numbers. Soon those first Derby men, including Albert Turley, who had been killed in their first real action with the battalion, would only add to the thousands of faceless names on the 3rd Worcestershire 'Roll of Honour'.

Yet on that blood-drenched hillside in front of the village of Thiepval lay the remains of some of the finest young men from those old county regiments. Some would be found and receive a decent burial, many more would be buried as unidentified, and others would remain as fragments of humanity disinterred forever.

Through this reconstructed 'diary', it is hoped these soldiers, and one soldier in particular, can now give up their faceless image and live once more as representatives of those who fought, fell and lie there still, unknown, 'somewhere' on the battlefields of the Somme.

FOUR

Soldiers' Tales

Albert's reconstructed diary was now as complete as I could make it. I had the chronological events from the regimental histories, interleaved with Johnston's diary entries and other sources. Philip Gibbs' story had provided an initial eyewitness account of the 3rd Worcestershire going over the top, in the late afternoon of 24 August, to take the Hindenburg Trench. From the soldiers taking part, however, there was silence; even Johnston could only describe the start and the aftermath of the attack. I knew there must have been as many experiences and stories of that day as there were soldiers. Of course, some were lost forever with each fatal casualty, Albert's among them: but had anything else, I wondered, survived the passage of time?

It was practically certain that there were no living survivors to provide their own personal stories. But there was one other contemporary source of information that could speak for the soldiers after eighty-five years – the newspapers of the day. The new Defence of the Realm Act had effectively censored detailed newspaper coverage of events on the Western Front. Instead, newspapers had to rely on official despatches and stories from *bona fide* war correspondents (such as Philip Gibbs). Names of units involved were generally omitted or given in terms of the regiment rather than an individual battalion. The appearance of a long casualty list in a provincial newspaper was the best indication that a county regiment had taken part in a battle. Often such a list pre-dated published details of the action that had been responsible for the casualties.

Soldiers' Tales

Despite the lack of direct news from France, the newspapers received indirect news from soldiers who had been wounded in action and returned to England for treatment and convalescence. As long as names of individual battalions or participants were not revealed, these stories could be published. Furthermore, relatives of serving soldiers would send in letters to the newspaper, received from the front. Soldiers' letters were ruthlessly censored, while officers' letters on the other hand often relied only on the honesty of the sender for censorship.

The attack of the 3rd Worcestershire on Hindenburg Trench had resulted in over a hundred wounded soldiers, many of whom were men local to Worcester, who were transported home to convalesce. After such an attack, there was invariably a surge of letters home from the survivors, keen to inform their families that they were safe, knowing that they may well have heard the news of the attack.

Newspaper editors had a difficult task in trying to piece together exactly what happened in any particular action. Stories would have arrived from various sources over several days, and many such were published as soon as they were received, with little regard to checking the factual content or chronological sequence. The writing style was demonstrably patriotic, although both contemporary and modern eyes could and can see through this 'fog of war'.

It seemed logical to look through the Worcester papers from late August and into early September 1916. Although many soldiers would still have been available to give their stories after this period, it would be unlikely they would be reported, especially since 15 September 1916 had seen the opening of the Battle of Flers-Courcelette where 'tanks' were used for the first time in warfare. Once these 'secret weapons' had been revealed, every paper rushed to get more details (and would pay huge amounts for a photograph). An attack on the Thiepval Ridge the previous month, no matter how successful, would by then have been 'old news'.

Today the city of Worcester is a pleasant mixture of the old and the new. One of its newest attractions is its History Centre, which contains the county archives, ranging from fragile parish records to modern Internet terminals in a well laid out setting, with very helpful staff. What is more, it is free of charge! As part of our summer holiday, my wife and I decided to spend a few days in the city and make the most of the city's heritage, particularly in respect to finding traces of the Worcestershire Regiment's history.

During the First World War the *Worcester Daily News* and *Berrows Worcester Journal* served the city; the latter was in fact a weekly compilation of the best of the *Daily News*. In theory, then, the search for information would be simple; in practice the opposite was true.

Scrolling through the microfilmed editions revealed the life of the city at this time. There was a mixture of war news (always dominant) and local events, making interesting reading of life on the home front. The war news was very limited, being a mixture of recycled news from the nationals including the events from the remoter parts of the fighting; for example, the Middle East (where other battalions of the Worcestershire Regiment were heavily involved) and the Eastern Front. *Berrows* of Saturday 1 July had gone to press *without* the news of the opening of the Somme offensive. The *Daily News* had only picked up the story in the following days, details being sketchy, but there was certainly no mention of the 57,000 British casualties who had fallen on that first day.

Passing on through July and August the news consisted of stories of the Somme battle – each article detailing the taking of a village or wood, the lack of large gains in territory being offset by the promise of better things to come in the next attack. The casualty lists grew longer for the Worcestershire Regiment as battalion after battalion arrived on the Somme to take its turn in the 'Big Push'.

The news of the successful 3rd Worcestershire attack on Thiepval Ridge had been reported in editions of the *Daily News* and *Berrows* on and after 26 August. As this event had been particularly mentioned in one of Haig's despatches, and the Worcestershire Regiment specifically named, the Worcester newspapers seized on this to try to provide as much detail as it could to its readers. Given this zeal, the accounts published resulted in a complex mixture of official disclosures and war correspondents' and soldiers' accounts. There was little or no chronological framework, with events of 24 August often being published after those of 25 August (if indeed a date were given at all). The following represents a compilation of these reports, rearranged for convenience in chronological order of the events.

The 2 September edition of *Berrows*, under the heading '*The Gallant Worcesters*', provided two different accounts of the attack on 24 August by a participating officer and a private soldier of the 3rd Worcestershire:

Well it is over – a brilliant little success, 500 yards in depth, 300 yards in breadth, two German trenches taken and many prisoners. Our bombardment before the show for two hours was perfectly terrific and B and C companies simply walked over with very few casualties. A company went over third, in support and I had my company [D company, assumed] up in reserve. The reserve company usually has the worst of it as it has to come through a German barrage of shells, and the barrage that afternoon was terrific. I constantly thought none of us would possibly survive and shells burst all around me; if I was nearly outed once, I must have been hundreds of times. One piece of whizzing shell grazed my coat on the right shoulder. The barrage was the worst thing of all for my company as when we got up to the front we obviously found B and C already firmly established in the first and second German lines and digging in and improving the trenches with all speed. They lost some men from German shrapnel but the total casualties of the Battalion was only 180 (15 killed and most of the wounded very slight). Not a German machine-gun was to be seen or heard; destroyed by the bombardment, I suppose, or else they had fled. I sent my four platoons where they were needed, to different parts of the captured trench. Little ? was absolutely dead beat and blown up by a shell; he went down early and will perhaps go to England, but he will soon be alright. The great blot on the whole thing was that poor ? was badly wounded and is not expected to live, several other officers got slight wounds – lucky devils, as I expect they will get to

England. The great event was that I caught two prisoners myself! I had been up in the farthest captured Hun trench directing matters and was returning over the top with my orderly to the front captured trench, and was stooping down to do up my puttee, when out of a shell hole crawled two unfortunate young Huns shrieking for mercy. My orderly ? a very strong lad ups his rifle and bayonet and shouts, 'Come on Fritz'. I did take the trouble to undo my revolver, but I pointed my electric torch at them and said, 'Haude poch [sic]'. Up went their hands and they came back most willingly with us to the old English front line where I handed them over to someone else. I was quite dead beat even when the show started, as we have had little rest last week, but it is amazing how success keeps one going, and it is the greatest success the Battalion has had since Gheluvelt in October 1914. The Brigadier, Corps and Army Commanders have all sent their heartiest congratulation and are very braced about it. At present we are all fearfully tired but tremendously bucked with life.

Interestingly, *Berrows* retracted this story on 16 September, because, they said, the account described an earlier action by the officer. This notwithstanding, I feel the first part almost certainly relates to 24 August: the description of the capture of the two Germans to an electric torch may have come from another letter by the same officer.

A letter from Private George Mills of Evesham followed this account. He had joined the 3rd Worcestershire in April 1916 and had gone to France five weeks afterwards: he was probably in the same draft of reinforcements as Albert Turley. George Mills had been wounded in the knee and was convalescing at home. His account lacks the flair of the previous officer's account, but provides the ordinary soldier's view of the battle – something Albert Turley probably could have identified with:

The charge I was in on Thursday [24 August] was awful. About 4.15 our artillery started; that is enough to drive any man mad. Then our officers gave us the order to charge. Over the top went the Worcesters and Wiltshires and took the German trench, about 200 yards with very few casualties. After we got into the trench, the German artillery commenced and then we had some casualties. We were repairing the trench which our artillery had blown level and I got my wound while I was digging. At 5 o'clock, I crawled about 180 yards to a dugout and there remained till 11 with five more of our chaps. We were in a pickle, with blood and mud then our stretchers arrived and got us away.

Here were the types of account I had been hoping to find. The first tied in well with Gibbs' description, that is, with three waves of attack up the Thiepval Ridge, B and C to storm the trenches with A in close support, D to follow on with supplies and to take over the defence of the captured trenches in preparation for the expected German counter-attack. The fact that the German barrage came too late to stop the initial attack would indeed make life difficult for those behind the leading waves. This German barrage would have been deliberate: a concentrated barrage on the British front line would aim to prevent further reinforcements and supplies getting up to the captured trenches and would isolate the tired attacking troops. It was then hoped that these isolated attackers could be wiped out by a successful counter-attack. The German barrage would not have been directed initially on the disputed trenches as this would run the risk of killing their own men who might still have some chance of holding off the British attackers (although Gibbs does mention some German troops running towards the British lines to escape their own shell-fire). Only when it was clear that these trenches had been definitely given up could a German barrage be directed on their own lost trenches. Indeed, it was this second barrage that had been responsible for wounding Pte George Mills – who was probably one of the wounded soldiers seen by Philip Gibbs coming back down the hill to safety from the captured Hindenburg Trench.

On Tuesday 29 August the *Daily News* reported how the news of the attack had been received at Norton Barracks, the Worcestershire regimental HQ. The commander, Col C.M. Edwards, had gathered all available soldiers together and addressed them:

I think it is only right that we in this Depot, the home of the Worcestershire Regiment, should show our appreciation of the good work performed by the brave lads of the Worcestershire Regiment, aided by another county regiment, the Wiltshire, in defeating the most famous of all German Regiments, the Prussian Guards. The county Regiments have proved themselves equal to the best Regiments of the British Army, and they still retain the fighting spirit of our forefathers and continue by their gallant fighting and determination to uphold the grand tradition of the Regiment, and always true to the good old motto 'Firm'. It is our duty to let the brave lads at the front know that we who are at home send them our encouragement in the great and difficult work they are undertaking.

I do not know what battalion put up such a splendid fight, together with a good old county Regiment, whether a regular or service battalion but, anyhow, it is a battalion of the Worcestershire Regiment. You know that the Worcestershire Regiment are always to the fore in all sport and fighting which takes place, and always hold their own against allcomers whether Scotch, Irish or English. They have proved themselves worthy to be classed with the best of all 'working' or 'fancy' Corps. I do not know what battalion it was which carried out this gallant work, but as soon as I do, I shall not lose any time in writing to their C.O. and inform him of how proud the depot is of their work.

It is reported that the troops at the barracks gave three cheers, played the Regimental march and took the news to the sick and wounded convalescing in the barracks.

Clearly secrecy had its part to play within the army at home too. In fact, Col Edwards would have had to get his congratulatory letter off to the CO 3rd Worcestershire very quickly if he was to receive it, as Acting Lt Col W.B. Gibbs was himself killed only a matter of days later, on 3 September.

In the days that followed, more stories were printed. On 2 September *Berrows* gave three further accounts. The first was a story of the attack of 24 August and the aborted German counter-attack entitled, 'The 'Firm's Stand – Dauntless Worcester Runner'. This report had originated in Philip Gibbs' despatch of 28 August, which had now been much circulated in the wider press, but Berrows still thought it worth re-telling, especially as the runner mentioned in it belonged to the 3rd Worcestershire. In addition, this account fills in more detail of the fighting for the gap in the Hindenburg Trench inadvertently left between the attacking Wiltshire and Worcestershire companies, again partly taken from Gibbs' despatch of 28 August:

One special correspondent says: 'The best of the British soldier is that he never feels himself a hero.' You would have thought that the old county troops who fill trenches and beat the Prussian Guard, would be conscious of some exultation, but most of them chiefly felt pride, I think, in the individual feats of others. One of these (from that desperate artillery fighting south of Thiepval on 25 July [sic]) was one of the strangest of the war. It's the tale of a runner.

There is, I suppose, no one man more calmly persistent in doing his job than the English runner. On this night one of them was sent back from our newly taken trench with an important message at a time when the German bombardment was particularly fast and furious. The Wiltshires and Worcestershires from whose ranks he came, were being provided with all the weight of metal the enemy could command, and his artillery had never been stronger.

The runner passed through unscathed and presently returned with an answer. He had twice passed through the curtain of howitzer fire. Indeed the shells had fallen in such profusion during his absence that the landscape had quite changed. The trenches that had been signposts had been battered to the state of confusing pits and paths. The runner thought that his journey was unduly prolonged, but he went on – that was his business – and in reward presently came to a trench. Being cautious as well as courageous he looked in before leaping, saw not good kind Englishmen but crouching Prussians packed tight beneath a frise of bayonets. The sight was enough to sate his curiosity, and he returned again in safety.

His experience was instantly reported to the artillery and immediately our heavy shells followed the example of the runner and also looked into the Prussian trench. It was the very moment that the Guard – the 28th Regiment of Prussian Fusiliers – had decided to charge. One wave came over the parapet and as it came was broken, here, there and everywhere. Its last ripple faded out into flatness 50 yards from the trench. A second followed. The last surviving unit of it may have travelled 50 yards. No more made the adventure. The attack was broken. Since they caught the Prussian Guard north-east of Contalmaison, our heroes never did more thorough work.

The original attack on 24 July [sic] which first won these trenches has no incident that stands out in clearer definition than this English runner peering over the parapet onto the avenue of Prussian bayonets but every step of the advance was an adventure and single-handed deeds abound. Since we were advancing up and parallel with the old German front line, only his old communication alleys made a right-angled barrier. One of these, our men entered at two points, with a gap of 50 yards between them. This interval was full of Germans who hesitated a moment. To scatter their doubts, a Wiltshire officer ran at them alone, discharging his rifle as he went. He shot four. The rest hesitated no longer but dived for the dugouts to await 'the ferrets'.

The trenches on our left – up the old German front line – were a tangled maze, and most of the trenches were broken and traversed. But in one of them was a perfectly straight line of some 250 yards raked by protected machine-guns. In spite of its deadly appearance, we won it in a pitched battle of guns. Our snipers and Lewis guns challenged the German machine-guns and beat it, winning a noble success in minor tactics. Before the eyes of those who fought is the picture of the irresistible sergeant who took to the open and bowled the German before him over a long reach of trench. Another is of a South African sniper who somehow found himself in these ranks. As in the old romances, they said of him that 'he bore a charmed life'. He sought no cover and sniped with the accuracy of a marksman in the 'Last of the Mohicans'. Between his rounds, he shouted and shrieked in a sort of battle ecstasy and at the end of the fight took six prisoners to his own gun. The rushing of the German strong point – at the junction of the trenches known as the Lemberg and Konigstrasse – saved many lives. But incidents tread on one another's heels in such an attack that the full tale would be interminable, short and 'slick' though the victory was. I am assured that the first group of prisoners were back in Battalion headquarters ten minutes after the attack developed. Though in the first attack I had seen many prisoners surrender and return, I had hardly dared to believe that the speed was quite so great as this. It seems our county troops are quick as well as sure when the need arises. But it is their surrender that will finally defeat the Germans, as the Germans hereabouts, at any rate, begin to feel.

The second account on 2 September by *Berrows* was an edited version of Philip Gibbs' despatch of 25 August, giving his eyewitness account of the attack on the 24th (provided in full in an earlier chapter).

The third account told of the German counter-attack on the newly won positions on 25 August under the headline, 'Enemies Frantic Endeavours'. In fact, this account was taken from Philip Gibbs' despatch of 26 August (also provided earlier).

The importance attached by the enemy to the Thiepval sector of his line is shown by the great efforts he is making to recover his lost ground in the Leipzig Salient. He has recently been effecting a great concentration of guns in this area to oppose our progress and support his attacks.

Last night he delivered an attack in considerable force on our trenches south of Thiepval village.

The attack was made by the Prussian Guard and was preceded by a very heavy bombardment, which commenced at 7 p.m.

The attack was launched at 7.30 p.m. and was pressed with determination, but was everywhere repulsed with heavy losses to the enemy, and we maintained all our positions.

The success of our defence is largely due to the steady and determined gallantry of the Wiltshires and Worcesters who, in spite of being subjected to a very heavy bombardment, steadily maintained their position and repulsed the determined assault of the enemy.

This series of articles had been preceded in the *Daily News* of 31 August by a piece called 'Worcesters Wonderful Dash', which gave three accounts of this counter-attack, two by officers, the other by a sergeant:

1) It was hot, hotter than anything I have ever been in. Our attack on the enemy's position was child's play to what we had to go through when they hurled their masses of packed troops against us. We had settled down in our new quarters when we got our second peep into hell. A furious bombardment began. As suddenly as it began the bombardment ceased. The enemy began to mass in front for the attacks. Before the foe could widen out into wider formation, they came under fire from our big guns. Their losses must have been appalling. We could see great gaps torn through and through their ranks. Then the attack broke down.

2) The odds against our lads were great – at least 6 to 1, at times nearer twice that. There was one terrible moment when the dead and wounded were so numerous that the living found it impossible to advance further. The onward rush of the Huns came to a dead stop. The great machine was clogged up, choked by its own dead. Behind a barricade of their own dead, the Huns laid and tried to return our fire.

Our grenade men stole out and made things hot for the Hun. Enemy reinforcements pressed forwards adding to the congestion on that narrow front. An officer rose and gave an order. Before he could finish, he was shot down. His men had half risen to resume the advance. A deluge of fire swept across the ground where they lay. The continual pressure on to a small front of reinforcements from behind forced the enemy to press on despite themselves. They rose suddenly and took another plunge into the sea of lead. They looked groggy as they waded through. Men went down at every step. The survivors kept pressing on, probably finding the pressure from the rear as the reinforcements came up too much for them. At last they reached our parapet. With an exulting yell, they leapt into our trench. Our chaps sprang forward with the bayonet. The grenade men let fly. The enemy fought furiously. Tenaciously they clung to the few yards of trench they occupied. Our lads never gave them rest. They kept peppering and bayoneting the Huns without ceasing. Grenade and machine-gun men dashed forward and seized a position from which they were able to play hell with the Hun troops being hurried up to strengthen those who had fought their way into our trench.

The hand-to-hand struggle that followed was deadly. The band of Germans were speedily being thinned out, the survivors seemed to have the courage of demons. The struggle became so fierce that it became impossible to use ordinary weapons. Sparring and wrestling became the order of the day. Many a Midland man laid out his foe with his fists. At times men could be seen in deadly grapple, trying to choke the life out of each other. The fight only ended when the last Hun was put out of action.

3) I have had my share of most samples of hell that have been going on from Mons onwards, you can take my word for it that this attack from the Prussian Guards was the most desperate affair of the war. They fought like men possessed by all the devils heard of. Every German struck me as a

living incarnation of the 'Hymn of Hate'. Fury and ungovernable rage and unfathomable passion blazed from their eyes as they closed with us. They showed their venom with every thrust of the bayonet. Some of them were so mad that they would stoop over a fallen Worcester and stab him again and again to make sure that there was no life left in him or to gratify their lust for slaughter.

Having pieced these different accounts together, I realised that, together with the unit histories and the Johnston diary, I had about as complete a picture of the events of an individual attack within the Battle of the Somme as it was possible to have. In terms of planning, execution and aftermath this attack was typical of the Battle of the Somme. There had been a bombardment, an infantry attack in waves, the capture of the enemy trench and a defence against an enemy counter-attack. The main differences between this attack and many of the countless others that made up the Battle of the Somme was both the success itself and the relatively small number of fatalities to the attacking British troops. This was due to the surprise factor (short bombardment and rapid advance), new technology (the 'push pipe'), attention to detail ('mopping up' of the German dug-outs) – but above all to the courage of the attacking troops. Good fortune had played a part too, as when the runner noted the deployment of the counter-attacking German troops bringing forth a devastating barrage to help break them up.

Despite the official censorship and the style of writing used, the soldiers' tales speak volumes about what it must have been like to take part in the initial attack and German counter-attack on Thiepval Ridge – something no dry official history could give. The information gained had been well worth the search.

When thinking about the Battle of the Somme today, the mental picture is one of long lines of British troops going over the top only to be machine-gunned to a standstill in No Man's Land; of survivors being defied by belts of uncut barbed wire, only to be picked off and left to rot, hanging there as a testament to human courage and to the futility of war. We read of the mud and the shelling, of poison gas and flamethrowers – this all adds to our horror of the First World War. Yet in all this, we rarely consider what happened when an attack on an enemy trench was a success, when the attackers and defenders of a trench actually came together face to face. Here, at such close quarters, the artillery, the cause of the majority of casualties in this war, was of little use. Fighting was no longer impersonal and at a distance, since a man would be able to look into the eyes of the enemy. Only previous training, physical strength and luck could save a man. Let no one now be in any doubt about what lies behind those simple phrases: *'captured the trench'* or *'held the trench'*, found in all soldier's accounts of the Great War. This is the ultimate horror of war in the trenches, in this or in any other war.

Inevitably I thought again of Albert, of what he must have seen and taken part in. I thought, too, of what my own emotions would have been had I been there in his stead; and soon this turned into a waking nightmare. The fear, the exhaustion after the original charge, the fact of being too physically weak to parry a thrusting bayonet during the counter-attack, the agonising pain as vital organs were brutally torn apart, the eyes of a stranger driven equally mad with terror for the loss of his own life – it was too horrible to contemplate further. As I mentally returned to the modern security of the Worcester History Centre, I fervently hoped that Albert had been killed in the rush up the hill towards the Hindenburg Trench by an all-engulfing shell-burst – cleanly, to escape what happened to other wounded men of the 3rd Worcestershire only a few hours later.

FIVE

'Yea, though I walk through the Valley of the Shadow of Death . . .'

I was pleased to have found some contemporary accounts in the Worcester newspapers of the attack of the 3rd Worcestershire on the Hindenburg Trench. On the same pages as the war news were, inevitably, the casualty lists, beginning (naturally) with the Worcestershire Regiment. Looking for Albert's name, my eyes saw a familiar text, which soon led me into another avenue for research.

Berrows Weekly News carried a letter from the widow of 20050 Pte George Harris of Droitwich. This, in turn, contained another letter from the Regimental Chaplain, Revd G.M. Evans, giving Mrs Harris details of her husband's death and burial: this was the only news of her husband she and her five children would receive. I quote the chaplain's word in full:

It is with the deepest regret and sympathy that I have to give you the news of the death in action of your husband, which took place on 23 August. Your husband was in the trenches when he was hit by a piece of shell and only lived a few moments. He thought of you to the end, as his last words were 'Oh, my poor wife and children'. I am very sorry to say that owing to conditions there at the time, it was necessary to bury him where he fell, but you can be sure that if it becomes possible later on to mark his grave, this will be done. The Commanding Officer and Company Officers and comrades all send you their sincerest sympathy. I know what a terrible blow this must be to you, but I pray that God may give you the strength to bear it and that you may be comforted by the thought that your husband died nobly for King and Country.

Revd G.M. Evans.

It was almost an exact copy of the letter that Mrs Turley had received about her son Albert.

Such letters of condolence were common – this much I already knew. The emphasis was almost always on the painless death. Death in action was usually reported instead as being the result of accurate sniper fire (usually to the head or heart) or a direct hit by a shell. If a soldier died of wounds, he had received the best of care, and in any case suffering was minimised by drugs, which resulted in a 'peaceful death'. Looking at a selection of such obituaries on any one page of a contemporary newspaper, one is struck by both the consistent accuracy of the German Army and the minimal pain involved in being killed while on active service. I wondered if, as late as 1916, people at home could still be fooled in this way? Surely there would have been a sufficient number of soldiers discharged on grounds of disability to provide the real details behind the term 'killed in action' or 'died of wounds'?

I then remembered two things. First, a First World War veteran I had once known had returned on leave from the Somme only to be bombarded by visits from neighbours asking about missing relatives. He had kept secret from these people what he really knew, only lifting his burden some seventy years later, when he divulged his stories to me. Secondly, I remembered the look of relief on my aunt's face when she had first read Revd G.M. Evan's letter revealing that Albert had been killed instantly by a shell and had suffered no pain. It seems that even today we prefer to hold on to any consolation rather than think more deeply about what may really have happened.

My search of the casualty lists continued. It was only another two editions before the now familiar words were printed once more. This time it was to the widow of Pte Clay of Worcester, quite probably the same Pte Alfred William Clay who had been killed alongside Albert in the attack on the Hindenburg Trench. Again I quote the letter verbatim.

> Pte Clay was in the trenches when he was killed by a shell. His death was instantaneous and he could have suffered no pain. I am very sorry to say that owing to the conditions there at the time, it was necessary to bury him where he fell, but you may be sure that should it become possible later to mark his grave, this will be done. His Commanding Officer, his company officers and comrades all send their sincerest sympathy. I know what a terrible blow this must be to you, and I pray that God may give you the strength to bear it. You may be comforted by the thought that your husband died nobly for King and Country.
>
> Revd G.M. Evans.

I now felt angry. Today, with word processors, we have the benefits of 'cut and paste' for duplication of parts of text – there is even the option of mail merge, which can generate duplicate letters to many people, suitably personalised. Here, in 1916, was someone who would have appreciated this modern technology! The Revd G.M. Evans had sent near-identical letters to three (and probably more) recipients giving the news of the death of their loved ones in a very short space of time. The grieving relatives may initially have been comforted by knowing that death had been virtually painless and that their son/husband must have been well thought of as so many officers and comrades sent their best wishes. But what if they had seen that an identical letter had previously been published in the local paper from another grieving family? The 'comforting' words of the Revd G.M. Evans would then have sounded very hollow and caused the family even more grief, since they would probably now start to think the worst. I began to wonder what had happened to the Revd G.M. Evans, Chaplain, attached to the 3rd Worcestershire.

'The Valley of the Shadow of Death'

Turning again to Stacke's *Worcestershire Regimental History*, I discovered there was no Revd G.M. Evans in the index, but there was a Revd E.M. Evans. I quickly found the entry. It referred to events involving the 3rd Worcestershire on 11 August 1917:

> Two great losses befell the Battalion during that morning, which deeply affected all ranks: the Revd E.M. Evans M.C. who had been attached to the Battalion as Chaplain for more than two years was killed, and the not less devoted Medical Officer, Captain H.D. Willis, was mortally wounded.

Clearly there was a mistake over the first initial; nevertheless, the Revd G.M. Evans too had been killed in action. I had thought that chaplains had a more or less 'cushy' time, keeping out of the way. Here was one who had not only been awarded the Military Cross, but also had given his life. Now I felt I wanted to know more.

I went back to *Berrows Weekly News* for August 1917 believing that such an officer would have merited a reasonable obituary. I was not to be disappointed: on 25 August 1917 it appeared:

> The Reverend Geoffrey Maynard Evans CF attached to a battalion of the Worcestershire Regiment, was killed by a shell in the front-line trenches on Sunday 12 August. He was the son of the late Dr Samuel Evans and of Mrs (Eleanor Sophie) Evans now of Cartref, Dovercourt and was born in 1882 and educated at Marlborough. On leaving school in 1901, he had intended to offer himself for ordination but the South African War had still a year to run and he obtained a commission in the militia, and went to the Front. On the conclusion of Peace, he was offered a commission in the Welsh [sic] Regt. and held it for nearly 10 years. After this he went to Bishop's College at Chislehurst and in 1913 was ordained and joined the clerical staff of his old school's mission (St Mary's) Tottenham. In the Spring of 1915 he went to the Front as Chaplain. He was awarded the MC last June. The Colonel of his Battalion, to which he was attached, says 'He was an ideal Chaplain to troops, and was simply worshipped by the men.'

It seemed ironic that the obituary appeared on the first anniversary of the 3rd Worcestershire taking and holding the Hindenburg Trench. There was a discrepancy in the date of death (11/12 August) from the two accounts. The Revd Evans had certainly led an interesting life, having fought in the Boer War and now finding himself caught up in an even greater conflict. I looked up in Stacke how he had gained his MC. It was not listed – only that it had been awarded in June 1916, which was only just within the fifteen months he had served with the 3rd Worcestershire. I can only assume that the action must have taken place between April 1915 and June 1916, when he was serving elsewhere. Indeed he had received one of the first Military Crosses to be awarded.

Even more ironic was the phrase in the obituary 'killed by a shell in the front-line trenches'. I checked in Stacke as to what the 3rd Worcestershire were doing on 11/12 August 1917. The battalion was involved in the 3rd Battle of Ypres, more commonly known as the 'Battle of Passchendaele'. It had taken part in the capture of Westhoek Ridge, a low rise situated in an ever-worsening morass of Flanders mud. Stacke's account reads:

> Next day (11 August) the defence of the captured ridge was continued. Lewis-gun teams of the Regiment went forward over the ridge to assist the 13th Cheshire. Word came to send help to the right flank against an enemy counter-attack. All movement was perilous under the hail of shells, but Sergeant G.H. Tucker bravely led his men forward through the fire to the threatened flank. There he established his Lewis-guns in positions from which their fire checked the enemy's movement . . .
>
> On the next day (12 August) the 3rd Worcestershire moved back through Ypres to Vlamentinghe and thence by bus to Steenvoorde to rest.

The battalion was under heavy shell-fire. I could imagine both the chaplain and the medical officer working together, trying as best they could to look after the wounded troops: possibly they were both hit by the same shell. I was left to wonder whether, in his letters to bereaved relatives, Evans's consistent use of *'killed instantly by shell-fire in the front-line trenches'* had been some form of premonition for his own demise almost exactly a year later.

I now felt ashamed of my earlier thoughts. It would have been an awful job to write seemingly endless numbers of letters to bereaved relatives, each time hiding the truth (if he had ever known it) behind a 'white lie' in order to spare them. I thought of my own position. I had now found contemporary accounts saying that very few of the 3rd Worcestershire had fallen to shell-fire crossing No Man's Land between Lemberg and Hindenburg Trenches. There had been some retaliatory shell-fire while the 3rd Worcestershire had held Hindenburg Trench, which had caused some casualties, which would have made the chaplain's letter quite accurate. However, there had also been the account of the Prussian Guard's counter-attack, ultimately beaten back by brutal hand-to-hand fighting. Could *I* have told anyone, even in a letter, that their son or father had died in agony having been repeatedly bayoneted to death? Could *anybody?* I now felt an empathy with the Revd G.M. Evans, and was relieved that the exact manner of Albert Turley's death will never be known.

Finally, I looked up the Revd Geoffrey Evans on the Commonwealth War Graves Commission website database. Unlike the majority of the fallen of the 3rd Worcestershire from their attack on the Hindenburg Trench, Revd Geoffrey Evans does have an individual grave. He is buried in plot II, row E, grave 12 at Divisional Collecting Point Cemetery, Ypres. The next time I go to Ypres, I will visit his grave. May he also rest in peace.

SIX

A Needle in the Haystack

Nearly half the 1,146,844 soldiers of the British Empire killed in the First World War have no known grave. These soldiers have their names inscribed on large memorials at strategic points along the Western Front and elsewhere. There are many, and some obvious, reasons for this lack of identification: some soldiers were blown into unrecognisable fragments by shell-fire; others were required to remove their identification prior to an action; sometimes grave markers were lost; and graves that were prepared were sometimes destroyed by subsequent events. Moreover, many of the 'missing' do have graves, although if identification of the body for burial (or re-burial) proved impossible the inscription on the headstone may only read 'An Unknown Soldier of the Great War'.

The actual identity tagging system used for soldiers in the First World War had not been fully thought through, particularly in respect to the effects of conditions on the Western Front. In 1914 soldiers were issued with a single compressed fibre tag with name, regiment, number and religion stamped on it. When a soldier died, this would be removed and passed on as confirmation of death, which would leave the corpse unidentifiable if it were later moved or the grave marker were lost. In 1916 soldiers were given *two* identity tags. One was removed on death, while the other was left on the body to aid future identification. Unfortunately the same compressed fibre material was retained. With time and exposure to moisture, these tags rotted, again making identification of bodies difficult (as is generally the case when bodies from this war are discovered today). Soldiers privately procured aluminium identity tags to be worn as a bracelet (some of these can be seen in the photograph of the 3rd Worcestershire parading their trophies after the capture of the Hindenburg Trench). Some even made their own from stamped copper or silver coins and a length of watch chain.

Where no individual identification was possible, partial identification could be achieved using other artefacts that survived, such as the soldier's metal shoulder-title or collar badge. In such cases a headstone could read, for example, 'An Unknown Soldier, Worcestershire Regiment'.

Albert Turley is commemorated, along with the other 73,000 'Missing' soldiers of the Somme, on the Thiepval Memorial. For Albert, this is particularly fitting, as he was killed in an attack at Thiepval, only a few hundred yards from the Memorial itself. The majority of the soldiers whose names appear on this Memorial were killed many miles from Thiepval, from Gommecourt in the north to Maricourt in the extreme south of the Somme battlefield.

The Thiepval Memorial is large and impressive, as it rightly should be, designed by the architect Sir Edwin Lutyens. The sight of the thousands of names inscribed on its walls leaves the visitor with an emotion impossible to describe or, more importantly, to forget. It is said that every family name in Britain is represented here. Despite the constant care of the Commonwealth War Graves Commission staff, this Memorial (and all other 'Memorials to the Missing') will always lack the individual poignancy that one feels when standing by a named (or unnamed) headstone of the fallen.

There was still an unanswered question at the back of my mind: would it be possible to find Albert's grave after all this time? Using twenty-first-century DNA testing, identification of unknown bodies is now possible using comparisons with living relatives (for example, the skeletons believed to belong to the assassinated Russian royal family were identified using DNA from the present British royal family), but given the number of unknown soldiers buried on the Somme, and the many branches of descendants and relatives alive today, DNA testing for identification purposes will in all likelihood remain in the realms of fantasy.

My aim was now to narrow the search, to enable future visitors to the Somme to see Albert's name on the Thiepval Memorial, find where he was killed and then to visit a particular cemetery, to lay flowers at the grave of an 'Unknown Soldier, Worcestershire Regiment', who just might be Albert himself.

In order to start this more sensitive form of search it was first necessary to understand a little more about what could happen to a body when a soldier was 'killed in action'. Clearly this would depend on individual circumstances, but in Albert's case the circumstantial evidence was plentiful and the potential reward in pursuing this avenue of research could outweigh its seemingly macabre nature.

In all the accounts I had traced on the 3rd Worcestershire for 24/25 August, there was no mention of what happened to the bodies of the soldiers killed in action that day. The letter from the Revd G.M. Evans to Mrs Turley declared that Albert had been killed by 'shell-fire in a trench'; his body was 'buried where he fell' and 'would be marked, should it become possible'. This may indeed have been true: the 3rd Worcestershire did take casualties from shell-fire when they were holding the Hindenburg Trench before the German counter-attack. The grim hand-to-hand fighting during both the capture and the counter-attack would have added to the number of bodies in this trench.

Following unsuccessful attacks casualties were usually left in No Man's Land until such time as they could be recovered (the wounded usually at night, either by their own painful efforts or by those of brave comrades). Some informal truces are recorded, enabling the recovery of the dead, but these are exceptions. Many of the fallen from the attacks on the Somme on 1 July had to be left in No Man's Land until early in 1917, when the Germans had withdrawn to the east. The condition of the bodies by then may only be inadequately imagined by modern minds.

However, the attack on the Hindenburg Trench had been successful and the ground had been captured and held. This would have enabled more rapid recovery of the wounded and dead, particularly in No Man's Land; in fact Gibbs' account mentions stretchers bearing the wounded being carried 'shoulder-high' after the attack. The dead lying in No Man's Land would naturally have taken a lower priority.

The surviving soldiers holding the Hindenburg Trench on the evening of 24 August would have had more pressing matters to worry about than taking proper care of their dead comrades. Johnston mentioned that clearing-up operations ('reversing the fire-step', for example) were well under way by the time he visited the newly captured trench late on the 24th, as they expected a counter-attack at any moment. The remains of dead soldiers are likely to have been cleared away by putting their bodies into nearby shell holes, unusable dug-outs or using them 'practically' to repair broken defences. Bodies for interrment could be covered over either immediately (if convenient) or later, as circumstances dictated. Under such conditions the dead soldiers would have their identity tags (and personal effects, if practicable) collected for onward transmission.

The German counter-attack on 25 August was repulsed, adding to the 3rd Worcestershire's casualties, and new bodies would have been dealt with in the same way by the surviving soldiers. When the 3rd Worcestershire were relieved on 26 August it is unlikely that they took their dead with them this time, as was the case when they had held the 'quiet' trenches in front of Beaumont Hamel. Carrying the many wounded soldiers using the limited number of stretchers along winding trenches was difficult enough, especially against the flow of relief troops. It would simply be pointless for tired troops attempting to carry large numbers of dead bodies under the same conditions. Those bodies they couldn't cover over (or collapse the dug-out over) would have to be left to the fresher incoming relief troops to deal with as best they could. It was also likely that some bodies were only fragmentary and it would not be practical to deal with these further other than to place the parts in a sandbag.

The capture of the Hindenburg Trench was not the end of the attacks on Thiepval from these positions. Indeed, the 3rd Worcestershire and 1st Wiltshire returned for another attack on 3 September. Following this unsuccessful attempt there were subsequent attacks on this ridge by other troops. Thiepval itself was taken by way of the Thiepval Ridge on 26 September 1916. Clearly operations in and around the Hindenburg Trench after 24 August had the potential to disturb and obliterate the soldiers' graves (particularly by shell-fire). However, after the end of September 1916 the fighting would concentrate on the Schwaben Redoubt to the north of Thiepval, leaving the Ridge comparatively quiet.

In the spring of 1917 the German withdrawal eastwards allowed the partial clearance of the Somme battlefields. A number of cemeteries (Lonsdale and Blighty Valley cemeteries, among others) were set up near the Leipzig Salient, to which soldiers' bodies could be removed for proper and formally registered burial. This clearance may have included only those bodies found in the open, and not previously marked graves. Unmarked graves are likely to have been missed, and some of them would only be found in later years as the land was returned to its previous agricultural use.

The fighting in 1918 swept across the 1916 Somme battlefields twice, but as the movement of armies was rapid in this area little further disturbance occurred in this part of the battlefield. After the war there was an intensive programme of battlefield clearance, which took many years to complete. Where possible, individual graves and smaller cemeteries (those with less than forty graves) were concentrated into larger ones nearby. The land was returned to surviving refugees from the area. As they cleared the cratered wilderness and rebuilt their homes, it was inevitable that more soldiers' bodies would be found. The farmers were encouraged to report such bodies and were financially rewarded for doing so. These were then buried wherever convenient, often in a military cemetery then under construction. This could result in soldiers being buried many miles from where they had fallen. This practice continued until quite recently. Today newly discovered bodies are buried in a military cemetery as close to their point of discovery as practicable and preferably next (or near) to a fallen comrade from the same regiment (if identification is possible).

It was clear from the battalion diary that Albert had been one of many fatalities for the 3rd Worcestershire that day. What if Albert's body hadn't been blown to bits, but had been rapidly interred along with other casualties? What if some of these bodies had been later recovered and identified? Might it be possible that

Albert's body, if not actually positively identified, had been buried alongside them in a grave marked 'Unknown Soldier, Worcestershire Regiment'?

At the outset it seemed a tenuous possibility. However, the reward of finding such a grave alongside that of a named 3rd Worcestershire soldier known to have fallen on 24 August would be a close second to finding Albert's grave itself. Despite the difficult work I knew would be ahead, I felt this just had to be worth a try.

After the war the multi-volumed *Soldiers Died in the Great War* was published. Each volume represented one or more regiments, with entries ordered by surname and battalion. This is now available on a single CD-ROM, and the database is fully searchable on all fields. Following a request to my friend Victor Piuk, who lives on the Somme, I received a print-out of the 3rd Worcestershire fatalities for 24/25 August 1916. The poignancy of receiving this casualty list, actually posted from the battlefields of the Somme, albeit eighty-five years later, was not lost.

In total, one officer and forty-one other ranks of the 3rd Worcestershire died on 24/25 August 1916. Although this may seem high, this total was significantly smaller than most battalions on the opening day of the Somme offensive. It was reassuring to find Albert's name there, with all details correct.

The next task proved to be both one of the most sobering and saddest parts of my researches. Thanks to the Internet, finding the burial details of named soldiers has now been simplified: the database can be found on the Commonwealth War Graves Commission website (www.cwgc.org). I spent three evenings on this website, entering each of the names in turn, knowing that I would eventually find an exact match, and that this was no blind search.

I was now recreating the aftermath of a battle that took place more than eighty-five years ago, and discovering what physical remains of that action could still be found on a visit to the Somme battlefields today. The names I was uncovering had once been real people with hopes and expectations, and linked to most of them were family members, each of whom had spent the rest of their lives without their son, husband, father or brother.

In all, thirty-three of the forty-one 3rd Worcestershire to die on 24/25 August 1916 have no known grave and are commemorated on the Thiepval Memorial to the Missing, Albert Turley among them. This represented some 80 per cent of those fallen – a significant statistic, summarising the tragic aftermath of this successful Somme action.

Despite my negative findings in respect of Albert, I had found eight soldiers of the 3rd Worcestershire who did have individual graves. I now began to look at these in more detail. They were as follows:

PTE HARRY WESTWOOD
Died of wounds 25/8/16, buried in Puchevillers Military Cemetery, plot III, row E, grave 24

Puchevillers was one of the villages the 3rd Worcestershire had marched through on their way to the Leipzig Salient only days before the attack on the 24th, and was many miles from Thiepval. Unlike Albert Turley, Harry Westwood 'died of wounds'. The register of burials related that a Casualty Clearing Station (CCS) had used the Puchevillers cemetery, the purpose of a CCS being to provide either emergency attention or minimum care (rebandaging and pain relief) before passing the casualties on down the line for further treatment in base hospitals in France or England. It was quite probable that Harry Westwood had been wounded in the attack on the Hindenburg Trench.

PTE ROBERT REEVES AND CPL ARTHUR CALDERWOOD
Both killed in action 24/8/16, buried in Lonsdale Military Cemetery, plot III, row A, graves 8, 9

Lonsdale cemetery, Authuille, is now the nearest cemetery to the Leipzig Salient. I expected that if any named burials had survived from the 3rd Worcestershire action on 24/25 August, then they would be found here. The present cemetery (then denoted Lonsdale No. 1) was one of the original cemeteries set up in 1917; the ninety-six graves in plot I belonged to it. After the war both individual graves and smaller cemeteries in the vicinity – Lonsdale No. 2 (Authuille), Nab Road (Ovillers-la-Boisselle), Paisley Avenue and Paisley Hillside (Authuille) – were removed and the bodies reinterred here. In total there are now 1,542 graves, of which 816 are unidentified. As both Robert Reeves and Arthur Calderwood are in plot III, this means that they were buried here as part of this concentration process. The care demonstrated in this work is indicated by the fact that these identified soldiers, from the same regiment, were finally buried side by side.

PTE HUGHSIA RUDDOCK AND SGT JOHN GRIFFIN

The former killed in action 24/8/16; the latter killed in action 25/8/16, buried in Serre Road No. 2 Cemetery: plot XXVIII, row G, grave 12 and Plot XXVII, row D, grave 7 respectively.

The village of Serre is many miles to the north of Thiepval and is synonymous with the near-annihilation of the 'Pals' battalions in their attack on the village on 1 July 1916. Serre Road No. 2 cemetery is the largest on the Somme battlefield, with 7,126 graves of which 4,943 are unknown. This was also a concentration cemetery and was still under construction in the late 1920s. The high plot numbers again indicate that the bodies of these soldiers were buried here long after the war. Although not actually adjacent to each other, they were sufficiently close to indicate that they were found at a similar date.

SGT FREDERICK POCOCK

Died of wounds 24/8/16, buried in Ovillers Military Cemetery: plot XV, row G, grave 12

Ovillers Military Cemetery is only a little to the south of the Leipzig Salient. It is another concentration cemetery with 3,439 graves of which 2,479 are unknown. Frederick Pocock must have been very seriously wounded in the attack on 24 August. He may have died at a nearby first aid post, situated in the reserve and support lines and staffed by the battalion medical officer and a few orderlies (probably with the Revd G.M. Evans also in attendance). Here, a casualty would have received only enough treatment to enable him to be passed down the line to the field ambulance, as transport became available. At these first aid posts the most difficult decisions – whom to treat first and how much treatment should be given in hopeless cases – had to be taken.

PTE HARRY DAVIS AND PTE ROLAND ROSE

Both killed in action 24/8/16, buried in Bray Military Cemetery: both in plot III, row B, grave 4 and row C, grave 22

Bray is at the very south of the Somme battlefield, standing on the River Somme itself. This village was behind the lines for the whole of the 1916 fighting, but was involved in the battles of 1918. It is a small cemetery with approximately 900 graves of which over 100 are unknown. The cemetery details tell that the graves in plot III were laid there in 1924. As with Serre Road No. 2, it would seem that both Harry Davis and Roland Rose were found long after the war and taken to Bray to be buried.

This information accounted for all the named graves of the 3rd Worcestershire from the 24/25 August. They were widely scattered across the whole Somme battlefield, indicating that the identified bodies of the 3rd Worcestershire had been discovered some years after the war, as, possibly, had the unidentified ones as well, which would have been buried alongside them. Unfortunately it was not possible to determine from the databases whether any 'unknowns' in the above-mentioned cemeteries had been partially identified as belonging to the Worcestershire Regiment.

The answers to this last question could only be satisfied by a visit to the cemeteries themselves. Whether or not these soldiers were lone burials or part of a larger group of 'Worcestershire unknowns', we would still be able us to pay our respects to Albert's comrades, who had fallen with him in the attack on the Hindenburg Trench.

There was still one last hope: if only we could find just one 'Unknown Soldier, Worcestershire Regiment' buried next to one of these named graves, particularly in Lonsdale, Serre Road or Bray, then we might actually have found Albert Turley himself! We would never know for certain, and the odds would still be long – but all the effort in this search would have been worthwhile.

SEVEN

A Pilgrimage to the Somme

The winter of 2000 was drawing to a close: it was time to plan our now annual trip to France to visit the battlefields of the First World War. I had first visited the Somme over twenty years before. For me every visit had been special in its own way, but this visit to the areas in which Albert Turley had served and fallen would become one of the most memorable.

The Somme battlefield was an agricultural area before the war, and in the eighty-odd years since the Armistice the land has again reverted to its former use. All the villages have been rebuilt, and are now sufficiently aged to resemble their pre-1914 appearance. The roads too have been re-laid and metalled to follow their former courses, with only minor variations. The fields, once a barren moonscape, then a wilderness of rough vegetation, have now been smoothed over by farmers' efforts and the healing hands of time. The devastated woods have been replanted, again following the original boundaries; the trees are now sufficiently mature to belie the woods' former state through a walk within their dark confines still reveals the shell-riven terrain. The Somme battlefield again blends in with adjacent areas, as if untouched by warfare, in this quiet part of northern France – indeed the area now truly merits Sassoon's 'heavenly'.

However, although the pre-1914 Somme visitor would recognise many of the geographical features as 'unchanged', there are some very obvious differences. The villages are almost depopulated, many residents either weekend visitors to their country retreats from the city of Paris, or elderly: the young have moved away in search of work. The mechanisation of farming has reduced the number of agricultural workers and turned once small fields into prairies. Despite cars travelling along the narrow roads (at amazing speeds!), the region is very quiet, as it should be – the whole area is scattered with dozens and dozens of military cemeteries, mainly British. These range from the smallest, containing thirty or so graves, dotted around the former No Man's Land, to huge ones, containing many thousands of graves associated with villages or woods. These reflect their use as either battlefield casualty clearing stations or concentration cemeteries where isolated graves and smaller cemeteries were moved after the war. Each cemetery was designed by some of the best architects of the period under the supervision of Sir Fabian Ware, as head of the then Imperial War Graves Commission. Their layout reflects military precision in the lines and uniformity of the stones, combined with the homely, peaceful atmosphere of a well-kept British garden. With time the cemetery gardens have matured, to match the concepts of those original architects, and are now maintained by the Commonwealth War Graves Commission – the new name also reflecting the world's changes. Surmounting all this, and visible from practically the entire Somme battlefield, is the Thiepval Memorial to the Missing, containing the names of the 73,000 missing of the Somme with no known grave, Albert Turley's among them.

The casual visitor to the Somme who expects to see devastation and the remains of lines of trenches littered with the debris of war in some form of sepia-and-white landscape will be very disappointed. First, his colour vision will confuse him (would that he wait for nightfall!), and there are only a few trenches preserved from 1916 among the acres of rolling downs. The numerous piles of unexploded shells found at corners of fields, uncovered each ploughing, seem to have decreased in recent years. But the visitor could not but be impressed by the sheer number of cemeteries and graves therein, although without some knowledge of the history and geography of the battle he may soon weary even of these and pass on, shaking his head at the futility and waste of war. He will have missed a great deal; and understood less.

A Pilgrimage to the Somme

In recent years the numbers of people visiting the area has increased. This is due in part to the subject of the First World War entering the National Curriculum in schools, and for older visitors promises not kept by previous generations to visit graves of relatives are now being honoured as the Somme area is within easy reach of the Channel ports (1¼ hours on the French motorway system). Despite these factors the Somme battlefields cannot as yet be regarded as 'touristy' – and I sincerely hope they may never become so! Places to stay are few, the night-life is minimal, there are no tea shops (and few toilets!) and few locals rarely speak English. However, the genuine visitor doesn't come for such things. Using the few remembered French phrases from school always elicits a kind reply, since the locals are grateful that the British still return and remember the past.

Some things, however, have changed, and many for the better. A small number of British people now live 'on the Somme', acting as both guides and hosts to travellers. All these people have had their lives affected in some way by contact with the history of the First World War. They carry on the tradition of those old soldiers who chose to stay in France after the war to become the battlefield guides and cemetery gardeners of the 1920s. For a pilgrimage to the battlefields, there is no better place to stay – for here the '*comradeship of the trenches*' still lives on. The house of Victor and Diane Piuk in Hardecourt aux Bois is one such – and it became for us a welcoming home-from-home for our pilgrimage.

This is the story of that pilgrimage.

FOLLOWING ALBERT TURLEY AND THE 3RD WORCESTERSHIRE

The weather broke fine and clear for our first morning, as the May sun promised a hot summer's day ahead. We packed the car with maps, folders and cameras and set off for the north of the Somme battlefield. The natural place to begin the pilgrimage was Mailly Wood, where Albert had joined the 3rd Worcestershire on 24 July 1916.

The village of Mailly-Maillet was larger than the average Somme village, but seemingly just as deserted. The houses were a mixture of styles, from post-medieval structures to modern chalets, the village church still bearing scars of shelling and graffiti from British troops as they had once passed through. The village had been behind the lines and although damaged by long-range shells it had not suffered the total devastation inflicted on those nearer the front lines. Many buildings had not changed since before 1916, and would be recognisable to the soldiers of the day who had known it as a billet. However, we had come to find the 'wood'. After driving through the village there was a sign to 'Mailly Wood Cemetery'. We found a convenient place to park the car and followed the directions up a farm track. This led us around the edge of a large field towards Mailly Wood. Just in front was the military cemetery, a small one. From the visitors' book it was clear that visits here had been few in past years – this cemetery was well off the tourist route. We wrote down our names and the purpose of our visit. Mailly Wood stood dark and imposing, stretching westwards down into a valley, the tall mature trees giving a false impression of age. We did not venture into the wood itself, because the land was private, but we wondered if there remained any relics of the army camp that had once been here. Spending some time among the gravestones in the cemetery, we looked outwards to distant hills and villages, knowing that Albert too would have seen the same panorama.

Leaving Mailly Wood we returned to the car. Our next destination was to be Beaumont Hamel and the Newfoundland Memorial Park. Here Albert had done his first tour of duty in the trenches. We again drove through the village of Mailly-Maillet and onwards the few kilometres to Auchonvillers. Albert and the 3rd Worcestershire would have marched down this road under the cover of night, following the gun flashes to the front line. Auchonvillers is the home of Avril Williams, another British expat. Her house contains a cellar that was once a dressing station used in the Somme battle, and relics found here on its restoration are on display. This makes a good place to stop; a bowl of hot French onion soup and a generous bacon roll go down wonderfully well on a cold day! However, this day we had to promise ourselves a return trip as we pressed on the short distance to the Memorial Park. Leaving Auchonvillers, we went up a rise to see ahead the wooded park that marked the front lines of 1 July 1916.

The Newfoundland Memorial Park deserves a chapter in its own right: it is one of the focal points of any trip to the Somme battlefield. Maintained by the government of Canada, it contains several memorials and cemeteries and a new museum dedicated to the men of Newfoundland who fell here on that fateful day. As importantly, it contains the remains of the trenches from 1 July and subsequent actions. During the summer months the place is rarely without tourists, who keep the volunteer guides, all students from Canada, very busy.

This day we bypassed the coach parties and guides and walked down the path, across the former No Man's Land towards one of the small cemeteries. Many people would take the same path, as part of the guided walk. The path crosses over a small trench, generally overgrown. The guides take pains to point out that this trench was not part of operations on 1 July since it was dug later, and normally pass on; however, it was this forgotten trench that we had come to see.

Situated several hundred yards in front of the old British front line of 1 July this trench would fit in exactly with Johnston's (and Wallace Pratt's) description of the new trench that was constructed by the units of the 7th Brigade, including the 3rd Worcestershire. I had not been able to find a more detailed reference as to exactly which trenches had been occupied by Albert and his fellow reinforcements in the first week of August, as they received their baptism of fire in front of Beaumont Hamel. However, here, preserved by association with events relating to the 1 July operations, could be the very trench that Albert had helped dig and hold.

Effectively ignored by tourists keen to walk down the zigzags of the 1 July front line, this trench has escaped the sympathetic restoration afforded to other trenches in the park, where permanent duckboards have been placed. As such it is still fairly narrow, the twists and turns of bays and traverses being very apparent. Eighty-odd years have reduced its depth to only a few feet at most. Although sunny, the temperature was significantly lower than it was in August 1916, and it was hard to imagine what it was like to stand or sit in that trench surrounded by the stinking remains of the 1 July débâcle. But it was still impressive. Its proximity to the German lines made it easy to imagine the fear of those new soldiers who had dug that trench under the cover of nightfall, fearing that any noise would bring retaliation in the form of a bombardment or raid from the enemy trenches close by. We left this place quietly, passing by another group of tourists who would soon walk over 'Albert's trench' without realising its significance to us.

For the next part of the visit we retraced our steps through Auchonvillers and Mailly-Maillet, and headed westwards. We saw the sign to Bertrancourt to the right at the fork in the valley below Mailly Wood. Stopping the car, we looked back over the expanse of the wood and then carried on towards Bertrancourt.

We passed through the small village of Beaussart. At the end of this village it was possible to see the village of Bertrancourt on the hill on the opposite, western, side of the valley. I got out of the car, leaving my wife to drive on to Bertrancourt. I was effectively alone. There were no other cars about, nor people – all was very quiet except for the sound of birds and the wind rustling the leaves of nearby trees. As I started to walk along the road to Bertrancourt, I knew without doubt that Albert and the 3rd Worcestershire had walked along this same piece of road. The new metalled road surface and the presence of electricity and telephone poles were the only indications that any time had passed between August 1916 and the present. As they marched, they must have seen and heard exactly what I was now seeing and hearing. I did not feel lonely walking along that road, it was with a sense of pride that I continued onwards.

At Bertrancourt I rejoined my wife to find another quiet, practically deserted village. When Albert was here, the place would have been a thriving scene of activity with headquarters for all kinds of army units, transport lorries, horses and long lines of men passing through it. The contrast in sound could not have been more pronounced. Only old women and a few small children were visible on their hurried visits to one of the few shops. As with Mailly-Maillet, Bertrancourt had not been destroyed by shell-fire and even more of the buildings dated to before the First World War. If any old soldiers had returned, they would have recognised more here than at the Memorial Park, filled with its 'lawned' trenches and many memorials. In the centre of the village were still the old barns used as billets in 1916, timber-framed, now in-filled with bricks with here and there traces of the old daub remaining. Here too were farmhouses, like the ones described in all old soldiers' accounts of billets behind the lines. These comprised a single-storey extended cottage making up one side of a square of buildings with a gate opposite the front door. Soldiers had used the once-infested outbuildings as billets. All was as it had been, except that the storage buildings had their internal floors removed to house the working farm machinery. The high middens of stinking manure that once filled the central courtyards had long since gone. In their place were immaculately kept gardens filled with colourful flowers.

From Bertrancourt we had a longer drive. This would take us through the villages of Louvencourt and Vauchelles, past Marieux and finally to Sarton. We stopped at the first of these villages, Louvencourt. At the entrance to the village is a small British military cemetery in which is buried an officer of the Worcestershire Regiment, Lt Roland A. Leighton. Although he was killed before the Somme battle, his story was immortalised by his fiancée Vera Brittain in *Testament of Youth*. On his gravestone his family had inscribed the following epitaph: '*Goodnight though life and all take flight never goodbye*'. His brother officers had laid him to rest after a short service at the local church on 26 December 1915.

We arrived at Sarton in mid-afternoon. The village itself was very small, though the road passing through it was one of the busiest 'country' roads we had yet come across. Now a totally unremarkable stretch, it was easy to imagine the lines of soldiers from the 3rd Worcestershire and 1st Wiltshire on the morning of 12 August. As another car sped off, I wondered whether the driver or any of the local inhabitants knew that once the King of

England and the Prince of Wales also passed this way (a little more slowly!) receiving cheers from throngs of troops.

From here we rejoined the old Roman road to Amiens and drove south through the village of Raincheval to Puchevillers. This quiet village borders the main road passing through it. Most of the houses stretch up the hillside to the church situated on top of a hill. Here again, the majority of the houses and buildings dated to before the First World War and it was as if no time had passed at all. Leaving the car, we walked up the main street to look at the church. A tiled spire surmounted the square limestone tower: perhaps Albert had admired this structure – after all, he was a stonemason. We found the sign to Puchevillers Military Cemetery and started to follow the directions. After a while we wished we had taken the car, and were forced to turn back, having failed to find it; we still had a long way to go.

The next journey would follow Albert and the 3rd Worcestershire the 8 miles back up the line from Puchevillers to Hedauville on 17 August. We too set off in the late afternoon, as they had. The car allowed us to follow their route through Toutencourt, Harponville, Varennes and finally to the outskirts of the village of Hedauville. Despite the relatively short distance it took much longer than we had expected. The road twisted and turned, right and left, up and down, through each of the above villages. The road signs and even the modern Michelin road map proved to be of less use than the 1916 British trench maps I had brought with me. If we had got lost once and been forced to turn back, we must have done so many times. We began to understand why it had taken the rest of the afternoon, the evening and into the night before the 3rd Worcestershire finally found themselves at Hedauville, shattered (and wet through).

We had followed Albert and the 3rd Worcestershire from his arrival at Mailly Wood and his joining the battalion, through his baptism of fire at Beaumont Hamel and back down the line through Bertrancourt, Sarton and Puchevillers for training, finally to arrive at Hedauville. This proved to be a natural break for us to go back to our comfortable billet at Hardecourt aux Bois, and for Albert and the 3rd Worcestershire a final night before going back into the trenches.

A Pilgrimage to the Somme

The following morning again broke fine and clear: it would be another hot sunny day. Unlike the 3rd Worcestershire we returned to Hedauville mid-morning, much later than the 5 a.m. that they had left it on 18 August 1916. This village had been much nearer the front line and had therefore been practically destroyed. Many of the houses and buildings are now modern, and there is a central grassed area reminiscent of an English village green. During our pilgrimage the road through it to Albert was quite busy; there were also several people about, again mainly old women who clearly had lived there all their lives. Although the sight of a British car on the Somme is no longer a novelty, in the villages behind the lines it is still uncommon. However, they knew the reason we were here and politely wished us 'Good morning'; we replied politely in French, glad to carry on the tradition of Anglo-French cordiality in this area which dates back to the Battle of the Somme.

We took the road down the hill from Hedauville through to Bouzincourt and the village of Aveluy on the River Ancre. Rising over the crest of Bouzincourt Ridge we stopped the car. From here stretches one of the best panoramas over the Somme battlefields. That morning the sun glinted off the golden virgin atop the basilica in the town of Albert to the south. Further down the straight road, to the east, lay the village of Aveluy. Across the valley stood the battle lines of the Somme. To the north-east, on the highest part, towered the Thiepval Memorial – our ultimate destination. On the slopes leading up to the crest were Thiepval and Authuille Woods. At the time Albert and the 3rd Worcestershire passed this way, the dawn would have been breaking and gunfire flashes would have helped light up the eastern horizon. We stayed here a while admiring the view, knowing that in 1916 it would have been very dangerous to linger there. Under direct observation from the German lines on the far crest, the nearby Bouzincourt Ridge Military Cemetery was filled with the soldiers caught by German artillery fire. At our feet were rusting pieces of shell fragments, testament to less peaceful mornings.

Driving down the hill, we passed through the village of Aveluy and crossed over the fast flowing but narrow River Ancre. The modernised bridge is in the same place as the original –

photographs taken here of the crossing accurately match those taken over eighty years ago. We stopped here at the far side where, looking into the trees, one's eyes soon became accustomed to the gloom, and observed a tall crucifix. In 1916 there was a similar crucifix here too – indeed this was still Crucifix Corner. Here Albert and the 3rd Worcestershire would have entered the trench system leading towards the Authuille Wood defence lines and thence to the Leipzig Salient. Looking around the area behind the crucifix the traces of trench systems can still be found along with shell craters and the remnants of concrete emplacements. Here was the place the 3rd Worcestershire had been relieved by the 1/6th West Yorkshire after their first tour in the Leipzig Salient in July 1916. Again, although it would have been interesting to walk through the wood, the land was private. On the right-hand side of the crucifix there is a small trackway that skirts the edge of the wood, it follows the exact route taken and so well described by Corporal Henry Ogle. Eventually this leads to the Nab, Blighty Valley and the Leipzig Salient. It would have made a nice walk, but this day we had much to do. Instead we took the car and drove northwards through the village of Authuille and onwards to Thiepval village, the sheer size of the Memorial to the Missing now becoming very evident.

We parked the car at the entrance to the Memorial and entered. The wide pathway is laid with gravel, and the crunching sound as we made our way along it seemed much too loud for a place such as this. After a short distance, on the right, open the wide lawns leading to the Memorial itself. Fittingly there is no continuation of the gravelled path at this point – the manicured grass now ensures the silence of the many feet that pass this way. However, for us it was not yet time to visit the Memorial itself.

The gravel path led on through the Memorial grounds southwards. It ends abruptly at the edge of the park, a surprise to modern visitors, though a farm track carries on from here. This track, once a road, bisects the once infamous Leipzig Salient.

Before our pilgrimage I had spent many hours poring over maps of the Leipzig Salient – copies of original 1916 trench maps, hand-drawn sketches reproduced in the *History of the Worcestershire*

Regiment in the Great War and modern French maps (1:25000 Series Bleu). Using the first two sources I had located not only the trenches the 3rd Worcestershire and 1st Wiltshire had held but also the German defences on 24 August 1916. By careful manipulation of the zoom control on a simple photocopier, I had altered the scale of the modern French map to match that of my copy of a 1916 trench map. Using a needle I pierced through the latter, accurately laid over the former, to trace over these trenches. Final inking in gave me a 'modern' trench map.

We started out on this track heading southwards. Shortly the whole panorama of the Leipzig Salient opened up. Standing here, on the site of the Hindenburg Trench, it was possible to see for miles. All the British positions were visible: from Ovillers Spur on the left, carrying on through Blighty Valley, the Nab to Authuille Wood, with Lonsdale Military Cemetery in the fields before it, and finally away on the right, out of sight, Authuille village. The hours spent in preparing my improvised map had left an indelible mental picture – everything was as I had expected to find it. This sense of recognition seemed to electrify the atmosphere.

To the unprepared visitor the Leipzig Salient comprises just two more fields in the patchwork landscape. In fact, both fields had recently been ploughed and rain had softened the furrows. Sometimes in these circumstances it is possible to see the white chalk scars of old trenches and shell-craters, backfilled after the war and smoothed over by years of subsequent farming. From ground level these scars can be hard to discern unless one is actually standing on the trench line, when the chalk 'scar' zigzags away from the observer. Today, there seemed to be no such lines. However, among the brown earth flecked with flints and chalk were lumps of a different hue: here were the fragments of the thousands of exploded shells that must have fallen on this hillside. At the corner of the field was a small pile of complete shells – just a small sample of those that didn't explode, many more of which remain under that now peaceful brown earth, probably forever.

Walking ever downwards along this track, with the Thiepval Memorial to our rear, generated strange emotions: a sense of utter isolation from the modern world and of being very conspicuous in this open landscape. This is a common feeling when walking on the Somme battlefield, and reduces a visitor to silence. Yet the place was far from silent, and the wind coming from the south that day was quite stiff. The differing sounds of the wind over this open countryside will haunt a pilgrim for the rest of his life. When strong, they remind him of barrages fired long ago; when gentle, of the swaying poppies in rich cornfields, the flowers in neat military cemeteries and rustling leaves in now peaceful woods. No country walk over moors or along peaceful lanes at home can ever be the same again. The sound of the wind, even in these homely places, triggers a distant memory and the walker mentally walks the Somme once more.

Soon the track entered a rough crater, not generated by a tumultuous shell or mine detonation, but rather the remains of an old quarry. Until recently this place was surrounded by trees, their stumps still in evidence among carelessly dumped rubbish. It was heartening to see that new trees had been planted here, though it will be many years before the remains of the Leipzig Redoubt will be hidden again. Still a piece of tortured ground, it is not difficult to imagine the bitter fighting that once took place on this spot during July and August 1916. The trenches here changed hands many times, even on a single day; enemies were only yards from each other. Disturbed crows made clear their objection to our presence. We carried on over the rubble of buildings placed to level the track, and to cover the undiscovered dead – a mockery of the neat white stones laid in ordered rows to cover more fortunate comrades only a few hundred yards away.

From here the track widened as it joined the road. We turned to our left and walked downwards. Among the jetsam at the roadside was a long length of twisted iron pipe, its thickness and method of fracture indicating that it was no piece of discarded car exhaust pipe. Being effectively unrecognisable and worthless, it had been overlooked by 'collectors' who prefer more easily identifiable artefacts from the battlefield. Yet here, possibly, was a piece of the actual 'push-pipe' that was used to such good effect prior to the attack of the 1st Wiltshire and 3rd Worcestershire in August 1916. We left the object as we found it, hoping it would be reburied and remain there.

After a short walk another farm track appeared on our left. This was the one we had come to find. Narrower and clearly less used, it headed northwards back up the Thiepval Ridge almost parallel to the first track. On our right ran the edge of the Bois de la Haye, partly obscuring Blighty Valley. On our left the ploughed field stretched away to the quarry and the line of the first track, which now became the western skyline. On our left front, standing behind trees, was the Thiepval Memorial on top of the ridge. Ahead the track could be seen to bend to the right, revealing a derelict farm building – a modern wreck – too far along the track for our visit.

With a heart that grew heavier with each step we started northwards along the track. Looking right and left we lined up the northern limit of the quarry and the dogleg on the western edge of the Bois de la Haye. Here we stopped and put down our belongings. Once again isolated from the main road, we knew we could count on our not being disturbed. For this was the site of the Lemberg Trench, the British front line of 24 August 1916, held by the 3rd Worcestershire – one of whom had been Albert Turley. Now pleasantly warm and sheltered, the sound of the wind was gentle and made even more tuneful by the larks singing in the nearby wood. As I looked right and left chalk marks in the soil that had previously looked indistinct and random were now resolved into the scar of the battered Lemberg Trench. This was the place we had come to visit – here was the last place that we knew Albert had been for certain. Looking up the Thiepval Ridge the ground rose to a crest a few hundred yards away, the site of the Hindenburg Trench. As the sun shone on that hillside, a sobering thought struck home – this same view was possibly the last many soldiers of the 3rd Worcestershire had had on that fateful day. Here, on this spot, Albert and his comrades had spent their last moments trying to compose themselves as they prepared to go 'over the top' on that afternoon long ago. Looking again right and left it was possible to imagine the lines of men fixing bayonets, crouching down or standing in front of scaling ladders. Ahead the hillside was baking in the afternoon sun, dust was being blown up from the field over the crest, a modern smoke screen; the wind now suddenly stronger echoing a bombardment in our ears. Yes, this place was indeed once a battlefield, and to those who come afterwards it still is – if only in the mind's eye.

I looked behind, into the distance. Framed between the edges of the Bois de la Haye on the left and Authuille Wood to the right stood a small bank, in the centre of which was a bush. Here was the Nab – Philip Gibbs had watched the attack from this very place. Time seemed to stand still here: all the many hours spent trying to piece together Albert's service on the Somme in 1916 had come to fruition in this place. All the hard effort had become worthwhile. Our feelings and emotions would have been incomprehensible to an outsider simply watching two people standing on a path in the middle of seemingly uninteresting farmland.

We stayed there for quite a while, fixing the view into permanent memory. We read Johnston's account of the action of the 3rd Worcestershire and 1st Wiltshire in the days leading up to the attack, knowing we were at the very place where all the events he described actually took place. We then remained alone in our thoughts. I had originally planned to walk up the hill to the Hindenburg Trench from here – but simply standing there, knowing what had happened all those years ago, made this task now seem inappropriate, one day perhaps. . . .

Retracing our steps, we went back to our car at the Thiepval Memorial. Walking back up the Thiepval Ridge from the site of the Leipzig Redoubt, we were indeed retracing the path of lines of 1st Wiltshire men who had gone over the top here. It was a steady climb; looking westwards we could imagine the long line of men going steadily up that ridge towards the Hindenburg Trench. Somehow the return journey didn't seem quite so lonely.

The last visit on this part of the pilgrimage was to the site of the Nab. Although well within walking distance of the Lemberg Trench position, we had taken the car. Standing against the grassed bank, in front of the bush, we had a clear panorama of the Thiepval Ridge across Blighty Valley. This view confirmed my earlier deduction of exactly where Philip Gibbs had stood that afternoon to witness the attack by the 3rd Worcestershire and 1st Wiltshire. From several hundred yards we could see the point on the farm track below us where we had stood on the site of

A Pilgrimage to the Somme

Lemberg Trench. Right and left of this we could see the whole of this trench and hence all of the 3rd Worcestershire attack. Using a pair of binoculars, as Gibbs undoubtedly had done, the view was much improved.

Before the trip I had planned to visit this place and to read Philip Gibbs' account on the very spot where he had stood. Realising that as written it would be much too long, I had made a précis. Reading it now the character of the entire piece had changed. It had somehow regained its immediacy, the events witnessed by Philip Gibbs now standing out even more clearly, and with them the horror of the attack on the distant ridge. The account, now, left one breathless.

I stood with my eyes glued to the binoculars as my wife read out the piece:

> Yesterday I saw them take the Hindenburg Trench and its strong point, which is almost the last of the defensive works barring our way to the south entrance of the village . . . on the skyline at the top of a ridge which slopes up from the Leipzig Salient there still stand a hundred trees or so, which are all that is left of Thiepval . . . an officer came along the trench and said, 'Good afternoon. The show begins in ten minutes' . . .

> The leisurely bombardment continued . . . then suddenly . . . A great orchestra of death crashed out . . . when hundreds of heavy guns are firing upon one small line of ground and shells of the greatest size are rushing through the sky in flocks and bursting in flashes, all description is futile . . . the shells tore up the German trenches and built up a great wall of smoke along the crest of the ridge . . . a voice at my elbow, speaking breathlessly said, 'Look they're away' . . . Out of our front-line trenches scrambled long lines of men. They stood for a moment on the parapet, waited for a second or two until all the men had got into alignment and then started forward . . .

> Our men had a big climb to make and a long way over open country . . . the enemy was not long in flinging a barrage in the way of our men . . . but they were too late to

do any damage there . . . he raised his barrage on to ground nearer his own lines . . . now and again they seemed to fall into the middle of a bunch of our men in a way frightful to see, but when the smoke cleared the group was still going forward . . . on the right of the line one great shell burst with an enormous crash, and this time there was no doubt that it had caught some of our men . . . nothing checked the advance of the long line of figures going through the smoke . . .

The men had to cross one of those narrow strips of grassland between the earthworks before they came to the first line of German trenches . . . they were not in close formation, they went forward after the first few moments of advance, in small parties, widely scattered but keeping the same direction . . . sometimes the parties themselves broke up and separated into individual figures, jumping over shell holes, running first to left or right as the shriek of an enemy shell warned them of approaching death . . . I saw how easy it was to lose all sense of direction in an attack like this . . . we watched the single figures, following the fortunes of each man across the fire-swept slope . . .

For a little while the men were swallowed up in smoke . . . I could see nothing of them . . . the wind drifted the smoke away from the Thiepval Ridge and there were the lines of our men swarming up, some of them already on the highest ground . . . [they] then jumped down and disappeared, they were in the German trenches.

In the centre of the German trenches was a strong point . . . I could see that our men were all around it . . . one single figure was a heroic silhouette against the blue of the sky. He was bombing the redoubt . . . a German shell burst close to him and he was engulfed in the upheaval . . . I did not see him again . . .

New sounds of an explosive kind came through the fury of gunfire . . . I knew it was bomb fire . . . our men were at work in and about the German dug-outs . . . there were Germans there who were not surrendering without a fight . . . one fight took place on the top of the parapet . . . a man came up and stood on the sky-line – whether an English soldier or a German it was impossible to see . . . another man came up as chasing him . . . the first man turned . . . both had revolvers and fired, and disappeared . . . other men were running along the parapets of the German trenches, they were ours, and they were flinging bombs as they ran . . .

Only in the ground near to me could I see any sign of life now . . . here some of our wounded were walking back . . . it was a perilous way of escape for wounded when the enemy was flinging shells all over the ground . . . then for more than an hour as I watched, other figures came back from the high ground . . . they were our lightly wounded men, with here and there a German [prisoner] . . . one of them would jump down from the sky-line and come at a quick run down the slope . . . I could see that he was out of breath . . . he would stumble . . . I would see him crawl on his hands and knees . . . he would reach our lines of trenches and jump down . . . safe cover at last . . . so it happened with man after man . . . trying to dodge death . . . it was horrible to see . . .

So I watched, and knew, because our men did not come back from the trenches on the Thiepval Ridge, that they had been successful.

The emotions I felt in the few minutes it took to read this account simply cannot be described, and the memory of that afternoon will stay with me for as long as I live. We had followed Albert Turley and the 3rd Worcestershire across the Somme battlefield to the very place he fell during the attack on the Hindenburg Trench. We knew we could follow him no further.

In parallel to visits to the sites mentioned above, we endeavoured to find the more personal side to this story – the search for Albert Turley's comrades – and to leave behind a tribute to all those who fell that day.

CEMETERIES AND MEMORIALS

During our pilgrimage we had passed many cemeteries, each with its own unique character, but all with a common serenity. Following previous researches we visited several of these.

First, we travelled to the north of the Somme battlefield to the areas in front of the village of Serre. For my wife and me this place is very special. Our home town is Bradford in Yorkshire and it was at Serre that both battalions of the Bradford Pals (16th and 18th Prince of Wales's Own West Yorkshire Regiment) attacked on 1 July. Both were effectively destroyed in the opening hours of the battle, along with many other Pals battalions from other northern towns and cities. Amid the numerous small cemeteries scattered along No Man's Land, there are two much larger ones, Serre Road Nos 1 and 2. These were originally established on the old British front line of 1 July and after the war were enlarged to contain many thousands of graves recovered from all over the Somme battlefield. In fact Serre Road No. 2 is the largest cemetery on the Somme, containing over 7,000 individual headstones, mostly of 'unknowns'.

The day was a hot one when we arrived at Serre Road No. 2. The huge square cemetery spreads out over a hillside, the highest corner resting on the site of a German strongpoint then known as the 'Quadrilateral'. A brick-and-flint wall surmounted by finely cut Portland stone surrounds the whole cemetery. At the entrance is a large pillared portico in the same material, housing the box containing the cemetery register and visitors' book. The rows of graves in square plots seem endless. An accurately cut border surrounded each row, each grave having a well-kept flowering bush or plant in front of the stone. Towards the top of the cemetery was the Cross and Stone of Sacrifice. The best English walled gardens could not have looked so fine as did this cemetery under the dazzlingly bright early summer sun that day.

Given the sheer size of the cemetery, we had to consult the cemetery register to identify the plot numbers and the order of the rows within each plot. Having identified plots XXVII and XXVIII, we walked up the slope towards the top of the cemetery, and easily identified the rows and the graves we had come to visit. In fact the two graves were quite close together. We had found the first of the 3rd Worcestershire who had fallen in the attack on the Hindenburg Trench on 24/25 August 1916. Here were Pte Hughsia Ruddock, killed on the 24th, and Sgt John Griffin, killed on the 25th. We sat there for a time while the soft breezes rustled the leaves in the bordering trees and thought about this pilgrimage and the countless other pilgrimages made to this place by past generations to visit the graves of sons, husbands and fathers. We wondered if the relatives of these two soldiers had once come here; clearly the relatives of Hughsia Ruddock had paid for an inscription on the bottom of his stone: 'Greater love hath no man than this, that he lay down his life for his friends' – an all-too-common epitaph in this and all other military cemeteries on the Somme. We did our best to take photographs, but the white stone and the high angle of the sun made it difficult to get good pictures.

We collected our belongings and began the long walk back to the entrance. Suddenly we spotted among the many graves to unknown soldiers not far from Hughsia Ruddock and John Griffin a similar grave to 'A Soldier of the Great War, Worcestershire Regiment'. At this our hearts leapt, for this was the first we had seen – and it was one such as this that we had come to find. Our feeling was 'well, this one just might be Albert'. As we left Serre Road No. 2, we felt a sense of inner peace that is impossible to describe in words.

In our walks in and around the Leipzig Salient we spent quite some time in Lonsdale Cemetery. On a second hot sunny day we sat quietly by the graves of Cpl Arthur Calderwood and Pte Robert Reeves of the 3rd Worcestershire. Both these had fallen in action on 24 August, alongside Albert. Now they are buried side by side. On Arthur Calderwood's gravestone his relatives had included the inscription: 'Thy duty nobly done.' This cemetery was the nearest one to the scene of the attack on 24 August, and thus this place had the highest probability of containing the body of Albert Turley as one of the 'unknowns'. The graves were from many regiments representing the actions from 1 July through into September 1916. All too many of the stones bore the inscription,

'*A Soldier of the Great War, Known unto God*'; indeed this was the case with an adjacent grave on the right of Arthur Calderwood. Any of these may have been Albert Turley. By chance, another couple entered the cemetery when we were there: they too had come to visit a relative's grave, a deferred promise kept, at last, by a grandson. We left the place to them.

On the evening of the same day we travelled to Ovillers Military Cemetery. This large post-war concentration cemetery stands at the head of the formerly infamous Mash Valley, in front of the village of Ovillers-la-Boisselle. As we stood at the grassed entrance to the cemetery looking towards where the sun would soon be setting, the basilica in Albert with its now restored golden virgin statue stood out as a sharp silhouette. In the foreground the field sloped downwards towards a small road crossing the valley about 500 yards away. Behind this was a small hill, Usna Hill. Of all the places to stand on the Somme battlefield this is one of the most poignant for anyone who knows something about the events of 1 July 1916. This cemetery entrance stands effectively on the German front line of that day. The small road crossing the valley below was the site of the British front line. On 1 July, behind Usna Hill, stood the main body of British troops. The plan was that both attacking and reserve troops would go over the top together in a series of waves. Success relied on the German wire being effectively cut and on minimal German resistance. However, the wire was not cut and German resistance was strong. With such distances between the lines, the leading waves were practically annihilated by machine-guns from both Ovillers-la-Boisselle and La Boisselle villages. Survivors were held up at the wire, only to be cut down by rifle fire from the now fully manned German lines. The reserves coming in waves over the crest of Usna Hill and down its forward slope made perfect targets. Approximately 75 per cent of the attacking 12,000 men would be casualties that morning. Standing on this spot provides the German machine-gunner's viewpoint that day facing the remnants of the 2nd Devonshire: one dare not imagine the view seen by a British soldier coming over the crest of the Usna Hill, looking into that perfect Hell. It was said there was not one square yard of ground in this valley that was not carpeted in a sea of crimsoned khaki.

We entered the cemetery and turned left to the domed portico which contained the cemetery register. We quickly found the name we were looking for, and walked up the hill following the cemetery wall. The cemetery was undergoing some restoration, and the French graves in the centre of the cemetery were all being re-laid. The new stone crosses were in place, but at all angles. The scene was reminiscent of Sir Stanley Spencer's painting, the *Resurrection of the Dead on Judgement Day*. We found the grave of Sgt Frederick Pocock, of the 3rd Worcestershire, who had died of wounds on 24 August. For once, the angle of the sun was more than perfect. Not only was the inscription highlighted by shadow, but the entire surface of the Portland stone shone the palest powder blue against the deepening blue of the sky. The newly planted trees rustled their leaves in the summer's breeze, ready for a lifetime of guardianship in this peaceful place.

From here it was but a short drive to the Thiepval Memorial itself. By now the evening sun was nearly setting; there were only a few clouds and the huge expanse of sky was the deepest blue that I could ever remember seeing. It may be only coincidence, but whenever we have made a special trip to the Thiepval Memorial, we have found ourselves there alone, despite the thousands of visitors it receives each summer. This was not to be an exception. For this pilgrimage we had purchased a poppy wreath from the Royal British Legion. We had made a laminated sheet and attached it to the base of the wreath. On the sheet was written:

In Tribute to the following Officer and Men of The 3rd Battalion Worcestershire Regiment, who fell during the successful attack on Hindenburg Trench 24/25 August 1916 within a few hundred yards of this memorial, the majority of whom have no known grave.

Underneath we had placed a copy of the photograph of Albert Turley we had found in Cinderford Library and a modern map of the Leipzig Salient, complete with both the Lemberg and the Hindenburg Trenches in relation to the Thiepval Memorial. Alongside was the list of names of the soldiers of the 3rd Worcestershire who had fallen.

At the bottom were our own simple words of tribute to just one of these:

Albert, your story once long forgotten, now forever remembered.

We found the panels to the Worcestershire Regiment. We looked up at the wall, here and there a now-familiar name stood out. However, one name shone out for us that evening: 'TURLEY A.E.'. One name among the 73,000 names that will remain forever, long after ours are forgotten. We gently laid the wreath with the several others already laid there against the Stone of Sacrifice. The names of the organisations represented on the other wreaths showed that many other individuals and groups of people were similarly remembered that day.

The sun was now setting, and its orange glow lit the west front of the Memorial, turning it a honeyed yellow against the near-purple of the sky. Binyon's words could never have been more appropriate than they were at the Thiepval Memorial that evening: '*At the going down of the sun, and in the morning, we will remember them.*'

Another family had come to the Memorial. They had given us time to complete our laying of the wreath and for some quiet time afterwards. It was now their turn to experience the atmosphere in this special place. As we passed each other we smiled in greeting and gratitude. There was no need for words – we each knew why we had come. As we looked back the huge Memorial seemed to engulf the silhouettes of the family. Eastwards the shadow of the arch stretched away before us, out into the fields beyond the Memorial grounds. We had laid our tribute, thought our own private thoughts, and wished we could have done so much more.

We left the last cemetery at Bray-sur-Somme to our final day. By now the warm sunny weather had given way to cloud and a strong wind was blowing. It seemed a long drive along the quiet, narrow country roads to the very south of the Somme battlefield. It made me think about the organisation for the burial of bodies discovered after the war, in 1924 – it seemed such a pity that they had to be brought such a long way from the place they had fallen.

Bray Military Cemetery is situated among fields with an adjacent modern farm complex, down a very narrow track. Of the cemeteries we had visited so far, this proved to be one of the smaller ones and the most intimate. The cemetery layout consisted of two squares attached to each other, the smaller seeming to be an extension to the larger. We did not need to use the cemetery register to find the graves we were looking for, as they proved to be quite near the entrance. Technically, despite being in different rows, the two 3rd Worcestershire graves were almost next to each other, with only the cemetery path dividing them. Here were Pte Harry Davis and Pte Roland Rose, both killed on 24 August. We could not see any personal inscriptions; closely packed plants, bursting forth with purple flowers, carpeted the base of each gravestone – it did not seem right to ease them away for simple curiosity.

Here, at last we had found what we had been only daring to hope to find from the start of this visit to the Somme battlefields. On the right of Harry Davis were two graves to 'unknowns', both of the Worcestershire Regiment. Further down the row there were even more, and behind were some graves to the Wiltshire Regiment. This grouping seemed to indicate that these burials had indeed been the result of the discovery of bodies of soldiers of the Worcestershire and Wiltshire Regiments on the Thiepval Ridge in approximately 1924. Sadly we realised that not even this number of stones could account for all the missing of these regiments from the 24/25 August attack.

But for us, just these few were enough. We knew that it would never be possible to identify beyond doubt Albert Turley's final resting-place. But here, standing by the graveside of these unknown Worcestershire soldiers, the high probability that they were associated with the attack of 24 August was all that we could have hoped for. For all we would ever know, one of these 'unknowns' was indeed Albert Turley himself.

Our pilgrimage had turned out to be all that we could have hoped it would be, and so much more besides. We had followed Albert on his journey of approximately 50 miles over the Somme battlefield to possibly his final resting place. Our lasting memories would be many and rich.

I have been to battlefields of the First World War many times; each visit had brought a personal reward beyond price. This pilgrimage was no exception. All the effort put into the research before the trip was repaid many, many times over.

A PROMISE FULFILLED

The search for Albert Turley had been a fascinating one. I had not only been able to recover the story of a First World War soldier who fell in one of the many actions that made up the Battle of the Somme, but I had also found out a great deal about myself in the process. Over the years I had amassed much information from many sources, met many kind and helpful people and proved a trouble to several members of my family, especially my wife. Yet, in all this time, I had not found one single piece of information, an action or letter, that was uniquely attributable to Albert Turley himself, nor did I find out how he had died or exactly where he now lies. I guess now it will ever be so.

It was true that I had managed to piece together some details of the actions of the 3rd Worcestershire during the Battle of the Somme, in which Albert had taken part, leading to the attack on the Hindenburg Trench, when he was killed. This may seem enough for some; indeed, when relating Albert's story to a fellow Somme pilgrim, I was heartened when he said: 'I cannot believe you can find out so much after all this time. I came here to see where my grandfather had been wounded in 1916, and I was content just to find the Somme battlefield – I never realised that it was possible to practically stand on the very blade of grass where a particular soldier fell!'

Yet I still felt that more was due to Albert, his comrades and all the people involved in this story, and in deciding to write a book about him I knew that at least I would be preserving some part of him. This decision was confirmed when my wife showed some photographs we had taken of another 'faceless name' on the Thiepval Memorial and the site of where he had fallen to a friend. Earlier the lady had given me a signed field postcard from a soldier dated 1916 – she had no idea who the person was who signed it.

A Pilgrimage to the Somme

At the sight of the photographs she was totally overwhelmed, saying, 'He is now no longer just a name, you have made him live again, and now we can remember him better.' The result is this book, which is now nearly complete.

However, there was one final act if my earlier promise, seemingly made so long ago, was to be fulfilled. From our pilgrimage to the Somme, where we followed Albert's journey, we had taken away more than our photographs and memories. On the site of the Lemberg Trench, the last place we knew that Albert had been for certain, and where he came to make his final peace before going over the top, we took a jar and filled it with soil. Whether this earth contained any remaining atoms of Albert's body lost in that place didn't matter, since for us it would contain part of his spirit. We brought this jar, with its precious contents, back to England and gave it to my aunt.

On 24 August 2001, exactly eighty-five years after Albert was killed, his niece scattered this soil onto the grave of Moses Richard and Mary Turley, Albert's parents, at Viney Hill churchyard, Blakeney. We had at last 'brought Uncle Albert home'. May he now rest there in peace, finally reunited with his family in the beautiful Forest of Dean.

Epilogue

Some time later my wife and I once again found ourselves on the Somme. This holiday was an organised walking tour of parts of the battlefield, covering a little over 30 miles in the broiling sunshine. As a group we were much older than the soldiers of 1916. Thankfully this was not to be a serious route march and we were not encumbered by 66 pounds of equipment on our backs. These latter 'comforts' and the pride generated by being able to walk in the footsteps of those soldiers ensured that no one 'fell out' en route. Still, it was a relief to find rest (and a drink!) in a modern equivalent of a 1916 *estaminet*.

One evening Vic and Diane joined us for a meal and they gave us some interesting news. Vic had spent the day guiding a (coach-bound) group and had ended the day at the Thiepval Memorial. During this visit a couple had come up to him and excitedly asked, 'Vic, where is this Hindenburg Trench then? We're from Worcester, we didn't know that people from Worcester were here.' They pointed towards the Stone of Sacrifice. Vic then looked at the pile of poppy wreaths and found our wreath still there. 'You might not believe this,' Vic replied, 'but I know the people who laid this, and I shall be seeing them tonight!'

We had laid the poppy wreath at the end of May. Vic informed us that all the wreaths on the Thiepval Memorial were removed towards the end of each June and the place especially spruced up. Each 1 July, on the anniversary of the opening of the Somme battle, there is an official ceremony and the 'great and good' lay their wreaths followed afterwards by many Somme pilgrims, keen to be here on this 'special' day. We concluded that the gardeners at the memorial must have thought a great deal of our wreath and kept it safe until it could be put back in its rightful place, after the official ceremony.

The following day our holiday schedule ended with a trip to the Thiepval Memorial. We were anxious to see what had in fact become of the wreath we had laid there.

The morning was sunny with high clouds and the temperature was a little cooler. The thirty of us walked up the long green lawn and climbed the steps into the heart of the Memorial where the Stone of Sacrifice lay. The stone and the surrounding steps were carpeted with poppy wreaths from the 1 July ceremony. There were some huge and colourful ones from many dignitaries and lots of smaller ones from organisations and families of the fallen.

In one corner was a single faded wreath, the material of the poppies tattered and spotted with marks from rain. Still firmly attached was the laminated sheet with the names of the fallen of the 3rd Worcestershire, the coloured inks now also faded. Albert's photograph and the map showing the trench systems were still bright and clear. None of the party knew that we had laid it there earlier in the year.

It was quiet and peaceful. In ones and twos the party looked up at the named panels and read the dedications on the many poppy wreaths. Maybe it was because our wreath looked the odd one out among the sea of fresh scarlet poppies, maybe because there was a photograph – whatever it was, everyone in the group came to look at our wreath: a polite queue even formed to read the names and look at Albert's photograph. A couple who had been among the first to see it had by now found the panel nearby on the memorial dedicated to the Worcestershire Regiment. 'Look, there he is – there's his name, TURLEY A.E., up there,' one said. More people came to see it. Eventually the whole party had seen it. By now some had worked out the orientation of the map and were pointing towards where the Lemberg/Hindenburg Trenches once lay. 'If only we had more time here, I would love to walk to it,' I heard one say. Yet we never told them who had placed the wreath there.

Occasionally in my life I have felt genuine pride. I realised that this group's actions in looking for Albert's name had been totally spontaneous, without any prompt. Similar occurrences may have happened many times since we had laid the wreath in May, and would continue as long as the wreath survived. Given the number of daily visitors the Memorial has during the summer months, many hundreds of people would have seen Albert's photograph and found his name on the wall – others too, would have had the time to find the site of the Hindenburg and Lemberg Trenches, only a few hundred yards away.

To many visitors that summer at the Thiepval Memorial, Albert Turley was more than just one of the 73,000 faceless names of the 'Missing of the Somme'. He now had an identity, he was someone who was still remembered and cared for. Our simple tribute had shown that all the others commemorated on the walls of both the Thiepval Memorial and countless cemeteries were more than just long-forgotten faceless names.

Each too had his story, simply waiting to be discovered and told.

. . . .

So ended the original edition of this book. Today, visitors still flock to the Somme in large numbers, stand wondering at the Thiepval Memorial and simply stare in awe at the thousands of names upon its walls. In recent years, there have been many new memorials erected to individuals, units and actions on the Somme. Perhaps the finest is the Franco-British Thiepval Visitor's Centre close to the site of the memorial itself. Of modern construction, it has been carefully designed and sited not to intrude on the landscape. Many times have I found myself trying to help casual visitors to the Somme to come to terms with the many cemeteries and what happened in particular areas. Hopefully, this visitor's centre will also be able to provide such information, and now, much more – for year on year, more people are coming. Many looking for traces of their own relatives, in much the same way as I did several years ago. At the centre are audio-visual aids to the comprehension of what happened here and computer terminals are available with access to various databases of records.

Monies from the sale of this book helped in a small way to equip this centre, as a lasting tribute to Albert Turley. On my first visit, after the centre opened, I was struck by what is perhaps the most poignant display feature – a huge mural consisting of 600 photographs of the 'Missing of the Somme', whose names are on the walls of the Thiepval Memorial. This is part of an on-going project to trace all the 73,000 soldiers on those walls. For these are now no longer 'faceless names'. The wreath with Albert's photograph on the steps of the memorial itself may have gone – however, Albert's photograph is indeed here, preserved, to be found among those 600. . . .

. . . I leave it to you, maybe on your own pilgrimage to the Somme, to find it among the sea of fresh young faces, cut down in their prime. By doing so, you will have fulfilled the purpose of this book and ensured that Albert, and all those other soldiers of 1914–18, are *never* forgotten.

Appendix

ROLL OF HONOUR

This true story had originally been the search for one man, Albert Turley. However, it became also the story of all the men who found themselves part of the 3rd Worcestershire and 1st Wiltshire battalions fighting in the Battle of the Somme in August 1916. This Appendix aims to provide some further details of all the men of these battalions who died during the period of Albert's service on the Somme, both as a source of information for others and as a tribute to that generation of soldiers who have now passed away.

The information was derived from both the Commonwealth War Graves Commission Internet database and the CD-ROM entitled *Soldiers (and Officers) died in the Great War*. Depending on the sources of the original records themselves, some information is fragmentary (particularly for officers) while other parts appear contradictory. However, alternatives have been included here.

In most cases the place of enlistment is given but the date of enlistment is not recorded in either database. Generally, it can be assumed that the lower the regimental number, the earlier the date of enlistment. Albert Turley joined the 3rd Worcestershire in approximately January 1916 with the number 31327. Almost all those listed have a number lower than this and hence would have enlisted in 1914/15. I would suggest that those with four-digit regimental numbers might well be survivors of the pre-war soldiers who had served with the battalion in France since 1914. A similar story would be found with those from the 1st Wiltshire.

The format follows the main periods of the earlier reconstructed diary. This is further subdivided by battalion, then by date of death and finally in alphabetical surname order. As with the war cemeteries, there is no division by rank.

Although the majority of these soldiers came from the counties in which regiment they served, many did not. Some living in distant parts of the country either returned to their home county to enlist or somehow effected a transfer after enlisting. Many soldiers who had been wounded and were returning to active service found themselves in these regiments only by chance. Many county towns and villages in Worcestershire and Wiltshire are represented here. A similar list derived from New Army battalions (for instance, 10th Cheshire or 8th Loyal North Lancs. in this brigade) would show tighter groupings from individual towns and cities. Heavy casualties in these latter 'Pals' battalions would be more apparent, as smaller localities would be devastated (such as Accrington, Bradford and Leeds on 1 July 1916). This is one reason why the actions of the Pals battalions dominate histories of the Somme offensive. It is all too easy to forget that regular county battalions taken from a wider background also fought and suffered on the Somme in 1916.

These lists are now more than just simple names: each of these fallen soldiers now has a background, and most have family members listed. This compilation is simply the tip of an iceberg: further research would identify other family members (particularly children, who are not listed in these databases). In looking through this Appendix, one now sees the real human tragedy of the First World War, or indeed of any war. This is not only a reminder of young lives cut down in their prime, it is also the beginning of a lifetime of grief for the families involved, which will continue for as long as people remember the war itself.

24 JULY TO 6 AUGUST 1916

From 24 July to 1 August the 3rd Worcestershire were at rest in Mailly Wood. The records list three soldiers who died of wounds in this period. It therefore seems evident that these soldiers were wounded in actions that preceded 24 July.

From 1 to 6 August the battalion was holding the front-line trench in front of the village of Beaumont Hamel. It is probable that most of these men fell during the construction of the new front-line trench as mentioned in the diary entries of Brigade Major A.C. Johnston. From their burial records, those soldiers 'killed in action' appear to have been given formal burials on two separate occasions (rows B and E) by their comrades in the nearby Knightsbridge Cemetery at Mesnil-Martinsart. This cemetery must be one of the loneliest on the Somme and receives few visitors, because of its isolation. The cemetery is located 2 kilometres north-east of the village of Mesnil. Access is along a farm track, the first kilometre being metalled, the remainder being impassable to cars. The cemetery is located a further 200 metres from this latter track in a field with no direct access. Pte H. Sinclair's burial in Ancre British Cemetery indicates that his body was only discovered during postwar battlefield clearances, as this is one of the large concentration cemeteries in the vicinity.

Those soldiers who 'died of wounds' are buried in cemeteries associated with the dressing station at Mesnil Station (later removed to Mesnil Communal Extension Cemetery) and the Base Hospital at Couin.

3rd Worcestershire

Ashman, Pte Henry, 9265
Born: Netherton, Worcs.
Enlisted: Worcester
Residence: Birkenhead
Died: Killed in Action 1/8/16
Place of Burial: Knightsbridge Military Cemetery, Mesnil-
    Martinsart, row E, grave 49

Haywood, Pte Alfred, 34040
Born: Dudley, Worcs.
Enlisted: Dudley
Died: Killed in Action 1/8/16
Place of Burial: Knightsbridge Military Cemetery, Mesnil-
    Martinsart, row E, grave 46

Note: Alfred Haywood's regimental number is higher than Albert Turley's, indicating that he joined the 3rd Worcestershire after January 1916. It is probable that he too was part of the draft of new recruits sent to the regiment on 24 July, along with Albert. Clearly he had been killed only a matter of hours after entering the front line for the first time. The effect of this news on the rest of the Derby men may only be guessed.

Portman, Pte Solomon, 19414
Born: Netherton, Worcs.
Enlisted: Dudley
Residence: Netherton
Died: Killed in Action 1/8/16
Place of Burial: Knightsbridge Military Cemetery, Mesnil-
    Martinsart, row E, grave 47

Read, Cpl Edgar, 8967
Born: Birmingham
Enlisted: Birmingham
Died: Killed in Action 1/8/16
Place of Burial: Knightsbridge Military Cemetery, Mesnil-
    Martinsart, row E, grave 50
Biographical: son of J. and Clara Read of 5/20 College Street,
    Spring Hill, Birmingham
Age: 18

Pemberton, L/Cpl Frederick, 13395
Born: Birmingham
Enlisted: Birmingham
Died: Died of Wounds 3/8/16
Place of Burial: Mesnil Communal Cemetery Extension, plot II,
    row D, grave 10

Sinclair, Pte Henry, 6948
Born: Tipton, Staffs.
Enlisted: Dudley
Residence: Dudley

Died: Killed in Action 3/8/16

Place of Burial: Ancre British Cemetery, Beaumont Hamel, plot
  VII, row C, grave 6

Biographical: husband of Mrs M. Hocknell (formerly Sinclair),
  59 Sedgeley Road, Woodsetton, Dudley

Callaway, Cpl Frederick James, 6560

Born: Birkenhead

Enlisted: Worcester

Residence: Worcester

Died: Killed in Action 5/8/16

Place of Burial: Knightsbridge Military Cemetery, Mesnil-
  Martinsart, row B, grave 20

Biographical: son of James and Sarah Callaway of Worcester;
  husband of Frances Emily Callaway, Gainborough [sic] Terrace,
  Campden, Gloucestershire

Age: 30

Clarie, Pte John Edward, 23723

Born: London

Enlisted: Birmingham

Residence: Birmingham

Died: Killed in Action 5/8/16

Place of Burial: Knightsbridge Military Cemetery, Mesnil-
  Martinsart, row B, grave 21

Biographical: son of Joseph and Isabella Clarie of Birmingham;
  husband of Ellen Jane Clarie, 4 Buck Street, Dale End,
  Birmingham

Age: 39

House, Pte William, 23281

Born: Weston-super-Mare

Enlisted: Bristol

Residence: Weston-super-Mare

Died: Died of Wounds 6/8/16

Place of Burial: Couin British Cemetery, Pas-de-Calais, plot II, row
  B, grave 19

Appendix

Biographical: son of Nicholas and Sarah House, 124 Moorland
   Road, Weston-super-Mare, Somerset
Age: 26

The 1st Wiltshire had spent the period from 24 July to 1 August
in the trenches in front of Beaumont Hamel and from 1 to 6
August 'at rest' in Mailly Wood – that is, in opposition to the 3rd
Worcestershire. They also experienced fewer casualties. Like the
3rd Worcestershire, the 1st Wiltshire endeavoured to recover the
bodies of the fallen and give them a formal burial behind the front
lines: thus L/Cpl Morse is buried in an original grave in Hamel
Military Cemetery. Unfortunately this was not the case with Sgt
Robbins, who has no known grave and is commemorated on the
Thiepval Memorial to the Missing. The remainder of these
casualties died of their wounds at the Field Ambulances, Casualty
Clearing Stations and Base Hospitals through to the coast at
Étaples. More details regarding this system are given in later
sections of this Appendix.

After 6 August the 3rd Worcestershire and the 1st Wiltshire
effectively served together.

1st Wiltshire

Roff, Pte Edwin, 3/9995
Born: Grafton, Wilts.
Enlisted: Devizes, Wilts.
Residence: Marlborough, Wilts.
Died: Died of Wounds 25/7/16
Place of Burial: La Neuville British Cemetery, plot I, row D, grave
   54
Biographical: son of C. and F. Roff, Wilton, Marlborough, Wilts.
Age: 21
Note: also listed as Roffe.

Messer, Cpl Maurice George, 9153
Born: Handley, Dorset
Enlisted: Tidworth, Wilts.

Residence: Salisbury
Died: Died of Wounds 26/7/16
Place of Burial: Louvencourt Military Cemetery, plot I, row D,
    grave 8
Biographical: son of George and Sarah Messer, Handley, Dorset
Age: 24
Note: listed as a member of 'A Company'.

Nicholls, Pte Arthur Frederick, 12330
Born: Bradford-on-Avon, Wilts.
Enlisted: Pentre, Glam.
Residence: Llwyn-y-pia, Glam.
Died: Died of Wounds 28/7/16
Place of Burial: Couin British Cemetery, plot II, row B, grave 4
Biographical: son of Alfred and Mary Nicholls, Trowbridge, Wilts.;
    husband of Ethel Nicholls, 5 Tyntyla Avenue, Llwyn-y-pia,
    Glam.
Age: 22

Morse, L/Cpl Thomas, 8398
Born: Swindon
Enlisted: Swindon
Residence: Barton, Lincs.
Died: Killed in Action 29/7/16
Place of Burial: Hamel British Cemetery, plot II, row E, grave 21

Robbins, Sgt David, 9085
Born: Devizes, Wilts.
Enlisted: Devizes
Residence: Swindon
Died: Killed in Action 29/7/16
Place of Commemoration: Thiepval Memorial to the Missing, Pier
    and Face 13A
Biographical: son of Sarah and Lt David Robbins, husband of
    Elizabeth Gertrude Robbins, 19 Britannia Place, Old Swindon,
    Wilts.
Age: 35

Vizard, Sgt Arthur, 9099
Born: Southall, Middlesex
Enlisted: Devizes, Wilts.
Residence: Southall
Died: Died 29/7/16
Place of Burial: Gezaincourt Cemetery and Extension, plot II, row
    B, grave 4

Wiseman, Pte Sidney, 23298
Born: Southampton
Enlisted: Southampton
Residence: Southampton
Died: Died of Wounds 30/7/16
Place of Burial: Couin British Cemetery, plot II, row B, grave 6

Watson, Pte Leonard Percy, 22733
Born: Trowbridge, Wilts.
Enlisted: Trowbridge
Residence: Bradford-on-Avon, Wilts.
Died: Died of Wounds 7/8/16
Place of Burial: Etaples Military Cemetery, plot IX, row C, grave 17
Biographical: son of Alice and Lt Alfred Watson, Hartley, Winsley,
    Bradford-on-Avon, Wilts.
Age: 23

18 TO 23 AUGUST 1916

Following a period of training in the back areas of the Somme,
the 3rd Worcestershire and 1st Wiltshire were again in the front-
line trenches before the Leipzig Salient. The following casualties
reflect the more hazardous conditions here. For the 3rd
Worcestershire, these casualties would have been the result of
shelling and sniper fire from the German trenches that overlooked
the British positions, as noted in Johnston's diary entries. In
addition to such losses, the 1st Wiltshire took part in a successful
attack on the 21st (the 22nd according to their battalion diary),
seemingly with few fatalities.

Once again, in 'quieter' periods – i.e. from 18 to 22 August – efforts appear to have been made by the 3rd Worcestershire to bring back the bodies of those killed for formal burial in Authuille Military Cemetery, as the three adjoining graves are in their original locations.

On 23 August, when both battalions were making hurried preparations for the attack on the following day, those killed were likely to have been buried near where they fell, out of necessity. Such graves were subsequently lost, most of these soldiers being now commemorated on the Thiepval Memorial to the Missing, but one of them must have been found after the war and reinterred in the concentration cemetery at AIF Burial Ground near Flers, several miles to the south-east. The soldiers killed on the 23rd and buried at Blighty Valley Military Cemetery may have been original burials (they are in plot I), although from the cemetery records this is not certain. This cemetery also acted as a concentration cemetery for nearby isolated graves and the relocation of bodies from the Quarry Post dressing station situated in Authuille Wood.

The soldiers who were to die of their wounds had been taken back to Puchevillers and Forceville field hospitals, where they succumbed, and are buried close together.

3rd Worcestershire

Bishop, Pte Herbert James, 29074
Born: Bristol
Enlisted: Bristol
Died: Killed in Action 18/8/16
Place of Burial: Authuille Military Cemetery, row I, grave 2
Biographical: son of Mr A.B. Bishop, 15 Edward Street, Eastville, Bristol

Tristram, Pte Charles, 29594
Born: Quarry Bank, Staffs.
Enlisted: Stourbridge, Worcs.
Residence: Cradley, Staffs.

Died: Died of Wounds 19/8/16
Place of Burial: Forceville Communal Cemetery and Extension,
    plot 2, row E, grave 11

Harding, Pte John Lewis, 31416

Born: Gloucester
Enlisted: Gloucester
Died: Killed in Action 21/8/16
Place of Commemoration: Thiepval Memorial to the Missing,
    panels 5A, 6C

Jefferies, Pte William, 31378

Born: Bristol
Enlisted: Bristol
Died: Killed in Action 21/8/16
Place of Commemoration: Thiepval Memorial to the Missing,
    panels 5A, 6C
Biographical: brother of Albert Jefferies, 78 Chambercombe Road,
    Ilfracombe, Devon
Age: 21

Powell, Pte John Joseph, 9002

Born: Birmingham
Enlisted: Birmingham
Died: Killed in Action 21/8/16
Place of Burial: Authuille Military Cemetery, row I, grave 1
Biographical: son of Mrs Jane Emma Powell, 158 Latimer Street,
    Edgbaston, Birmingham
Age: 21

Keyte, Pte Charles Hubert, 27819

Born: Broadway, Worcs.
Enlisted: Worcester
Residence: Broadway
Died: Killed in Action 22/8/16
Place of Burial: Authuille Military Cemetery, row I, grave 3
Biographical: son of Joseph and Emma Keyte, Broadway, Worcs.;

husband of Lillian Annie Keyte, 'The Busy Bee', Broadway, Worcestershire.
Age: 25

Griffiths, Pte Daniel, 27903
Born: Codsall, Staffs.
Enlisted: Hollywood, Birmingham
Residence: Birmingham
Died: Killed in Action 23/8/16
Place of Commemoration: Thiepval Memorial to the Missing, panels 5A, 6C
Biographical: son of Mrs Griffiths, Bewdley, Worcs.; husband of Polly Griffiths, 'The Chestnuts', Alcester Road, Wythall, Alvechurch, Birmingham
Age: 22

Harris, Pte George, 20050
Born: Droitwich, Worcs.
Enlisted: Worcester
Residence: Droitwich
Died: Killed in Action 23/8/16
Place of Commemoration: Thiepval Memorial to the Missing, panels 5A, 6C

Hunt, Pte Arthur Henry, 18474
Born: Birmingham
Enlisted: Birmingham
Died: Killed in Action 23/8/16
Place of Burial: Blighty Valley Military Cemetery, plot I, row C, grave 23
Biographical: son of Joseph and Sarah Hunt, Birmingham; husband of Mary Olive Hunt, 26 Chain Walk, Lozelles, Birmingham
Age: 42

Hunt, L/Cpl William, 14983
Born: Kidderminster

Enlisted: Worcester

Residence: Kidderminster

Died: Died of Wounds 23/8/16

Place of Burial: Forceville Communal Cemetery and Extension, plot 2, row E, grave 9

Biographical: son of Mr and Mrs T.H. Hunt, 82 Broad Street, Kidderminster

Age: 21

Note: listed as being a member of 'B Company, machine-gun section'.

Lovell, L/Cpl Horace Stanley, 14983

Born: Clapton, London

Enlisted: Stratford, London

Residence: Leyton, Essex

Died: Killed in Action 23/8/16

Place of Commemoration: Thiepval Memorial to the Missing, panels 5A, 6C

Biographical: son of James and Jane Lovell; husband of Martha Yeldham (formerly Lovell), 'The Lodge', Saville Lane, Thurlstone, Penistone, Sheffield

Note: listed as served in the Boer War (1899–1902) and at Gallipoli, formerly wounded. The non-local addresses would suggest that Horace Lovell was assigned to the 3rd Worcestershire after recovering from wounds received while serving with another regiment. The fact that the 3rd Worcestershire did not serve in Gallipoli serves to corroborate this suggestion.

Marsh, L/Cpl Fred, 27679

Born: Walsall, Staffs.

Enlisted: Stourbridge, Worcs.

Residence: Walsall

Died: Killed in Action 23/8/16

Place of Commemoration: Thiepval Memorial to the Missing, panels 5A, 6C

Biographical: son of Isaiah and Phoebe Marsh, 31 Kinnersley Street, Walsall, Staffs

Age: 30

1st Wiltshire

Short, L/Cpl Frederick, 7722
Born: Salisbury
Enlisted: Salisbury
Residence: Salisbury
Died: Killed in Action 20/8/16
Place of Burial: Blighty Valley Military Cemetery, plot I, row C, grave
   22

Brooks, Sgt Frederick Sydney, 18208
Born: London
Enlisted: Devizes, Wilts.
Residence: Chumleigh, Devon
Died: Killed in Action 21/8/16
Place of Burial: Blighty Valley Military Cemetery, plot I, row C,
   grave 32
Biographical: son of Frederick Thomas and Elizabeth Brooks,
   3 Ennismore Gardens, Mews North, South Kensington, London
Age: 22
Note: listed as being a member of 'D Company'; also listed as being
a resident of Cromer, Norfolk

Rogers, Pte Frederick John, 25396
Born: East Cowes, Isle of Wight
Enlisted: Cowes, Isle of Wight
Residence: Cowes
Died: Killed in Action 21/8/16
Place of Commemoration: Thiepval Memorial to the Missing, pier
   and face 13A
Biographical: son of Mrs Elizabeth Rogers, 7 Almera Terrace,
   Albert Road, Gurnard, Cowes
Age: 26
Note: listed as previously serving as 22755, Somerset Light
   Infantry.

Dredge, Pte Frank William, 24142
Born: Salisbury
Enlisted: Salisbury
Residence: Salisbury
Died: Killed in Action 22/8/16
Place of Commemoration: Thiepval Memorial to the Missing, pier
    and face 13A

Bowsher, Pte Henry Charles, 23742
Born: Chippenham, Wilts.
Enlisted: Chippenham
Residence: Chippenham
Died: Died of Wounds 23/8/16
Place of Burial: Puchevillers British Cemetery, plot III, row E,
    grave 7
Biographical: son of Henry and Mary Ann Bowsher, Lower
    Swinley Cottage, Sutton Benger, Chippenham
Age: 36
Note: listed as being a native of Kington Langley, Chippenham.

Farley, Pte Tom, 6725
Born: Warminster, Wilts.
Enlisted: Warminster
Residence: Warminster
Died: Killed in Action 23/8/16
Place of Commemoration: Thiepval Memorial to the Missing, pier
    and face 13A
Biographical: son of Albert Edward and Sarah Jane Farley,
    27 Fore Street, Warminster
Age: 27
Note: listed as being a member of 'A Company'.

Pearce, Pte William Harold, 24182
Born: Warminster, Wilts.
Enlisted: Devizes, Wilts.
Residence: Warminster
Died: Killed in Action 23/8/16

Place of Commemoration: Thiepval Memorial to the Missing, pier and face 13A

Robertson, Pte William Rowland, 23191
Born: Sholing, Hants.
Enlisted: Brokenhurst, Hants.
Residence: Lymington, Hants.
Died: Killed in Action 23/8/16
Place of Commemoration: Thiepval Memorial to the Missing, pier and face 13A
Biographical: son of Annie Norris (formerly Robertson) and Lt John Robertson, Plot Cottage, Pilley, Lymington
Age: 21

Saunders, Pte Verney, 24133
Born: Sherston, Wilts.
Enlisted: Malmesbury, Wilts.
Residence: Malmesbury
Died: Killed in Action 23/8/16
Place of Commemoration: Thiepval Memorial to the Missing, pier and face 13A
Note: Listed in error as Verney Neal on the Sherston War Memorial, but correctly on a second memorial within the parish church.

Stevens, Pte Frederick, 14214
Born: Tisbury, Wilts.
Enlisted: Salisbury
Residence: Salisbury
Died: Killed in Action 23/8/16
Place of Burial: AIF Burial Ground, plot XIV, row D, grave 13
Biographical: husband of Elsie A. Stevens, Bee Farm, Old Castle, Salisbury
Age: 25

Appendix

24 TO 25 AUGUST 1916

This period covers the attack on the Hindenburg Trench by the 3rd Worcestershire and 1st Wiltshire Regiments. Given the nature of the fighting and understandable confusion in the surviving accounts of this action, it would be too simplistic to say those casualties of the 24th were due to the attack and those of the 25th due to the German counter-attack. Many soldiers would have fallen during the night of 24/25 August because of the intensive German shelling prior to the actual counter-attack.

The final casualty lists could only have been made up following a roll call when the regiment was out of the line a few days later. Here soldiers would have been lined up to answer their names and provide details of what happened to those not present. Surviving witnesses to particular events may have subsequently been killed, resulting in some soldiers being denoted as 'missing in action'. In this case the attack had been so successful that only eleven soldiers were missing out of the 205 casualties noted in the 3rd Worcestershire diary.

The majority of the fallen from both the 3rd Worcestershire and the 1st Wiltshire have no known grave and are thus commemorated on the Thiepval Memorial to the Missing. It would have been impossible to bring back the bodies of their fallen comrades during the relief through the trenches on the 26th. Hurried burials may have taken place in and around the captured Hindenburg Trench and the graves left to the fortunes of war, as mentioned in Revd G.M. Evans's letters. As discussed in earlier chapters, identified graves seem only to be the result of postwar battlefield clearances with fortuitous survival of identification discs.

3rd Worcestershire

Allcock, Pte William, 19434
Born: Netherton, Worcs.
Enlisted: Worcester
Died: Killed in Action 24/8/16

Place of Commemoration: Thiepval Memorial to the Missing, panels 5A, 6C

Biographical: son of William James Allcock, 24 Cinder Bank, Netherton, Dudley, Worcs.

Age: 22

Amos, Pte William, 20801

Born: Dudley, Worcs.

Enlisted: Worcester

Residence: Dudley

Died: Killed in Action 24/8/16

Place of Commemoration: Thiepval Memorial to the Missing, panels 5A, 6C

Archard, Pte Frederick John, 22888

Born: Birmingham

Enlisted: Devonport

Residence: Birmingham

Died: Killed in Action 24/8/16

Place of Commemoration: Thiepval Memorial to the Missing, panels 5A, 6C

Biographical: son of Mrs Mary M. Archard, 1/40 Ellen Street, Brooksfield, Birmingham; husband of Bertha Archard, 1/40 Ellen Street, Brooksfield, Birmingham

Age: 35

Berry, L/Cpl Charles Henry, 9431

Born: Gillingham, Kent

Enlisted: Gravesend, Kent

Residence: Old Brompton, Kent

Died: Killed in Action 24/8/16

Place of Commemoration: Thiepval Memorial to the Missing, panels 5A, 6C

Biographical: son of Lt Charles and Mary Berry, Chatham; husband of Mary E. Berry, Lydford, Devon

Age: 30

Calderwood, Cpl Arthur, 10593

Born: Marazion, Cornwall
Enlisted: Falmouth, Cornwall
Residence: Falmouth
Died: Killed in Action 24/8/16
Place of Burial: Lonsdale Military Cemetery, plot III, row A,
    grave 9
Biographical: brother of Mrs C.W. Uffen, 33 Lisson Grove, Mutley,
    Plymouth
Age: 29

Candlin, Pte Robert Heywood, 27888

Born: Pensnett, Staffs.
Enlisted: Dudley, Worcs.
Residence: Birmingham
Died: Killed in Action 24/8/16
Place of Commemoration: Thiepval Memorial to the Missing,
    panels 5A, 6C

Clay, Pte Alfred William, 27896

Born: Worcester
Enlisted: Worcester
Died: Killed in Action 24/8/16
Place of Commemoration: Thiepval Memorial to the Missing,
    panels 5A, 6C
Biographical: husband of Nellie May Coward (formerly Clay) of
    11 New Bank Street, Barbourne, Worcs.
Age: 27

Clayton, L/Cpl Arthur William, 25662

Born: Birmingham
Enlisted: Worcester
Residence: Redditch, Worcs.
Died: Killed in Action 24/8/16
Place of Commemoration: Thiepval Memorial to the Missing,
    panels 5A, 6C

Davis, Pte Harry, 27697

Born: Birmingham
Enlisted: Birmingham
Died: Killed in Action 24/8/16
Place of Burial: Bray Military Cemetery, plot III, row B, grave 4
Biographical: brother of Edwin Davis, 16 Bartholmew [sic] Street, Birmingham
Age: 33

Edwards, Cpl Arthur, 7026

Born: Newport, Mon.
Enlisted: Worcester
Residence: Stretton, Worcs.
Died: Killed in Action 24/8/16
Place of Commemoration: Thiepval Memorial to the Missing, panels 5A, 6C

Hadley, Pte Theophilus James, 27608

Born: Walsall, Staffs.
Enlisted: Dudley, Worcs.
Residence: Dudley
Died: Killed in Action 24/8/16
Place of Commemoration: Thiepval Memorial to the Missing, panels 5A, 6C
Biographical: son of James and Polly Hadley
Age: 32

Harper, Pte George Ernest, 17771

Born: Quarry Bank, Staffs.
Enlisted: Dudley, Worcs.
Residence: Old Hill, Staffs.
Died: Killed in Action 24/8/16
Place of Commemoration: Thiepval Memorial to the Missing, panels 5A, 6C
Biographical: son of David and Martha Harper, Spring Meadows, Old Hill; husband of Clara Ann Harper, 67 Waggon Street, Old Hill
Age: 24

Hepworth, Pte Benjamin Thomas, 27670
Born: Birmingham
Enlisted: Birmingham
Residence: Pershore, Worcs.
Died: Killed in Action 24/8/16
Place of Commemoration: Thiepval Memorial to the Missing,
    panels 5A, 6C

Keates, L/Cpl William, 11946
Born: Birmingham
Enlisted: Birmingham
Residence: Wolverhampton
Died: Killed in Action 24/8/16
Place of Commemoration: Thiepval Memorial to the Missing,
    panels 5A, 6C

Kenwrick, Pte Walter, 24905
Born: Birmingham
Enlisted: Birmingham
Died: Killed in Action 24/8/16
Place of Commemoration: Thiepval Memorial to the Missing,
    panels 5A, 6C

Murphy, Pte William Edward, 25224
Born: Birmingham
Enlisted: Birmingham
Died: Killed in Action 24/8/16
Place of Commemoration: Thiepval Memorial to the Missing,
    panels 5A, 6C

Oakley, L/Cpl Harold, 14114
Born: Tipton, Staffs.
Enlisted: Worcester
Residence: Tipton
Died: Killed in Action 24/8/16
Place of Commemoration: Thiepval Memorial to the Missing,
    panels 5A, 6C

Penny, Pte Arthur, 27087
Born: Bromsgrove, Worcs.
Enlisted: Bromsgrove
Died: Killed in Action 24/8/16
Place of Commemoration: Thiepval Memorial to the Missing, panels 5A, 6C

Perks, 2/Lt Wilfred Lawson
Died: Killed in Action 24/8/16
Place of Commemoration: Thiepval Memorial to the Missing, panels 5A, 6C

Peters, Pte Arthur, 27652
Born: Longdon, Worcs.
Enlisted: Upton-on-Severn, Worcs.
Residence: Longdon
Died: Killed in Action 24/8/16
Place of Commemoration: Thiepval Memorial to the Missing, panels 5A, 6C

Pitt, Pte Albert, 29783
Born: Kidderminster, Worcs.
Enlisted: Worcester
Residence: Worcester
Died: Killed in Action 24/8/16
Place of Commemoration: Thiepval Memorial to the Missing, panels 5A, 6C

Pocock, Sgt Frederick Charles, 8653
Born: Brighton, Sussex
Enlisted: Chichester, Sussex
Residence: Yapton, Sussex
Died: Died of Wounds 24/8/16
Place of Burial: Ovillers Military Cemetery, plot XV, row M, grave 2

Pratt, Pte Wallace Reginald, 29067

Born: Charfield, Glos.

Enlisted: Bristol

Residence: Charfield

Died: Killed in Action 24/8/16

Place of Commemoration: Thiepval Memorial to the Missing,
    panels 5A, 6C

Reeves, Pte Robert, 27664

Born: Pershore, Worcs.

Enlisted: Pershore

Residence: Worcester

Died: Killed in Action 24/8/16

Place of Burial: Lonsdale Military Cemetery, plot III, row A,
    grave 8

Robinson, Pte Sidney, 19624

Born: Longton, Staffs.

Enlisted: Longton

Died: Killed in Action 24/8/16

Place of Commemoration: Thiepval Memorial to the Missing,
    . panels 5A, 6C

Rollins, Pte John, 27809

Born: Allerton, Leics.

Enlisted: Kidderminster, Worcs.

Residence: Bewdley, Worcs.

Died: Killed in Action 24/8/16

Place of Commemoration: Thiepval Memorial to the Missing,
    panels 5A, 6C

Rose, Pte Roland George, 27932

Born: Birmingham

Enlisted: Birmingham

Died: Killed in Action 24/8/16

Place of Burial: Bray Military Cemetery, plot III, row C,
    grave 22

Biographical: son of B.C. and C. Rose, 145 Metchley Lane, Harbourne, Birmingham

Age: 20

Ruddock, Pte Hughsia, 27459
Born: Betws-y-Coed, Carnarvon
Enlisted: Dudley, Worcs.
Residence: Pontypool, Mon.
Died: Killed in Action 24/8/16
Place of Burial: Serre Road No. 2 Military Cemetery, plot XXVIII, row G, grave 12
Biographical: son of C.A. and A.G. Ruddock, 11 Osbourne Road, Pontypool, Mon.
Age: 27

Shilvock, L/Cpl John Henry, 24546
Born: Stourbridge, Worcs.
Enlisted: London
Residence: Stourbridge
Died: Killed in Action 24/8/16
Place of Commemoration: Thiepval Memorial to the Missing, panels 5A, 6C

Talbot, Pte Philip Ernest, 27397
Born: Kinver, Worcs.
Enlisted: Stourbridge, Worcs.
Residence: Oldswinford, Worcs.
Died: Killed in Action 24/8/16
Place of Commemoration: Thiepval Memorial to the Missing, panels 5A, 6C

Turley, Pte Albert Edward, 31327
Born: East Dean, Glos.
Enlisted: Lydney, Glos.
Residence: Blakeney, Glos.
Died: Killed in Action 24/8/16

Place of Commemoration: Thiepval Memorial to the Missing,
    panels 5A, 6C

Whitehead, Pte Richard Frank, 25071
Born: Birmingham
Enlisted: Birmingham
Died: Killed in Action 24/8/16
Place of Commemoration: Thiepval Memorial to the Missing,
    panels 5A, 6C
Biographical: son of Clara Jane and Lt Richard John Whitehead,
    299 Cooksey Road, Small Heath, Birmingham
Age: 28

Grealey, Pte Joseph, 7209
Born: Birmingham
Enlisted: Birmingham
Died: Killed in Action 25/8/16
Place of Commemoration: Thiepval Memorial to the Missing,
    panels 5A, 6C

Griffin, Sgt John, 8544
Born: Dudley, Worcs.
Enlisted: Dudley
Died: Killed in Action 25/8/16
Place of Burial: Serre Road No. 2 Military Cemetery, plot XXVII,
    row D, grave 7
Biographical: husband of Eliza Griffin, Swan Street, Dudley,
    Worcs.
Age: 27
Note: listed as being a member of 'D Company'.

Jakes, Pte Albert, 14074
Born: Birmingham
Enlisted: Birmingham
Died: Killed in Action 25/8/16
Place of Commemoration: Thiepval Memorial to the Missing,
    panels 5A, 6C

Biographical: son of Mr and Mrs Jakes, 43 Hanley Street, Summer
   Lane, Birmingham
Age: 20

Lowe, L/Cpl James, 10141

Born: Birmingham
Enlisted: Warwick
Residence: Birmingham
Died: Killed in Action 25/8/16
Place of Commemoration: Thiepval Memorial to the Missing,
   panels 5A, 6C

Morgan, Pte James George, 15942

Born: Berryhill, Glos.
Enlisted: Coleford, Glos.
Residence: Coleford
Died: Killed in Action 25/8/16
Place of Commemoration: Thiepval Memorial to the Missing,
   panels 5A, 6C

Tattersall, Pte George, 23809

Born: Bloxwich, Staffs.
Enlisted: Smethwick, Staffs.
Residence: Walsall Wood, Staffs.
Died: Killed in Action 25/8/16
Place of Commemoration: Thiepval Memorial to the Missing,
   panels 5A, 6C

Walker, Pte James, 27667

Born: Worcester
Enlisted: Worcester
Died: Killed in Action 25/8/16
Place of Commemoration: Thiepval Memorial to the Missing,
   panels 5A, 6C

Appendix

Westwood, Pte Harry, 27440
Born: Netherton, Worcs.
Enlisted: Dudley, Worcs.
Residence: Netherton
Died: Died of Wounds 25/8/16
Place of Burial: Puchevillers British Cemetery, plot III, row E, grave 24
Biographical: son of Harry and Louisa Westwood, Netherton, Dudley
Age: 26

Whitehouse, Pte James, 25054
Born: Darby End, Worcs.
Enlisted: Dudley, Worcs.
Residence: Darby End
Died: Killed in Action 25/8/16
Place of Commemoration: Thiepval Memorial to the Missing, panels 5A, 6C

1st Wiltshire

Many soldiers listed here as 'died of wounds' appear to have no known grave and are listed on the Thiepval Memorial to the Missing. This seems strange. Great care was taken with the wounded to preserve personal details as they were transported 'down the line' (to the point of written tags being attached to tunics, etc.). Hence, soldiers who died at Casualty Clearing Stations etc. had the highest chance of having identified graves. Soldiers who succumbed to wounds and who were buried in or near the front-line trench were usually listed as 'killed in action'.

Baker, Pte Albert Edward, 18225
Born: Trowbridge, Wilts.
Enlisted: Devizes, Wilts.
Residence: Trowbridge
Died: Killed in Action 24/8/16

Place of Commemoration: Thiepval Memorial to the Missing, pier and face 13A

Cleal, Pte Edward, 19151
Born: St Peter's Port, Guernsey, Channel Islands
Enlisted: Guernsey
Residence: Guernsey
Died: Killed in Action 24/8/16
Place of Commemoration: Thiepval Memorial to the Missing, pier and face 13A

Doughty, Pte George Howard, 22740
Born: Hindon, Wilts.
Enlisted: Warminster, Wilts.
Residence: Salisbury
Died: Killed in Action 24/8/16
Place of Commemoration: Thiepval Memorial to the Missing, pier and face 13A

Dunne, L/Cpl George Aloysius, 9080
Born: Athlone
Enlisted: Dublin
Residence: Dublin
Died: Killed in Action 24/8/16
Place of Burial: Serre Road No. 2 Military Cemetery, plot XXXI, row E, grave 1

Finnmore, Pte James, 25437
Born: Uplyme, Devon
Enlisted: Devizes, Wilts.
Residence: Uplyme
Died: Died of Wounds 24/8/16
Place of Burial: Puchevillers British Cemetery, plot III, row E, grave 12
Note: also listed as Finnemore, and saw previous service as 22813, Somerset Light Infantry.

Gerrish, Pte Reginald, 24135
Born: Westbury, Wilts.
Enlisted: Trowbridge
Residence: Westbury, Wilts
Died: Killed in Action 24/8/16
Place of Burial: Serre Road No. 2 Military Cemetery, plot XVIII,
    row A, grave 14
Biographical: son of Annie Maria Gerrish, 84 Warminster Road,
    Westbury
Age: 24

Gigg, Pte Francis Edward, 25403
Born: Wexcum, Wilts.
Enlisted: Salisbury
Residence: Wimbledon, Surrey
Died: Died of Wounds 24/8/16
Place of Burial: Puchevillers British Cemetery, plot III, row E, grave
    21
Biographical: son of Charles and Martha Gigg, Baydon, Wilts.;
    husband of Florence M. Gigg, Pundle View, Bartley, near
    Southampton
Age: 30
Note: previous service as 22290, Somerset Light Infantry

House, Pte Ernest Frank, 22113
Born: Salisbury
Enlisted: Salisbury
Residence: Salisbury
Died: Killed in Action 24/8/16
Place of Commemoration: Thiepval Memorial to the Missing, pier
    and face 13A
Biographical: son of Mrs. Ellen P. House, 46 Clifton Road,
    Salisbury
Age: 19
Note: listed as a member of 'C Company'.

Kent, Pte William Richard, 3/9852

Born: Wroughton, Wilts.

Enlisted: Swindon

Residence: Wroughton

Died: Died of Wounds 24/8/16

Place of Commemoration: Thiepval Memorial to the Missing, pier and face 13A

Biographical: son of Mrs Fanny Kent, 11 Perry's Lane, Wroughton, Swindon

Age: 20

Note: listed as a member of 'C Company'.

McCarthy, Pte Thomas James, 19689

Born: Birmingham

Enlisted: Birmingham

Residence: Birmingham

Died: Died of Wounds 24/8/16

Place of Commemoration: Thiepval Memorial to the Missing, pier and face 13A

Biographical: brother of Mr J. McCarthy, 24 George Arthur Road, Birmingham

Age: 22

Note: previous service as 8853, Ox. and Bucks. Light Infantry.

Reynolds, Pte Edward Arthur, 20138

Born: Malvern, Worcs.

Enlisted: Malvern

Residence: North Malvern, Worcs.

Died: Killed in Action 24/8/16

Place of Commemoration: Thiepval Memorial to the Missing, pier and face 13A

Note: previous service as 58199, Royal Field Artillery.

Weeks, Pte Harry Charles, 18740

Born: Berwick St John, Wilts.

Enlisted: Devizes, Wilts.

Residence: Salisbury

Died: Died of Wounds 24/8/16
Place of Burial: Warloy-Baillon Communal Cemetery and
    Extension, plot VII, row D, grave 53
Age: 28

Bannon, Pte Thomas, 22146
Born: Bradford, Yorks.
Enlisted: London
Residence: Bradford
Died: Killed in Action 25/8/16
Place of Commemoration: Thiepval Memorial to the Missing, pier
    and face 13A
Biographical: son of James and Alice Bannon, 73 Myrtle Street,
    Leeds Road, Bradford
Age: 18

Bullock, Pte Joseph, 18550
Born: Coate, Wilts.
Enlisted: Devizes, Wilts.
Residence: Devizes
Died: Killed in Action, 25/8/16
Place of Commemoration: Thiepval Memorial to the Missing, pier
    and face 13A

Butler, 2/Lt Eric
Died: Killed in Action 25/8/16
Place of Commemoration: Thiepval Memorial to the Missing, pier
    and face 13A

Empson, Cpl Henry, 11578
Born: Leafield, Oxon.
Enlisted: Swindon
Residence: Witney, Oxon.
Died: Killed in Action, 25/8/16
Place of Commemoration: Thiepval Memorial to the Missing, pier
    and face 13A

Biographical: son of Frederick and Sarah E. Empson, Leafield, Witney
Age: 27

Masling, Pte Frank, 10491
Born: Steeple Ashton, Wilts.
Enlisted: Steeple Ashton
Residence: Steeple Ashton
Died: Died of Wounds, 25/8/16
Place of Commemoration: Thiepval Memorial to the Missing, pier and face 13A
Biographical: son of Mrs Lydia Masling, Church Street, Steeple Ashton, Trowbridge, Wilts.
Age: 21
Note: also listed as Musling.

Prowett, Pte Charles, 19569
Born: Beeston, Notts.
Enlisted: Devizes, Wilts.
Residence: Beeston
Died: Died of Wounds, 25/8/16
Place of Burial: Puchevillers British Cemetery, plot III, row E, grave 41
Biographical: son of Joseph and Maria Prowett, Beeston
Age: 36

Salter, Pte John William, 13976
Enlisted: Salisbury
Residence: Bournemouth
Died: Killed in Action, 25/8/16
Place of Commemoration: Thiepval Memorial to the Missing, pier and face 13A
Biographical: son of Rose Robinson (formerly Salter) and Lt Thomas Salter, 5 Norwood Place, Southbourne, Bournemouth
Age: 20

Turtell, Pte Leslie Victor, 22341
Born: Bradford-on-Avon, Wilts.
Enlisted: Trowbridge, Wilts.
Residence: Bradford-on Avon
Died: Killed in Action, 25/8/16
Place of Burial: Serre Road No. 2 Military Cemetery, plot XXVIII,
   row A, grave 4

26 AUGUST TO 2 SEPTEMBER 1916

On 26 August the weary survivors of both battalions were relieved. For neither battalion was this without incident, and further casualties occurred. Again the bodies of the fallen seem to have been buried where they fell and most graves were subsequently lost, their names being found on the Thiepval Memorial. One identified body, probably found after the war, was interred in the AIF Burial Ground cemetery, mentioned previously.

In the attack of 24/25 August many more had fallen wounded than had been killed in action. In the days to come, some of these would succumb to their wounds as they were passed from aid posts immediately behind the front lines to field ambulances (as at Forceville, Puchevillers, and so on) and casualty clearing stations in villages further back (for example, Beauval, Contay). From here soldiers could be transferred to large base hospitals, as at Rouen, or, for the more fortunate, back to 'Blighty' via the main hospital at Étaples on the coast south of Boulogne. This last cemetery contains 10,769 burials of troops who so very nearly made it home. It is possible to discern the sad correlation between the date of death and the distance travelled back from the Somme battlefield.

One particular tragedy for the 1st Wiltshire was that two of its officers, being temporarily attached to the 8th Loyal North Lancs., were killed in the attack on the extreme left of the Hindenburg Trench on the 26th.

It would be almost impossible to trace further casualties from the attack on Hindenburg Trench on 24/25 August, as both battalions were involved in the much less unsuccessful attack in the Leipzig Salient on 3 September, resulting in new casualties that were then added to the records.

3rd Worcestershire

Banner, Pte Frederick, 8834. DCM
Born: Tipton, Staffs.
Enlisted: Birmingham
Residence: Tipton
Died: Killed in Action 26/8/16
Place of Commemoration: Thiepval Memorial to the Missing,
  panels 5A, 6C

Capewell, Pte Lewis Joseph, 25123
Born: Birmingham
Enlisted: Birmingham
Died: Killed in Action 26/8/16
Place of Commemoration: AIF Burial Ground, plot XV, row H,
  grave 33
Biographical: son of David Capewell, 56 James Turner Street,
  Winson Green, Birmingham
Age: 19

Emms, Pte William Joseph, 27695
Born: Birmingham
Enlisted: Birmingham
Died: Killed in Action 26/8/16
Place of Commemoration: Thiepval Memorial to the Missing,
  panels 5A, 6C
Biographical: husband of Beatrice M. Emms, 409 Garrison Lane,
  Bordesley Green, Small Heath, Birmingham
Age: 29
Note: listed as being a member of 'C Company'.

Appendix

Jenkins, Pte Albert, 14074
Born: Kingswinford, Staffs.
Enlisted: Stourbridge, Worcs.
Residence: Wollaston, Worcs.
Died: Killed in Action 26/8/16
Place of Commemoration: Thiepval Memorial to the Missing, panels 5A, 6C

Meere, Pte Alfred James, 14292
Born: Birmingham
Enlisted: Birmingham
Died: Died of Wounds 26/8/16
Place of Burial: Forceville Communal Cemetery and Extension, plot 2, row E, grave 3
Biographical: son of Lucy Jane and Lt Thomas James Meere, Selly Oak, Birmingham
Age: 19

Morley, Pte Charles Frederick, 20043
Born: Sherborne, Dorset
Enlisted: Ashford, Kent
Residence: Ashford
Died: Killed in Action 26/8/16
Place of Commemoration: Thiepval Memorial to the Missing, panels 5A, 6C

Nash, Sgt Frederick, 19664
Born: Stoke Prior, Worcs.
Enlisted: Birmingham
Residence: Birmingham
Died: Killed in Action 26/8/16
Place of Commemoration: Thiepval Memorial to the Missing, panels 5A, 6C
Biographical: son of Thomas John Steward Nash and Elizabeth Nash
Age: 26

Petford, Pte Frank, 19372
Born: Bradley Green, Worcs.
Enlisted: Redditch, Worcs.
Residence: Birmingham
Died: Died of Wounds 26/8/16
Place of Burial: Forceville Communal Cemetery and Extension,
   plot 2, row E, grave 2
Biographical: son of William and Emma Petford, Stockwood,
   Inkberrow, Worcs.
Age: 25

Sinar, Pte Thomas, 12843
Born: West Bromwich
Enlisted: Birmingham
Residence: West Bromwich
Died: Died of Wounds 26/8/16
Place of Burial: Forceville Communal Cemetery and Extension,
   plot 3, row B, grave 2
Biographical: son of Harriet and Lt Thomas Sinar, West Bromwich
Age: 27

Sparey, Pte William, 28861
Born: Frome, Somerset
Enlisted: Frome
Died: Killed in Action 26/8/16
Place of Commemoration: Thiepval Memorial to the Missing,
   Panels 5A, 6C

Whittington, Sgt Bob, 12133. DCM
Born: Leatherhead, Surrey
Enlisted: Guildford, Surrey
Residence: Effingham, Surrey
Died: Killed in Action 26/8/16
Place of Commemoration: Thiepval Memorial to the Missing,
   panels 5A, 6C
Biographical: son of Mrs Ellen Maria Whittington, 12 Victory
   Cottages, Effingham
Age: 21

Hincley, Pte Arthur, 14637
Born: Cradley, Worcs.
Enlisted: Worcester
Residence: Old Hill, Staffs.
Died: Died of Wounds 27/8/16
Place of Burial: Forceville Communal Cemetery and Extension,
     plot 3, row B, grave 9
Biographical: son of Harry and E. Hincley
Age: 31

Whitmore, Pte Albert, 9406
Born: Stourport, Worcs.
Enlisted: Worcester
Residence: Cookley, Worcs.
Died: Died of Wounds 27/8/16
Place of Burial: Beauval Communal Cemetery, row F, grave 23

Cruise, Pte William, 27810
Born: Bridgnorth, Salop.
Enlisted: Wolverhampton
Residence: Kidderminster
Died: Died of Wounds 28/8/16
Place of Burial: Forceville Communal Cemetery and Extension,
     plot 3, row B, grave 6
Biographical: son of George and Catherine Cruise, 12 Queen
     Street, Kidderminster
Age: 29

Fisher, Pte Leonard Walter, 23272
Born: Clevedon, Somerset
Enlisted: Bristol
Residence: Bristol
Died: Died of Wounds 28/8/16
Place of Burial: Etaples Cemetery, Pas-de-Calais, plot X, row A,
     grave 10A

Biographical: son of Walter Andrew and Kate Fisher, 63 St Luke's
 Road, Totterdown, Bristol

Age: 23

Surman, Pte Ambrose William, 27023

Born: Birmingham

Enlisted: Birmingham

Residence: Catshill, Worcs.

Died: Died of Wounds 31/8/16

Place of Burial: Contay British Cemetery, plot 1, row A, grave 10

Biographical: only son of Ambrose and Mary Louise Surman,
 Birmingham

Age: 20

Note: listed as being a member of 'C Company'.

Holliday, Pte Bruce Philip, 31437

Born: Gloucester

Enlisted: Gloucester

Died: Died of Wounds 1/9/16

Place of Burial: St Sever Cemetery, Rouen, plot B, row 24,
 grave 36

Biographical: son of Elizabeth Mary Millard (formerly Holliday)
 and Lt William Holliday; husband of Elizabeth Ann Holliday, 17
 Albert Street, Gloucester

Age: 27

1st Wiltshire

Martin, Temp 2/Lt Robert Douglas

Died: Killed in Action 26/8/16

Place of Commemoration: Thiepval Memorial to the Missing, pier
 and face 13A

Pigott, Temp 2/Lt Christopher Devonshire

Died: Killed in Action 26/8/16

Place of Commemoration: Thiepval Memorial to the Missing, pier
 and face 13A

Sharps, Pte James, 7135
Born: Swindon
Enlisted: Swindon
Residence: Swindon
Died: Died of Wounds 26/8/16
Place of Burial: Beauval Communal Cemetery, row F,
    grave 22
Biographical: son of Mrs J. Sharps, 1 Cheltenham Street,
    Swindon
Age: 28

Cook, Pte Norman Henry, 22844
Born: Andover, Hants.
Enlisted: Andover
Residence: Andover
Died: Died of Wounds 28/8/16
Place of Burial: Forceville Communal Cemetery and Extension,
    plot 3, row B, grave 11
Biographical: son of Henry George and Louisa Cook, 4 Orchard
    Cottages, Chute Lodge, near Andover
Age: 20

Porter, Sgt Frank, 4911
Born: Neston, Wilts.
Enlisted: Corsham, Wilts.
Residence: Chippenham, Wilts.
Died: Died of Wounds 28/8/16
Place of Burial: Puchevillers British Cemetery, plot III, row F,
    grave 9

Muddle, Pte Frank, 22730
Born: Manningford, Wilts.
Enlisted: Pewsey, Wilts.
Residence: Pewsey
Died: Died of Wounds 29/8/16
Place of Burial: Forceville Communal Cemetery and Extension,
    plot 3, row B, grave 11

Biographical: son of Samuel and Mary Ann Muddle, Manningford
    Bruce, Pewsey
Age: 21

Smart, Pte Walter, 9054
Born: Wyke, Dorset
Enlisted: Dorchester
Residence: Salisbury
Died: Died 2/9/16
Place of Burial: Forceville Communal Cemetery and Extension,
    plot 3, row B, grave 14
Biographical: son of Tom and Elizabeth A.A. Smart, Gillingham,
    Dorset

AND FINALLY . . .

These lists of soldiers of the 3rd Worcestershire and 1st Wiltshire
who were killed or died of wounds still represent a minority. Most
of the soldiers who attacked up the slopes of the Thiepval Ridge
on 24 August 1916 survived.

Sadly, the names of the survivors of actions in the First World
War are not recorded. Many of them would fall in subsequent
actions on the Somme and throughout the rest of the war. The
active strength of a battalion was 1,000 men, and many infantry
battalions lost at least five times this number during the course of
the war. By November 1918 there would be were very few
survivors of this attack on the Hindenburg Trench still serving.

To **all** who took part during this action, friend and former foe
alike, this book is most humbly dedicated.

Bibliography and Further Reading

REGIMENTAL HISTORIES

Edmonds, Brig Gen Sir J.E., *Military Operations France and Belgium – 1916*, vol. 2, Macmillan & Co., 1932.

Kincade-Smith, Lt Col M., *The 25th Division in France and Flanders*, 2nd edn (date unknown).

Stacke, Capt H.M. Fitz, *The Worcestershire Regiment in the Great War*, G.T. Cheshire & Sons, 1928.

Battalion War Diary – 1st Wiltshire Regiment, July/September 1916 (unpublished). National Archive reference: WO 95/2243

Battalion War Diary – 3rd Worcestershire Regiment, July/August 1916 (unpublished). National Archive reference: WO 95/2244

Diary of Brigade-Major A.C. Johnston, 7th Brigade, 25th Division, July/August 1916 (unpublished).

NEWSPAPERS

Berrows Weekly Journal, August/September 1916.

Dean Forest Mercury, August/September 1916.

Worcester Daily News, August/September 1916.

EYEWITNESS ACCOUNTS

Gibbs, P., *The Battles of the Somme*, William Heinemann, 1917.

Glover, M. ed., *The Fateful Battle Line – The Great War journals and sketches of Captain Henry Ogle*, Leo Cooper, 2003.

GENERAL HISTORIES

Gliddon, G., *The Battle of the Somme – A Topographical History*, Sutton 1994

Swinton, Maj Gen Sir E., ed. *Twenty Years After – The Battlefields of 1914–18 Then and Now*, Newnes *c.* 1938

IT SOURCES

Commonwealth War Graves Commission, Register of the Fallen, see www.cwgc.org

Imperial War Museum Trench Map Archive on CD-ROM, The Naval and Military Press

Soldiers Died in the Great War on CD-ROM, The Naval and Military Press

FURTHER READING

Although not specifically cited in this work, the following books still act as an inspiration to anyone seriously involved with the study of the First World War and the Battle of the Somme in particular. These books, and the many others written by the same authors, concentrate on the personal testimonies given by officers and soldiers who served in that war. Importantly, these works are still in print and are likely to remain so for many years to come. I can wholeheartedly recommend all of them:

Brown, M., *Tommy Goes to War*, J.M. Dent & Sons, 1978.
MacDonald, L., *Somme*, Michael Joseph, 1983.
Middlebrook, M., *The First Day on the Somme*, Allen Lane, 1971.

The following series of books specifically covers aspects of tracing the history of a First World War soldier:

Holding, N., *World War I Army Ancestry*, 3rd edn, Federation of Family History Societies, Birmingham, 1997.
——, *More Sources of World War I Army Ancestry*, 3rd edn, Federation of Family History Societies, Birmingham, 1998.

——, *The Location of British Army Records 1914–1918*, 4th edn, Federation of Family History Societies, Birmingham, 1999.

Swinnerton, I., *Identifying your World War I Soldier from Badges and Photographs*, Federation of Family History Societies, Birmingham, 2001.

There are an increasing number of excellent battlefield guides. The most detailed are from the series entitled 'Battleground Europe'. Each book covers specific actions of a particular battle, and the Somme is especially well represented. The most relevant ones in this case are:

Cave, N., *Battleground Europe – Beaumont Hamel*, Leo Cooper, 1994.

Reed, P., *Battleground Europe – Walking the Somme*, Leo Cooper, 1997.

Stedman, M., *Battleground Europe – Thiepval*, Leo Cooper, 1995.

In addition, the following is a must:
Major and Mrs Holts Battlefield Guide to the Somme, Leo Cooper, (2001).

Finally, I would recommend a novel written by a surviving soldier, which was originally published anonymously in the 1920s. This fictionalised account was heavily based on the author's own experiences during the middle of the Somme offensive. This book more accurately describes the day-to-day life of a private soldier on the Somme better than I or any other 'armchair historian' could ever do:
Manning, F., *The Middle Parts of Fortune*, Book Club Associates, 1977.

A much expurgated version of the same book was later released, as the original language used was not considered suitable for general issue. Interestingly, it is this second version that is the better known (and is still in print, under the above author's name). The original reference was:

Private 19022, *Her Privates We*, 1929.

Index

Index

Index

Index